Informatik-Fachberichte

Herausgegeben von W. Brauer
im Auftrag der Gesellschaft für Informatik (GI)

77

Programmiersprachen und Programmentwicklung

8. Fachtagung, veranstaltet vom Fachausschuß 2.1 der GI und der
Schweizer Informatiker Gesellschaft
Zürich, 8./9. März 1984

Herausgegeben von Urs Ammann

Springer-Verlag
Berlin Heidelberg New York Tokyo 1984

Herausgeber

Dr. U. Ammann
DISER AG, Haldeneggsteig 5, CH-8006 Zürich

CR Subject Classifications (1983): 4.0, 4.1, 4.2, 4.6, 5.23, 5.24, 6.21

ISBN-13: 978-3-540-12905-9   e-ISBN-13: 978-3-642-69393-9
DOI: 10.1007/978-3-642-69393-9

CIP-Kurztitelaufnahme der Deutschen Bibliothek. Programmiersprachen und Programmentwicklung:
Fachtagung / veranst. vom Fachausschuß 2.1 d. GI u. d. Schweizer Informatiker-Ges. – Berlin; Heidel-
berg; New York; Tokyo: Springer; Bis 7 (1982) veranst. vom Fachausschuß 2 d. GI. – Bis 7 (1982) mit d.
Erscheinungsorten Berlin, Heidelberg, New York – Bis 5 (1978) u.d.T.: Programmiersprachen 8. Zürich,
März 1984. – 1984.
(Informatik-Fachberichte; 77)

NE: Gesellschaft für Informatik / Fachausschuß Programmiersprachen; Gesellschaft für Informatik /
Fachausschuß Programmiersprachen und Programmentwicklung; GT

2145/3140 – 5 4 3 2 1 0

<u>Vorwort</u>

Der Fachausschuss "Programmiersprachen und Programmentwicklung" der
Gesellschaft für Informatik e.V. veranstaltet am 8. und 9. März 1984
seine 8. Fachtagung. Erstmals wird diese im zweijährigen Turnus
durchgeführte Veranstaltung in Zusammenarbeit mit der Schweizer Informatiker Gesellschaft organisiert. Tagungsort ist die Eidgenössi-
sche Technische Hochschule Zürich, jene Schule also, die dank dem
leider viel zu früh verstorbenen Numeriker Heinz Rutishauser ein
Jahrzehnt lang als Algol-Hochburg galt und heute, dank dem Wirken
des Informatikers Niklaus Wirth, als Geburtsstätte von Pascal und
Modula-2 in Fachkreisen bestbekannt ist - und damit der Fachtagung
einen hoffentlich würdigen Rahmen verleiht.

Dank der gemeinsamen Organisation der Tagung durch die beiden Ge-
sellschaften präsentiert sich das Programmkomitee in der folgenden,
erweiterten Besetzung:

<pre>
          N. Wirth, ETH Zürich (Vorsitz)
          U. Ammann, DISER, Zürich
          H. Ganzinger, TU München
          H. Gerstmann, IBM,Böblingen
          P. Gorny, U Oldenburg
          Ch. Haenel, Siemens, München
          W. Hesse, Softlab, München
          R. Marty, U Zurich
          G. Musstopf, M&T, Hamburg
          J. Nievergelt, ETH Zürich
          W. Ruisinger, Daimler-Benz, Stuttgart
          H. Sandmayr, BBC, Baden
          R. Schild, Landis+Gyr, Zug
          K. Wendler, DATEV, Nürnberg
          R. Wilhelm, U Saarbrücken
          H. Wössner, TU München
</pre>

Dieses Gremium hat sich die Auswahl von 15 aus total 63 eingegangenen
Beiträgen nicht leicht gemacht. Jeder Beitrag wurde von drei unabhängigen Referenten begutachtet und bewertet. Es versteht sich von
selbst, dass bei dieser Fülle der eingereichten Arbeiten leider eine
ganze Reihe von wertvollen Beiträgen unberücksichtigt bleiben musste,
insbesondere da am bewährten bisherigen Abwicklungsmodus - einer
zweitägigen Veranstaltung mit einigen eingeladenen Hauptvorträgen,
ohne Parallelsitzungen - festgehalten wurde.

Thematisch liessen sich die ausgewählten Vorträge grob in die vier
Gebiete *) Theorie, Programmiersprachen, Programmierumgebungen und
Applikationen einordnen, denen die Fachtagung nun je eine Sitzung
widmet. Jede Sitzung wird eingeleitet durch einen eingeladenen Vortrag, nämlich

C.A.R. Hoare	"Specification and Proof of Parallel Programs"
J.D. Ichbiah	"Modular Programming in Ada"
J.J. Horning	"The Cedar Programming Environment: Status and Prospects"
J.W. Schmidt	"Data Base Programming: Language Constructs and Execution Models"

Den Autoren aller Vorträge dankt das Programmkomitee ganz besonders
für ihre Bereitschaft, substantiell zum Gelingen der Fachtagung bei-
zutragen (wobei es natürlich bedauert, dass nicht alle Vorträge
fristgemäss zur Aufnahme in diesen Tagungsband eingegangen sind).

Unser Dank geht auch an die ETH Zürich und insbesondere an das Institut für Informatik und den Co-Tagungsleiter Herrn H. Hinterberger,
welche uns die für eine solche Tagung unerlässliche Infrastruktur
erschliessen und für deren Betrieb besorgt sind. Ferner danken wir
allen Helfern für ihren anonymen, aber nicht minder wertvollen Beitrag zum Gelingen der Tagung und schliesslich bedanken wir uns beim
Springer-Verlag für die gute Zusammenarbeit bei der kurzfristigen
Herstellung des Tagungsbands.

Zürich, im Januar 1984   Urs Ammann

---

*) Die ebenfalls zum Fachbereich gehörenden Gebiete Sprachimple-
   mentierungen, Interaktive Systeme und Personal Computing werden
   durch die am Vortag den 7. März 1984 stattfindenden Fachgruppen-
   treffen abgedeckt.

<u>Gutachter</u>

Das Programmkomitee dankt allen Gutachtern für ihre kompetente Mitarbeit bei der Begutachtung der eingereichten Arbeiten:

M. Bärtschi, Zürich
Th. von Bomhard, München
M. Broy, Passau
H. Burkhart, Zürich
E. Engeler, Zürich
M. Eulenstein, Saarbrücken
P. Fink, Zürich
G. Fischer, München
R. Frölich, München
K. Frühauf, Baden
R. Gall, Erlangen
R. Gnatz, München
H. Göttler, Erlangen
G. Greiter, München
J. Griese, Bern
J. Gutknecht, Zürich
U. Hill-Samelson, München
J.F. Jauslin, Zürich
S. Keramidis, Erlangen
S.E. Knudsen, Zürich
D. Konnerth, München
B. Krieg-Brückner, Bremen
T.A. Matzner, München
P. Meinen, München
B. Möller, München
U. Möncke, Saarbrücken
F. Muheim, Zürich
F. Müller, Saarbrücken
M. Nagl, Osnabrück
H. Oesterle, St. Gallen
H. Partsch, München
P. Pepper, München
P. Pircher, San Franzisco
M. Reitenspiess, Erlangen
H.J. Schneider, Erlangen
P. Schulthess, Zürich
F. Simon, Kiel
J. Stelovsky, Zürich
H. Stoyan, Erlangen
H. Sugaya, Baden
K. Tomica, Zürich
A. Ventura, Zürich
D. Weber, Nürnberg

Inhaltsverzeichnis

DATABASE PROGRAMMING:

LANGUAGE CONSTRUCTS AND EXECUTION MODELS

Joachim W. Schmidt

Fachbereich Informatik

Johann Wolfgang Goethe-Universität

Frankfurt am Main

Abstract

Relations are in the process of being accepted as a data structure adequate for a wide variety of applications. On the one hand this is due to the powerful and high level operators on relations, on the other it results from additional services   such   as   recovery management, concurrency control and expression optimization provided by relational systems.

This paper presents a database person's view of data definition and data processing, and outlines principles of database programming from a language person's point of view.   In addition, design aspects of Database Programming Languages and execution models for query evaluation and transaction management are discussed.

1.0 INTRODUCTION: DATABASE PROGRAMMING

A data management problem is sometimes called a 'Database Problem' if
- the definition of data objects covers properties of 'real world entities' and their relationships - and the entities are long-lived and large in number;
- the selection of data objects is based on object properties rather than on object identifiers; and
- the operations on data objects are defined and initiated (in parallel) by independent members of some user community.

Current algorithmic languages support these requirements only to a limited extent: records define properties of entities but record selection is done by declared names or via references; files and file systems cope with data quantity and longevity and, to some extent, with concurrency but do not support object relationships. These shortcomings stimulated the development of what might be called Database Programming Languages; examples are ADAPLEX [SmFL81], TAXIS [MyBW80], PLAIN [Wass79], Pascal/R [Schm77], or the approach followed by PS-ALGOL [AtCC81].

The main purpose of this paper is to present some of the language constructs found in Database Programming Languages. Furthermore, we want to show how these constructs interact with others which are designed for algorithmic work on data, thereby outlining some of the principles of Database Programming. Finally, we will discuss various execution models for Database Programming Languages.

2.0 A PROGRAMMER'S APPROACH TO THE RELATIONAL MODEL OF DATA

From a programmer's point of view a Database Model can be interpreted basically as an approach to structuring, identifying, and organizing large quantities of variables as required for solving Database Problems.

For traditional reasons, variables in databases are structured as records. What distinguishes, for example, Codd's Relational Model [Codd70] from Hoare's approach to Record Handling [Hoar66] is, in essence, the different ways both approaches deal with record identification; Codd's method has, as we will see, some far reaching consequences.

2.1 Naming Of Variables And Partitioning Of States

A *programmer* dealing, for example, with persons and houses will define types such as

```
TYPE      streetname   =     string; ...;

          person       =     RECORD      ... ;
                                         age  :  cardinal;
                                         sex  :  ... ; ...
                             END;

          house        =     RECORD      ... ;
                                         street: streetname;
                                         number: cardinal;
                                         value : ...; ...
                             END;
```

and declare variables such as

```
VAR        This-Person:    person;
           My-House:       house;
```

A *record handler*, expecting large quantities of record variables, organizes its state space by collecting all instances of the same type in one, say, *class*; he leaves the problems of record identification to someone else that provides unique references to records:

```
...
VAR        Persons:           CLASS OF person;
           Houses:            CLASS OF house;
           This-Person:       REF (Persons);
           My-House:          REF (Houses);
```

Finally, a *relationalist* groups records of the same type similarly in a set-like structure called *relation* . He starts, however, from the assumption that a property that is capable of identifying an entity, for example a person's name or the address of a house, is so important that it should be modelled explicitly by the type of the corresponding data object:

```
TYPE   personname =  string; ...;
       person     =  RECORD  name:     personname;
                             age:      cardinal;
                             sex:      ...; ...
                     END;

       house      =  RECORD  city:     cityname;
                             street:   streetname;
                             number:   cardinal;
                             value:    ...; ...
                     END;
VAR    Persons:    RELATION OF person;
       Houses:     RELATION OF house;
       This-Person: personname;
       My-House:    RECORD   city:     cityname;
                             street:   streetname;
                             number:   cardinal
                    END;
```

Roughly speaking, one can say that a programmer identifies variables by names, a record handler by references, and a relationalist trough the use of distinguished attribute values, i.e., properties, for record identification.

Both record handlers and relationalists can easily handle relationships between entities by defining, for example, ownership either through

```
TYPE   houseowner = RECORD ...
                        owner:     REF(person);
                        property:  REF(house);
                        purchasing-date: ...; ...
                    END;
```

or through:

```
TYPE    houseowner = RECORD   ...
                             owner:      personname;
                             property:   RECORD  city:    ... ;
                                                 street:  ... ;
                                                 number: ...
                                         END;
                             purchasing-date: ... ; ...
              END;
```

Ownership between several persons and houses is represented as above by a class or
a relation of houseowners respectively.

Record handlers and relationalists represent separate schools of database
people: these are, on the one hand, the adherents of the referential data models,
for example, network and hierarchy models, and, on the other, those preferring
associative data models, i.e., the relational one and the derived semantic data
models. This paper concentrates on the relational approach.

2.2 Consistency Of Identifiers

Using, for example, strings and cardinal numbers to represent identifiers, as
the relational approach does, is, of course, an open invitation to data
inconsistency, unless specific precautions are taken.

Values of type personname, for example, represent identifiers of persons only
if they are unique within their scope. In other words, the relation:

```
VAR Persons: RELATION OF person;
```

has to fulfil at all times the predicate:

```
ALL p,p' IN Persons ((p.name=p'.name) -> (p=p')).
```

Conditions of this kind are often called key constraints and are concerned with
entity integrity; we denote them shortly by listing the key attributes within the
relation's type definition:

```
VAR  Persons: RELATION name OF person;
     Houses:  RELATION city,street,number OF house;
```

While entity integrity guarantees that identifiers of relation elements are defined
uniquely, *referential integrity* ensures that identifiers are used properly. Proper
use means that identifiers have to be declared before they are used;   a person's
name that denotes the owner of some house is an identifier of some person only if
there is a record in the relation Persons identified by that name - otherwise it is
just a string of characters. A similar statement holds for houses identified by
their addresses. In other words, a relation Ownership with elements of type

houseowner has to meet, at all times, the predicate:

```
ALL o IN Ownership SOME p IN Persons ((o.owner=p.name) AND
        SOME h IN Houses (o.property = <h.city,h.street,h.number>)).
```

Codd calls only those database systems *fully relational* that support the two classes of constraints required for entity and referential integrity [Codd83].

2.3 Variability Of States

Database Programmers can change the state represented by the record variables of a relation in several ways: a new value can be associated with some identifier, a new <identifier, value>-pair can be introduced, or an existing one can be removed.

The Relational Model admits two substantially different perceptions: what a relation variable is, and how it is composed of its element variables. Both perceptions have their merits.

The set-like perception considers a relation as a set with members of type record constrained by some key condition. It provides a class of assignment operators for element insertion (:+), deletion (:-), and replacement (:&).

A new person, for example, is introduced by:

```
Persons :+ {<..., 'Klug', 33, ...>};
```

and is replaced by:

```
Persons :& {<..., 'Klug', 34, ...>};
```

using the person's name, in this case, 'Klug', as the identifier for the record to be replaced.

The alternative is an array-like or table perception. In this view an individual relation element is denoted by an array-like selection mechanism based on the relation's key, and the previous replacement is equivalent to a reassignment:

```
Persons ['Klug']:= <..., 'Klug', 34, ...>;
```

when perceived like arrays, relations usually are sparse, that is, there are no values associated with most keys. (A "no value" can be represented, for example, by the empty record constructor, < >). Such 'unassigned' variables do not contribute to the state as represented by the elements of a relation.

An insert in set-like perceptions corresponds to an assignment in the array-like picture, provided the selected element has not been assigned beforehand, and a delete corresponds to the assignment of the empty record constructor to an assigned relation element.

The definition of selectors for relations can be generalized, as in the case of arrays, to selectors denoting more than one relation element, i.e., a subrelation. Since data in a database are provided and processed by different members of a user community, powerful mechanisms for partitioning a relation variable are of particular importance. A discussion of this issue will form part of the subsequent section that extends the basic approach to relations through some high level constructs.

3.0 SOME HIGH LEVEL LANGUAGE CONSTRUCTS FOR RELATIONS

The evaluation of expressions with relations as operands requires mechanisms to refer to and operate on all of its elements. The immense cardinalities of the value sets that at times appear with key types (for example, strings) does not allow one, however, to step through relations by simply incrementing the key value, as we do with indexed arrays. In addition most of the selected relation elements would be unassigned anyway. With respect to element selection, the set picture itself does not help us at all since there is no selector mechanism defined for sets.

Hence, we start with some primitive access procedures for relations and use them to sketch solutions for some standard problems in database programming.

The uniqueness of key values provides a basis for accessing individual relation elements. Working under the assumption that the set of key values (not the relation!) is ordered we can define some standard procedures that access relations element by element. Procedure low (R,r), for example, assigns that element of the relation, R, which has the lowest key value to the record variable, r. Procedure next (R,r) accesses the element with the key value next highest to the one provided by r, and assigns it to r. The Boolean function, eor (R), becomes true if an access fails.

Each class of database problems addressed in this section will motivate some higher level language construct for relations that abstract from unnecessary implementational details [Schm77], [ScMa83]. This permits database programs to be more concise and accessible to optimization.

3.1 Query Expressions

Probably the most frequent and expensive operation on a database is querying, i.e., evaluating logical expressions that have relation elements as operands.

The case in which a Boolean expression, p, is evaluated for some relation element, R[kv], occurs frequently within loops that run over all the elements of a relation:

```
some-s := FALSE;
low (R,r);
WHILE NOT eor (R) DO
   some-s := some-s OR p(r);
   next (R,r)
END;
```

Such statements arise when testing whether an element variable in a relation makes a Boolean expression true - without knowing the variable's identifier. A situation like this sounds strange to an ordinary programmer, however, it occurs often in an environment with many thousands of variables shared with other database users. The above implementation of our test is unsatisfactory for several reasons: first, there is no indication that the order in which the program steps through the relation is optimal; second, there should be a loop exit as soon as an element is found that fulfils p; and, finally, the statement sequence is too long.

From predicate logic we know that the above program computes the same results for s as given by the first-order predicate:

SOME r IN R (p(r)).

The existential quantifier introduces a variable, r, that denotes arbitrary elements in relation R;   the predicate becomes true if and only if at least one element fulfils p.

In the given context, a predicate denotes more directly what we mean, and, ideally, its evaluation requires access to only one relation element that fulfils p and it is left up to some clever execution model to reach that optimum.

The universal quantifier can be justified and introduced in an analoguous way.

A variation of the above case arises when we want the values of all those relation elements that fulfil some selection predicate.

Relational queries generalize expressions consisting only of selected relation elements, {R[kv1], ..., R[kvn]}. Instead of selecting elements that match a specific key condition, relational queries ask for all elements of a relation that fulfil an arbitrary selection predicate, p:

```
result := { };
low (R,r);
WHILE NOT eor (R) DO
  IF p(r) THEN result :+ {r} END;
  next (R,r)
END;
```

Following similar arguments as with Boolean queries, we replace the above statement sequence by the relation-valued expression:

```
{EACH r IN R: p(r)}.
```

The quantifier EACH introduces the variable r that denotes arbitrary elements in relation R; the selection phrase EACH r IN R: p(r) selects all the elements that fulfil p; the relation constructor, {...}, finally turns the selected elements into a relation.

In their most general form relational queries introduce several variables, r, s..., which run over various relations, R, S...; they allow first-order selection predicates free in r, s..., and admit record constructors to structure the resulting relation elements:

```
{<..,r.f,..,s.g,...> OF EACH r IN R, EACH s IN S,...: p(r,s,..)}.
```

Note that relation expressions can be nested and that they can be combined with first-order predicates.

The selective power of the above relational expressions is equivalent to what Codd called a *relationally complete* query language [Codd71].

3.2 <u>Repetition Statements</u>

The above two classes of problems, element test and element selection, occur frequently in database programming; they are, however, special cases. In general, an arbitrary statement, S, is executed for all relation elements selected by some predicate:

```
low (R,r);
WHILE NOT eor (R) DO
  IF p(r) THEN S END;
  next (R,r)
END;
```

If the order in which relation elements are processed is irrelevant, element access by increasing key value is an unnecessary and often costly decision. As long as statement S is executed only once for each element of R that fulfils predicate p, any order will suffice, and the decision can be left up to the implementation. This is done by applying the principles of control abstraction, and allowing a selection phrase, i.e., EACH r IN R: p(r), for loop control:

```
FOR EACH r IN R: p(r) DO S END;
```

Nested loops with a common selection criterium, that is,

```
FOR EACH r1 IN R1: TRUE DO
   ...
   FOR EACH rn IN Rn: TRUE DO
      IF p(r1,...rn) THEN S END
   END
END;
```

can be replaced by one loop controlled by a compound selection:

```
FOR EACH r1 IN R1, ... EACH rn IN Rn: p(r1,...rn) DO S END;
```


3.3 Selected Variables

In practice several users contribute to the data integrated into the relations of a database. Consequently, individual users often do not require access to a complete relation variable but only to selected parts of it. In this section we will extend the notion of selected relation elements introduced above and outline the concept of generalized selected relation variables.

Let us assume that R is a relation with a key composed of two attributes, k1 and k2. If we switch from the array-like perception of relations to the set-like view, the assignment:

```
R[kv1,kv2] := <...,kv1, ..., kv2,...>;
```

converts into the assignment:

```
R := {EACH r IN R: NOT (<r.k1, r.k2> = <kv1, kv2>), <...,kv1,...,kv2,...>}.
```

Assignment of a record variable, rec, to a selected relation element:

```
R[kv1, kv2] := rec;
```

is equivalent to the following assignment to the entire relation, R, when controlled by a test:

```
IF <kv1,kv2> = <rec.k1,rec.k2> THEN
   R := {EACH r IN R: NOT (<r.k1,r.k2> = <kv1,kv2>), rec}
ELSE <exception>
END;
```

As a first generalization, the notion of an element selector can be extended, as for arrays, to a selector for subrelations. The following statement assigns a relational expression, rex, to a relation variable selected by a truncated key list:

```
    R[kv1] := rex;
```

Its semantics can be defined by an equivalent assignment to the entire relation:

```
    IF ALL x IN rex (x.k1=kv1) THEN
        R := {EACH r IN R: NOT (r.k1=kv1), EACH x IN rex: TRUE}
    ELSE <exception>
    END;
```

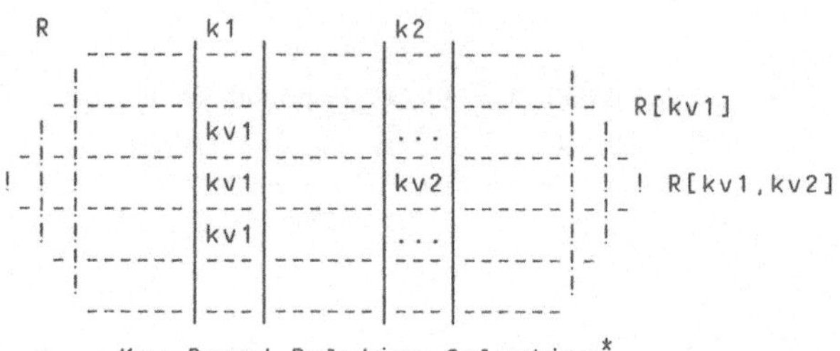

Key-Based Relation Selection*

The above selectors are based on specific selection predicates that depend on keys and key values only. We now want to generalize selectors and permit, as with query expressions, arbitrary predicates for relation selection.   The linguistic support for defining generalized selectors is provided by a language construct called a *selector generator*. We can use this generator to redefine, for example, the above selector for relation elements:

```
    SELECTOR sk (kf1:k1type; kf2:k2type) FOR rel: Rtype;
    BEGIN EACH r IN rel: (r.k1=kf1) AND (r.k2=kf2) END sk;
```

A selector definition introduces a selector name, may have parameters, and binds a selector to a formal relation of a given type. It includes the definition of a selection phrase, which introduces a selection predicate.

The use of a selector, for example, R[sk(kv1,kv2)], requires that the selected relation, R, is of type Rtype, as given by the selector definition, sk. The denotation R[sk(kv1,kv2)] is equivalent to the shorthand R [kv1,kv2] used above.

In its most general form a selector is based on an arbitrary selection predicate, p:

```
    SELECTOR sp (....) FOR rel: Rtype;
    BEGIN EACH r IN rel: p(r) END sp;
```

---

* The language constructs introduced so far are implemented on a DEC System/10 and have been in use since 1978/80 in a Database Programming Language called Pascal/R [Schm77], [ScMa80].

An Assignment

    R [sp(...)] := rex;

is equivalent to:

```
IF ALL x IN rex (p(x,...)) THEN
    R := {EACH r IN R: p(r,...), EACH x IN rex: TRUE}
ELSE <exception>
END;
```

and the value of a selected variable, R[sp(...)], is equal to that of the relational expression:

    {EACH r IN R: p(r,...)}.

Note that the selection phrase used in a selector definition (SELECTOR sp ...; BEGIN EACH r IN R: p(r,...) END sp) is the same as that already used in relation expressions ({EACH r IN R: p(r,...)}) and for loop control (FOR EACH r IN R: p(r,...) DO...).

In database literature selectors and selected relation variables are often called views [Ston75]. In subsequent sections we will demonstrate how selected relation variables can be used to control database integrity and support query evaluation and transaction handling.

4.0 SUPPORT FOR DATABASE INTEGRITY, RECOVERY AND CONCURRENCY

In some respects database users take their database for the "reality" it is supposed to describe and, therefore, are very concerned with data integrity. There are numerous reasons why the integrity of a database can get lost, however, there are some ways to keep database integrity under control.

First of all, programs may be incorrect and provide unintentional database input or output. Database programmers, being responsible for the data of a whole user community, are well advised to make use of whatever the state of the "Art and Craft, Science and Logic of Programming" offers in order to improve program correctness.

Some cases of unintentional input are detected because they violate one of the integrity constraints that are defined explicitly on the database, for example, a key constraint. In such a case subsequent statements and some previously executed ones usually become obsolete. Situations like these and similar ones caused by hard- or software malfunction call for recovery mechanisms that re-establish previous database states.

Finally, concurrent execution of database programs requires careful control of program dependencies to avoid additional problems with data integrity.

4.1 Statements For Database Integrity

The typical tasks a database program has to perform can be characterized as follows:
- local pre-processing of what is going to become the database input and transformation of the database into some new consistent state; and
- local evaluation of some consistent database state and post-processing of what happens* to be the database output.

Thus, the interactions between a program and database imply a structure of database programs where the operations on the database are concentrated in statement sequences, S, that begin and end in a consistent database state. We can express this by annotating a database program, i.e., by placing assertions (integrity constraints, ICs) around statements: {IC} S {IC}.

However, a database programmer usually knows - or should know - precisely what specific condition, Q, the output state of S has to fulfil. Following the approach of Hoare [Hoar69], Gries [Grie81] and others [Reyn81], [Hehn83], the postcondition, Q, should be taken as a starting point for developing the statement sequence, S, so that it guarantees the postcondition, provided execution begins in some precondition, P: {P} S {Q}.

Of course, any postcondition has to imply the integrity constraints. Furthermore, programmers must show that any precondition (the part that refers to the database) is a consequence of the postcondition established by the preceding statement sequence that operates on the database.

---

* In fact, database evaluation may be likened to "happening" because
- there are so many variables in a database that users might not remember what they put into them (probably a long time ago), and
- many of the variables in a database are likely to be created and assigned by others.

The following sketch of an annotated program includes explicitly the initial values, Rv, ..., of the relation variables, R, ..., used by S:

$$\{ \quad . \quad . \quad . \quad \} \ S^{j-1} \ ; \ \{Q^{j-1}\} \ ...$$
$$\{ \ P^j \wedge ((R^j=Rv^j) \wedge ...)\} \ S^j \quad ; \ \{Q^j\ \}$$

with Q^{j-1} --> IC ; Q^j --> IC ; and Q^{j-1} --> $P^j \wedge (...)$.

The omissions (...) between S^{j-1} and S^j refer to statements that work exclusively with local program variables and not with the database.

We will use pre- and postconditions to discuss some of the consequences that database recovery and concurrency impose on database programming.

4.2 Actions For Database Recovery

Provided S fulfils {P} S {Q}, we know that the following is true:

"If execution of S is begun in a state satisfying P, then it is guaranteed to terminate in a finite amount of time in a state satisfying Q" [Grie81].

This interpretation says nothing about the state of the variables referenced by S if, for one reason or another, the actions specified by the statements of sequence S cannot be executed.

Database Programming Languages enable a programmer to control actions on a database even under circumstances of failure. A database programmer may convert any statement sequence, S, into an action sequence, A, with the result that can be expressed best in terms of pre- and postconditions:

    if   {P ∧ ((R=Rv) ∧ ...)} S {Q}   holds for statement sequence S,
    then {P ∧ ((R=Rv) ∧ ...)} A {Q} ∨ {((R=Rv) ∧ ...)}   holds for the
    corresponding action sequence, A.

In other words, the postcondition of action sequences, A, is that of the underlying statement sequence, S, or it is, due to recovery actions, given by the re-established initial values of the database variables referenced by S.

Thus, database recovery leads to disjunctive postconditions of action sequences and, therefore, has an effect on database programming. The precondition of action sequence, Aj, now has to follow from a weaker postcondition:

$$Q^{j-1} \quad \lor \quad ((R^{j-1} = Rv^{j-1}) \land \ldots) \ --> \ P^j \land (\ldots) \ .$$

Converting statement sequences into action sequences not only maintains database integrity

$$Q^{j-1} \quad \lor \quad ((R^{j-1} = Rv^{j-1}) \land \ldots) \ --> \ IC,$$

but also extends its validity to cases that require database recovery[*].

4.3 Transactions For Database Concurrency

Up to now we assumed that all action sequences are part of the same database program, U. Converting action sequences, A, into transactions, T, allows two transactions, T_U^j and its predecessor, $T_{U'}^i$, to originate from independent database programs, U, U'. The consequences for database programming are obvious: the precondition of T_U^j has to follow from the postcondition of some $T_{U'}^i$.

$$Q_{U'}^i \lor ((R^i = Rv^i) \land \ldots) \ --> \ P_U^j \land (\ldots) \ .$$

Since concurrency models currently in use in databases exclude explicit communication between programs, U and U', there is very little the precondition of transaction T_U^j can learn from the postcondition of its predecessor, $T_{U'}^i$. All one knows for sure is that $T_{U'}^i$ re-establishes the integrity constraints:

$$Q_{U'}^i \lor ((R^i = Rv^i) \land \ldots) \ --> \ IC$$

and, therefore, T_U^j can rely upon them:

$$IC \ --> \ P_U^j \land (\ldots) \ .$$

In the context of a Database Programming Language the syntax of transactions may look like

```
TRANSACTION T(...);
IMPORT Rel[sp(...)], ... ;
BEGIN
    S
END;
```

---

[*] The language constructs introduced so far are implemented on the personal computer Lilith and are in use since 1982 in a Database Programming Language called Modula/R [KMPR83], [RRUZ83] with Modula/2 [Wirt82] as an algorithmic kernel.

The notion of a selected relation variable R[sp(...)] has been used to indicate that a transaction may demand access only to selected elements of a relation[*].

The weakening of conditions after actions and before transactions forces database programs to re-strengthen them through the explicit use of conditional statements. This is one of the reasons why Database Programming Languages need conditionals supported by powerful Boolean expressions, for example, first-order predicates.

In the remaining two sections we will outline some of the problems involved in implementing Database Programming Languages. We will concentrate on execution models for the two key areas: efficient evaluation of database queries, and concurrent execution of database transactions.

5.0 ON QUERY EVALUATION

Since the relational approach to databases is based on first-order predicates for data selection and evaluation, it depends, therefore, heavily upon efficient execution models for predicate evaluation.

A naive approach to evaluating a relational expression of the form:

{EACH r IN R: p(r,...)}

consists in testing the selection predicate, p(r,...), for each element, r, of the range relation, R:

```
result:= { };
FOR EACH r IN R: TRUE DO
    IF p(r,...) THEN result:+ {r} END
END;
```

With quantified predicates, for example,

SOME s IN S ALL t IN T (q(r,s,t))

further iterations over the ranges, S, T, of the bound variables, s, t, are required:

---

[*] Design and implementation of the language constructs introduced so far are under development in the DBPL-Project [SRPM83], [SRMK83] on a VAX, supported in part by the Deutsche Forschungsgemeinschaft (DFG) under grant numbers Schm 450/2,3.

```
result:= { };
FOR EACH r IN R: TRUE DO
   some-s:= FALSE;
   FOR EACH s IN S: TRUE DO
     all-t:= TRUE;
     FOR EACH t IN T: TRUE DO
       all-t:= all-t AND q(r,s,t);
        IF NOT all-t THEN EXIT END
     END;
     some-s:= some-s OR all-t;
     IF some-s THEN EXIT END
   END;
   IF some-s THEN result:+ {r} END
END;
```

Query optimization techniques aim at reducing the cost of query evaluation, which itself is primarily determined by the number of secondary storage accesses. Literature proposes numerous techniques for query evaluation [JaKo82], optimal only under specific assumptions. These assumptions can be grouped into three categories: long term assumptions already known by the compiling machine, medium term assumptions characterizing a set of target machines, and short term assumptions valid only for the executing machine.

In this section we shortly discuss these three categories of optimization techniques and apply them to the above procedure. We further outline how these techniques can be integrated within an optimizing DBPL compiler [KoSc83]

5.1 Query Classification

Amongst the decisions the compiling machine should make are definitely those based on long term assumptions (or permanently valid rules). Examples are the transformation rules of predicate logic that can be used to group semantically equivalent queries into classes. Individual members of an equivalence class may differ in number and complexity of their terms and, therefore, in evaluation costs. Query classification encompasses aspects of query simplification and query decomposition.

Simplification techniques include the elimination of redundancy in the presence of idempotency and common subexpressions [Hall76], and the propagation of constant values for the sake of reducing the number of (expensive) join terms [AhSU79]. They also make use of database invariants [King81] in order to derive a contradiction or tautology, which may drastically reduce the complexity of a selection predicate.

Structural decomposition is motivated by the insight that tree-structured queries,
that is, queries represented graphically as a tree describing range relations as
nodes and join terms as branches, can be evaluated stepwise following the branches
of the tree [BeCh81]. In contrast, cyclic queries usually imply a deeply nested
iteration, since the branches, and thus the corresponding subexpressions contained
in a cycle, cannot be processed independently of each other. For example, if the
predicate q(r,s,t) is a conjunction, q1(r,s) AND q2(r,t), then the query can be
represented by the graph:

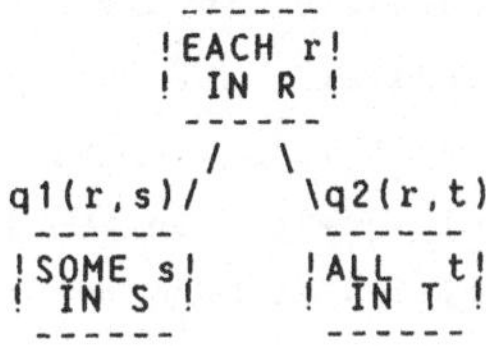

A Tree-Structured Query

and evaluated in a loop with a reduced nesting depth:

```
result := { };
FOR EACH r IN R:TRUE DO
  some-s := FALSE;
  FOR EACH s IN S:TRUE DO
    some-s := some-s OR q1(r,s);
    IF some-s THEN EXIT END
  END;
  all-t := TRUE;
  FOR EACH t IN T:TRUE DO
    all-t := all-t AND q2(r,t);
    IF NOT all-t THEN EXIT END
  END;
  IF some-s AND all-t THEN result :+ { r } END
END,
```

In this way, the upper bound of the number of element accesses has been reduced to
Card(R) + Card(R)*(Card(S)+Card(T)) as compared to Card(R) + Card(R)*Card(S) +
Card(R)*Card(S)*Card(T) in the completely nested loop.

5.2 Access Privilegation And Data Instantiation

The second category of optimization techniques exploits medium term
assumptions, which are often based on statistical information on data distribution
and data access. These assumptions lead to providing fast and selective access
paths such as direct access to single elements or subrelations via one- or
multidimensional indexes.

We can exploit our notion of a selector for a high level definition of access paths to relations. For example, an access path to those relation elements which have values, v1, v2,..., associated with attributes, a1, a2..., can be defined by:

```
SELECTOR sa (av1: atype1; av2: ...) FOR rel: Rtype;
BEGIN EACH r IN rel: <r.a1, r.a2,...> = <av1, av2,...> END sa;
```

which in turn abstracts from the specific implementation technique (ordering, hashing, indexing, grid files etc.) through which the support is actually provided.

The difference in access support for, say, arrays and relations is the degree of variability: array access usually involves one specific technique that is hard-wired into the compiler, for example, the use of dope vectors, while access to relations may be supported by several access paths that may vary over the lifetime of a relation and sometimes even disappear. In the latter case the value of the selected variable R [sa(v1,v2,..)] has to be computed by evaluating the equivalent query:

```
{EACH r IN R: <r.a1, r.a2,...> = <v1, v2,...>}.
```

Access paths select, in general, a superset of the result as specified by the query to be supported, for example, {EACH r IN R: p(r,...)}, and require, therefore, a further restriction:

```
result:= { }
FOR EACH r IN R [sp1(...)]: TRUE DO
   IF p2(r,...) THEN result: +{r} END
END;
```

In this case, the selection predicate, p(r,...), has been split into two components, p1(r,...) and p2(r,...), for which the equivalence p(r,...) = p1(r,...) AND p2(r,...) holds.

The third category of techniques for query optimization is based on characteristics determined by the actual data instances. Data instantiation defines database characteristics such as the cardinality of a relation, the selectivity of an attribute, and, of course, the existence or absence of elements matching a specific condition. These runtime characteristics determine, for example, the optimal execution sequence of loops on the same level, and decide whether - according to the principle of lazy evaluation - a loop has to be executed at all. (In one of our previous examples the loop for computing all-t had to be entered only if some-s was TRUE).

5.3 Robust Query Compilation

In general, however, data instantiation and - to a lesser extent - access privilegation are subject to change. Compile time decisions that exploit a specific access path or rely on statistical assumptions may become inadequate at query execution time. Recompilation becomes necessary, and together with the test on the validity of compile time assumptions, sometimes introduces a non-trivial overhead.

Therefore, the code to generate for query evaluation should be a mixture of both, operational terms (e.g., IF pi(r,...) THEN ... END) based on long term assumptions, and declarative terms (e.g., EACH r IN ...: pj(r,...)) coping with short term information available only at runtime. Reference to access paths leads to hybrid terms (e.g., R[spk(...)]) coping with medium term assumptions. When applied to the example of the previous section, this approach leads to the splitting of a predicate p2(r,...) into a component, p21(r,...), which is associated with decisions to be made at runtime, and p22(r,...), which represents compile time decisions according to long term assumptions. The conjunction of these components with the predicate, p1(r), from the hybrid term is equivalent to the original predicate, p(r,...):

```
result:= { };
FOR EACH r IN R[sp1]: p21(r,...) DO
    IF p22(r,...) THEN result: +{r} END
END;
```

This kind of code is robust in the sense that it remains valid under varying assumptions: it contains an operational skeleton only for the reliable compile time assumptions. Decisions based on data instantiation are left open for runtime interpretation by compiling them into the declarative selection phrase, EACH r IN...: p21(r,...), which is used for loop control. The code representing medium term assumptions can either be executed directly, leading to a privileged access if it exists, or it can be interpreted at runtime if the assumption does not hold. An extension of this approach to query compilation that is based on nested relational expressions is presented in [JaSc82], [JaKo83].

6.0 ON TRANSACTION MANAGEMENT

The notion of transaction as introduced above does not provide any primitives for the explicit synchronization of database programs [Gray81]; instead, these programs are synchronized implicitly by guaranteeing the effect of a serial execution of their transactions.

Based on the semantics of transaction, T, defined by:

$$\{ P \wedge ((R = Rv) \wedge \dots)\} \quad T \quad \{Q\} \vee \{((R = Rv) \wedge \dots) \}$$

we can discuss, however, principles of transaction execution models that do better than strict serialization.

6.1 Independence Of Transactions

Regardless of the specific statement sequences, S^i, S^j, two transactions, T^i, T^j, are based on, they can be executed concurrently if they are independent of each other in the sense that they cannot affect each others preconditions. Two transactions are clearly independent if they refer to different relation variables (or if access to common relations is read-only). Note, however, that the variables, R, ..., imported by a transaction are not always entire relations but are frequently sets of relation elements as, for example, given by selected relation variables, R[sp], ... For two selected relations, R[spi], R[spj], to be different means that they have no elements in common. Since relation elements are selected conditionally, the independence of transactions is by nature conditional, too.

For example, take the transaction definition

```
TRANSACTION T (kf : k1type);
IMPORT VAR R[kf];
BEGIN
   ...
   R[kf] := ...;
   ...
END;
```

The two transactions, T(kv11) and T(kv12), are independent if and only if kv11 $\neq$ kv12.

```
            |  k1  |        |  k2  |
  R  ------ |----- |------- |----- |------
     !
   --!----- |----- |------- |----- |------ !--  R[kv11]
   ! !      | kv11 |        |      |        ! !    imported
   ! !      | kv11 |        |      |        ! !    by T(kv11)
   --!----- |----- |------- |----- |------ !--
     !
   --!----- |----- |------- |----- |------ !--  R[kv12]
   ! !      | kv12 |        |      |        ! !    imported
   ! !      | kv12 |        |      |        ! !    by T(kv12)
   --!----- |----- |------- |----- |------ !--
     !
          ------- |----- |------- |----- |-------
```

Independent Transactions T(kv11) and T(kv12)

The various approaches to transaction scheduling differ by the 'how and when' the condition of independence is examined.

6.2 A-priori Enforcement Of Independence

A-priori scheduling strategies proceed with the execution of a transaction only as long as it is independent of other active transactions. Some strategies test and maintain independence by marking the individual relation elements accessed by a transaction; these strategies are often called "physical locking". Other approaches work on the level of selected relation variables and test independence of transactions by proving that selection predicates contradict each other; these strategies are called "predicate locking".

There is an inherit problem with physical locking called 'the phantom problem'. Phantoms may arise when a transaction, T1, evaluates a query, { EACH r IN R: p(r) } and draws conclusion from the assumption that it accessed all the elements of R fulfilling p. By just locking the n selected elements, T1 cannot exclude another transaction, T2, from inserting additional elements that also fulfil p. Thus, T2 may falsify T1's assumptions and, therefore, its conclusions. Predicate locking excludes phantoms [EGLT76].

A-priori scheduling strategies can be refined by teaching a compiler to use different lock modes and to time a lock application appropriately. Because of the disjunctive postconditions of transactions it is not wise, however, to unlock and reuse a relation as soon as it is no longer needed. In the event of failure a relation may, nevertheless, change its value and enforce cascading recovery actions.

6.3 <u>A-posteriori Validation Of Independence</u>

A-priori strategies expend a great deal of effort in lock management because they act under the pessimistic assumption that transactions are always in competition with others for the same data.   The opposite approach starts a transaction execution under the optimistic assumption that a transaction is independent of its competitors [KuRo81]. This assumption, however, needs to be validated.   A-posteriori strategies validate a transaction's independence after all its statements have been executed and before its results are made public.

If the assumption of independence holds, the computed results fulfil the intended postcondition, Q, and are entered into the database; if not, recovery is enforced leading to postcondition, $((R = Rv) \wedge \ldots)$, that enables a restart.

A-posteriori validation of T^i's independence with respect to transaction T^j amounts to demonstrating that T^i's precondition has not been changed by T^j. Provided Ti's variables, R^i, $\ldots$, are given by selected variables, R[spi], $\ldots$, it can be shown that T^i is independent of T^j if, for each variable, R[spi], $\ldots$, the predicate SOME r IN ΔR^j (pi(r)) becomes false; ΔR^j is the set of relation elements changed by T^j [Reim83], [BrRe83].

As with a-priori scheduling, a-posteriori strategies can also be improved by considering time and mode of data access.

Let us conclude with the remarks that since query optimization requires maintenance and evaluation of sets of interrelated data, and transaction handling results in predicate evaluation, implementors of database systems regard their task as being itself a Database Problem.

7.0 <u>CONCLUSION</u>

Relations are in the process of being accepted as a data structure adequate for a wide variety of applications. Earlier limitations, resulting primarily from insufficient implementations have been overcome.

The gain in programming productivity [Codd82] due to high level operators on relations and to additional services like recovery and concurrency management provided by relational systems, makes the relational approach attractive for many new applications. Examples are graphics, design applications and text processing [Lori81], [HaLo82], [ScPi82], [LaSc83], or program development systems [CeCr83]. Additional attractive features result from the fact that relations provide a sound basis for developing high level end user interfaces [Zloo77] up to the level of natural language [MaNe83].

These new applications stimulate, in return, extensions to the relational approach. To me the most promising ones are those that remove current restrictions imposed on relations, in particular limitations with respect to orthogonality between relations and other data structures, while trying to maintain the simplicity and the firm theoretical basis of the relational model.

Personally, I view the most serious practical problems that limit the use of the relational approach resulting from the inadequate design of most relational languages. This is due in art to the fact that only recently people from both camps, databases and programming languages, have developed a closer contact [BrZi81], [BrMS84]. A specific problem in this realm lies in the narrowness of interfaces between programming languages and database systems: it is not clear how programmers using the cleverly designed *New Languages* - or our old ones - can benefit from all the above advantages of relational systems by simply using external procedures and module libraries.

<u>Acknowledgement:</u>

I would like to thank the Computer Science Departement of Hamburg University for its continuous support during the past years, the Data Base Group, and in particular Jürgen Koch, Manuel Mall and Manuel Reimer.

8.0 <u>REFERENCES</u>

[AhSU79]   Aho,A.V., Sagiv,Y., Ullman,J.D.: Efficient Optimization of a
           Class of Relational Expressions. ACM TODS, Vol.4, No.4,
           December 1979.

[AtCC81]   Atkinson,M.P., Chrisholm,K, Cockshott,P.: The New Edinburgh
           Persistent Algorithmic Language. University of Edinburgh,
           Department of Computer Science, CSR-90-81, August 1981.

[BeCh81]   Bernstein,P.A., Chin,D.M.: Using Semi-Joins to Solve Relational
           Queries. J. ACM Vol.28, No.1, January 1981.

[BrMS84]   Brodie,M.L., Mylopoulos,J., Schmidt,J.W. (Eds.): Proc. Symp.
            on Conceptual Modelling: Perspectives from Artificial Intelligence,
            Databases and Programming Languages. Intervale, New Hampshire,
            June 1982, Springer-Verlag, 1984.

[BrRe83]   Brägger,R.P., Reimer,M.: Predicative Scheduling: Integration
            of Locking and Optimistic Methods. ETH Zürich, Institut für
            Informatik, Report Nr. 53, July 1983.

[BrZi81]   Brodie,M.L., Zilles,S. (Eds.): Proc. Workshop on Data Abstraction,
            Databases and Conceptual Modelling. Pingree Park, Colorado,
            June 1980, ACM SIGART / SIGMOD / SIGPLAN, 1981.

[CeCr83]   Ceri,S., Crespi-Reghizzi,S.: Relational Data Bases in the
            Design of Program Construction Systems. ACM SIGPLAN Notices,
            Vol.18, No.11, November 1983.

[Codd70]   Codd,E.F.: A Relational Model of Data for Large Shared Data
            Banks. CACM Vol.13, No.6, June 1970.

[Codd71]   Codd,E.F.: Relational Completeness of Data Base Sublanguages.
            Courant Computer Science Symposia 6, Prentice-Hall, May 1971.

[Codd82]   Codd,E.F.: Relational Database: A Practical Foundation for
            Productivity. CACM Vol.25, No.2, February 1982.

[Codd83]   Codd,E.F.: "Foreword" of [ScBr83].

[EGLT76]   Eswaran,K.P., Gray,J.N., Lorie,R.A., Traiger,I.L.: The Notions
            of Consistency and Predicate Locks in a Database System.
            CACM, Vol. 19, No. 11, November 1976.

[Gray81]   Gray,J.N.: The Transaction Concept: Virtues and Limitations.
            Proc. 7th VLDB Conf., Cannes, September 1981.

[Grie81]   Gries,D.: The Science of Programming. Springer-Verlag, 1981.

[Hall76]   Hall,P.A.V.: Optimization of Single Expressions in a Relational
            Data Base System. IBM J. Res. Development Vol.20, No.3,
            March 1976.

[Hehn83]   Hehner,E.C.R.: The Logic of Programming.
            Prentice-Hall, to be published, 1983.

[HaLo82]   Haskin,R., Lorie,R.: On Extending the Function of a Relational
            Database System. Proc. ACM SIGMOD Conf., Orlando, June 1982.

[Hoar66]   Hoare,C.A.R.: Record Handling. In F. Genuys (Ed.):
            Programming Languages. Academic Press, 1968.

[Hoar69]   Hoare,C.A.R.: An Axiomatic Approach to Computer Programming.
            CACM Vol.12, No.10, October 1969.

[JaKo82]   Jarke,M., Koch,J.: A Survey of Query Optimization in Centralized
            Database Systems. Tech. Rep. CRIS 44 GBA 82-73, New York University,
            November 1982.

[JaKo83]   Jarke,M., Koch,J.: Range Nesting: A Fast Method to Evaluate
            Quantified Queries. Proc. ACM SIGMOD Conf. on Management of
            Data, San Jose, June 1983.

[JaSc82]   Jarke,M., Schmidt,J.W.: Query Processing Strategies in the
            Pascal/R Relational Database Management System.
            Proc. ACM SIGMOD Conf., Orlando, June 1982.

[King81]   King,J.J.: QUIST: A System for Semantic Query Optimization in
            Relational Data Bases. Proc. 7th VLDB Conf., Cannes,
            September 1981.

[KMPR83]   Koch,J., Mall,M., Putfarken,P., Reimer,M., Schmidt,J.W.,
            Zehnder,C.A.: Modula/R Report. Lilith Version, ETH Zürich,
            Institut für Informatik, Februar 1983.

[KoSc83]   Koch,J., Schmidt,J.W.: Robust Query Compilation.
            Universität Hamburg, Institut für Informatik, November 1983.

[KuRo81]   Kung,H.T., Robinson,J.T.: On Optimistic Methods for Concurrency
            Control. ACM TODS, Vol.6, No.2, June 1981.

[LaSc83]   Lamersdorf,W, Schmidt,J.W.: Rekursive Datenmodelle.
            Proc. GI-Fachgespräch 'Sprachen für Datenbanken'. Hamburg,
            Informatik-Fachberichte Nr.83, Springer-Verlag, Oktober 1983.

[Lori81]   Lorie,R.: Issues in Database for Design Applications.
            IBM Research Report RJ3176, San Jose, July 1981.

[MaNe83]   Marburger,H., Nebel,B.: Natürlichsprachlicher Datenbankzugang
            mit HAM-ANS: Syntaktische Korrespondenz, natürlichsprachliche
            Quantifizierung und semantisches Modell des Diskursbereiches.
            Proc. GI-Fachgespräch 'Sprachen für Datenbanken', Hamburg,
            Informatik-Fachberichte Nr. 83, Springer-Verlag, Oktober 1983.

[MyBW80]   Mylopoulos,J., Bernstein,P., Wong,H.K.T.: A Language Facility
            for Designing Interactive Database-Intensive Applications.
            ACM TODS, Vol.5, No.2, June 1980.

[Reim83]   Reimer,M.: Solving the Phantom Problem by Predicative Optimistic
            Concurrency Control. Proc. 9th VLDB Conf., Florence, October 1983.

[Reyn81]   Reynolds,J.C.: The Craft of Programming. Prentice-Hall, 1981.

[RRUZ83]   Rebsamen,J., Reimer,M., Ursprung,P., Zehnder,C.A.,Diener,A.:
            LIDAS - The Database System for the Personal Computer Lilith.
            Proc. INRIA Workshop on Relational DBMS Design, Implementation,
            and Use on Micro-Computers, Toulouse, February 1983.

[ScBr83]   Schmidt,J.W., Brodie,M.L.: Relational Database Systems: Analysis
            and Comparison. Springer-Verlag, 1983.

[Schm77]   Schmidt,J.W.: Some High Level Language Constructs for Data
            of Type Relation. ACM TODS, Vol.2, No.3, September 1977.

[ScMa80]   Schmidt,J.W., Mall,M.: Pascal/R Report. Universität Hamburg,
            Fachbereich Informatik, Report No.66, Januar 1980.

[ScMa83]   Schmidt,J.W., Mall,M.: Abstraction Mechanisms for Database
            Programming. Proc. ACM SIGPLAN Symp. on Programming Language
            Issues in Software Systems, ACM SIGPLAN Notices, Vol.18,
            No.6, June 1983.

[ScPi82]   Schek,H.J., Pister,P.: Data Structure for an Integrated Data
            Base Management and Information Retrieval System.
            Proc. VLDB Conf., Mexico City, September 1982.

[SmFL81]   Smith,J.M., Fox,S., Landers,T: Reference Manual for ADAPLEX.
            Computer Corporation of America, Cambridge, January 1981.

[SRMK83]   Schmidt,J.W., Reimer,M., Mall,M., Koch,J.: Report on the Data-
            base Programming Language DBPL (draft version). Universität
            Hamburg, Fachbereich Informatik, 1983.

[SRPM83]   Schmidt,J.W., Reimer,M., Putfarken,P., Mall,M. Koch,J., Jarke,M.:
            Research in Database Programming: Language Constructs and
            Execution Models. IEEE Database Engineering 6, June 1983.

[Ston75]   Stonebraker,M.: Implementation of Integrity Constraints and
            Views by Query Modification. Proc. ACM SIGMOD Conf.,
            San Jose, May 1975.

[Wass79]   Wasserman,A.I.: The Data Management Facilities of PLAIN.
            Proc. ACM SIGMOD Conf., Boston, May 1979.

[Wirt82]   Wirth,N.: Programming in Modula/2. Springer-Verlag, 1982.

[Zloo77]   Zloof,M.: Query by Example: A Data Base Query Language.
            IBM Systems Journal, 4, 1977.

Programmverifikation in lauffähigen PASCAL-Programmen

Bernhard Hohlfeld

AEG-Telefunken
Forschungsinstitut Ulm

Zusammenfassung

Wir haben eine Sprache PASQUALE-L entworfen, mit der einige neuere Konzepte aus der theoretischen Informatik wie Programmverifikation und abstrakte Datentypen für lauffähige PASCAL-Programme verfügbar gemacht werden . Die Sprache ist in ein Verifikationssystem PASQUALE eingebettet, dessen Verification Condition Generator ·eine Implementierung der axiomatischen Definition von PASCAL ist. Die dort angegebene Verifikationsregel für Prozedur-Aufrufe wird mit Hilfe einer Transformationsregel realisiert.

PASQUALE-L erweitert PASCAL um ein Modulkonzept und um Sprachkonstrukte zur formalen Spezifikation von Programmen und Modulen. Ein PASQUALE-Modul besteht aus Funktionen und Prozeduren sowie internen Daten und ist auf der VAX unter VMS unabhängig übersetzbar . PASQUALE-L erlaubt so die Implementierung von abstrakten Datentypen in Modulen, die zu lauffähigen Programmen gebunden werden können.

1. Einleitung

Software wird zunehmend auch in sicherheitsempfindlichen Bereichen eingesetzt. Beispielsweise werden geheime Daten von Programmen verarbeitet oder persönliche Daten müssen vor unberechtigtem Zugriff geschützt werden, etwa um die Anforderungen des Bundesdatenschutzgesetzes zu erfüllen. Diesem Sicherheitsaspekt des Datenschutzes im weitesten Sinne, der dem administrativen Bereich zuzuordnen ist , stehen im technischen Bereich Sicherheitsanforderungen an programmgesteuerte Systeme gegenüber. Erinnert sei an Programme zur Steuerung von Kraftwerken und gefährlichen chemischen Prozessen sowie an Verkehrsleitsysteme und die Automatisierung von Bahn-Stellwerken. Fehler in dort eingesetzten Programmen können zur direkten physischen Gefährdung von Menschen führen , wie ein Programmfehler, der zwei Zügen gleichzeitig 'grünes Licht' für die Zufahrt auf eine Weiche gibt.

Der Einsatz von Software in sicherheitsempfindlichen Bereichen führt so zu hohen Qualitätsanforderungen an die verwendeten Programme : Die Programme sollen möglichst fehlerfrei sein; Fehler, die zur Verletzung von Sicherheitsanforderungen führen , dürfen unter keinen Umständen auftreten , selbst nicht um den Preis hoher Kosten für die Programmerstellung . Die an sich selbstverständliche Forderung nach Fehlerfreiheit ist bei Programmsystemen zur Steuerung von Prozessen (mehrere zehntausend oder gar hunderttausend Quellzeilen , geschrieben von mehreren Programmierern) gar nicht mehr so selbstverständlich zu erfüllen.

Die Qualität eines Programms hängt , neben dem Können des Programmierers , von den verwendeten Hilfsmitteln ab, und damit in erster Linie von der Programmiersprache, in der das Programm codiert ist. Neuere Programmiersprachen wie PASCAL /9/ bieten Möglichkeiten zur Strukturierung von Programm und Daten . Damit werden Programme übersichtlich und lesbar , der Entwurf von korrekten Programmen wird erleichtert, Fehler in inkorrekten Programmen werden schneller gefunden.

In diesem Beitrag wird ein System zur Programmverifikation vorgestellt, ein System also, das gestattet, mit formalen Methoden die Korrektheit eines Programmes nachzuweisen . Unter 'Korrektheit eines Programmes' verstehen wir die Erfüllung von Anforderungen (Spezifikationen) an das Programm durch das Programm, wir sprechen auch von 'Korrektheit eines Programmes bezüglich seiner Spezifikation' . Die Anwendung von formalen Methoden der Programmverifikation setzt die Formalisierung der Spezifikation des zu verifizierenden Programms in der Sprache der Logik, genauer der Prädikatenlogik erster Ordnung, voraus. Dazu ausgehend von Bild 1 ein kleines Beispiel . (Alle Abbildungen befinden sich am Ende des Beitrages.)

Das Bild zeigt eine Bahnanlage mit einer Weiche und drei Signalen . Auf die Weiche fährt von links ein Zug zu und soll über Strecke 1 oder Strecke 2 weitergeleitet werden , falls eine der beiden Strecken frei ist . Ist keine Strecke frei, soll der Zug an Signal 3 halten.

An die Steuerung von Weiche und Signalen ist folgende Sicherheitsanforderung gestellt : Die Stellung von Weiche und Signalen soll nach Ablauf des Steuerprogrammes stets so sein , dass keine Flankenfahrten möglich sind, d.h. wird der von links kommende Zug über die Weiche auf Strecke 1 weitergeleitet, darf kein anderer Zug auf Strecke 2 in die Weiche hineinfahren. Entsprechendes soll gelten, wenn der Zug über Strecke 2 weitergeleitet wird. Diese Sicherheitsanforderung formulieren wir präziser als 'Ist die Weiche auf Gerade gestellt , soll Signal 2 Rot zeigen, ist die Weiche auf Kurve , dann soll Signal 1 Rot zeigen. ' oder, in der Sprache der Logik :

```
((WEICHE = GERADE) impl (SIGNAL2 = ROT))
        and
((WEICHE = KURVE) impl (SIGNAL1 = ROT)) .
```

2. Programmverifikation mit dem PASQUALE-System

Systeme zur formalen Verifikation von PASCAL-Programmen wie der Stanford PASCAL Verifier /10/ basieren meist auf der Hoareschen Programmlogik /4/ und ihrer Anwendung auf die Programmiersprache PASCAL in /5/.

In der Axiomatischen Definition von PASCAL /5/ wird die Semantik (Bedeutung, Wirkung) der PASCAL-Anweisungen durch Verifikationsregeln formal definiert. Die Verifikationsregeln beschreiben die Wirkung einer Anweisung mit Hilfe des Programmzustands vor und nach Ausführung dieser Anweisung.

Die Aussage 'Ist die Vorbedingung P vor Ausführung der Anweisung S wahr, so ist die Nachbedingung Q nach Ausführung von S wahr, falls S terminiert.' wird kurz notiert als $P \{ S \} Q$.

Die Semantik der Wertzuweisung beschreibt das 'axiom of assignment' /4/ :

$$Q \, {}^{Y}_{X} \, \{ Y := X \} \, Q$$

Die Vorbedingung erhält man aus der Nachbedingung Q, indem man Y durch X ersetzt.

Die Verifikationsregel für die If-Anweisung if B then S1 else S2 lautet :

$$\frac{P1 \{ S1 \} Q , \quad P2 \{ S2 \} Q}{(B \text{ impl } P1) \text{ and } (\text{not } B \text{ impl } P2) \{ \text{ if } B \text{ then } S1 \text{ else } S2 \} Q} .$$

Aus den beiden Voraussetzungen $P1 \{ S1 \} Q$ und $P2 \{ S2 \} Q$ folgt : Gilt vor der If-Anweisung die Vorbedingung (B impl P1) and (not B impl P2) , so gilt nach der If-Anweisung die Nachbedingung Q.

Mit diesen beiden Regeln verifizieren wir das folgende Beispiel :

    true { if X >= 0 then Y := X else Y := -X } Y >= 0 ,

das heisst, bei beliebiger Vorbedingung gilt nach der If-Anweisung die Nachbedingung Y >= 0. Die Verifikationsregeln (mit B --> X >= 0, P1 --> X >= 0, P2 --> -X >= 0) besagen nun, dass diese Aussage genau dann wahr ist, wenn das folgende Korrektheitskriterium erfüllt ist :

    ((X >= 0) impl (X >= 0)) and (not(X >= 0) impl (-X >= 0)).

Der Beweis dieser sogenannten Verifikationsbedingung ist einfach, es werden nur elementare Regeln aus der Arithmetik und der Aussagenlogik benötigt. Allgemein werden mit Hilfe der Verifikationsregeln Aussagen über Programme auf mathematische Sätze (Verifikationsbedingungen) zurückgeführt . Die Aussagen über die Programme sind genau dann wahr, wenn die Verifikationsbedingungen wahr sind.

Sowohl die Erzeugung von Verifikationsbedingungen durch Anwendung von Verifikationsregeln als auch ihr Beweis erfordern schon bei relativ kurzen Programmen eine Vielzahl von im Einzelnen trivialen Schritten , eine Tätigkeit also, die der Mensch besser dem Computer überlässt.

Das PASQUALE-System (PAScal for QUALity softwarE) mit der Sprache PASQUALE-L ermöglicht Programmverifikation für lauffähige PASCAL-Programme (Bild 2). Die Sprache PASQUALE-L ist einerseits eine Untermenge von PASCAL, Programme in PASQUALE-L sind korrekte , lauffähige PASCAL-Programme . Andererseits umfasst PASQUALE-L Sprachelemente zur formalen Spezifikation von Programmen und ein Modulkonzept (vgl. Abschnitt 4). Die zusätzlichen Sprachelemente stehen als Formalkommentare in (*# Klammern #*) und werden von einem normalen PASCAL-Compiler überlesen. Der Vorübersetzer des PASQUALE-Systems überprüft dagegen die PASQUALE-L-Quellen , also PASCAL-Programm und formale Spezifikation, syntaktisch und semantisch, auch die gegenüber PASCAL zusätzlichen Sprachelemente, und baut eine baumförmige zwischensprachliche Darstellung (PASQUALE-Z) der Quelle auf. Der VCGEN (Verification Condition GENerator, /8/) ist eine Implementierung der axiomatischen Definition von PASCAL /5/ , er erzeugt durch Anwendung der Verifikationsregeln aus der zwischensprachlichen Darstellung die Verifikationsbedingungen.

Für die Wahl von PASCAL als Ausgangssprache gab es mehrere Gründe. Einmal bietet PASCAL schon eine Reihe von Strukturierungsmöglichkeiten wie Prozeduren und Funktionen sowie vom Programmierer aus Grundtypen selber definierbare Datentypen . Zum zweiten ist PASCAL zwar in der Anwendung noch nicht so verbreitet wie etwa FORTRAN , aber es ist Standardlehrsprache an Universitäten und Fachhochschulen und auf vielen Rechnern verfügbar . Die wachsende Bedeutung von PASCAL wird durch zwei neue Sprachentwicklungen unterstrichen : Die Programmiersprache Ada /1/ , auf eine Ausschreibung des US-Verteidigungsministeriums hin entworfen, und die Roboterprogrammiersprache SRL /13/ , entwickelt an der Universität Karlsruhe, basieren auf PASCAL.

PASQUALE-L umfasst, bis auf 'goto' und 'with', alle PASCAL-Anweisungen. Für die beiden weggelassenen Anweisungen gibt es keine Verifikationsregel , die ohne Einschränkung gültig ist . Durch das Verbot von 'goto' und 'with' wird PASCAL aber nicht wesentlich eingeschränkt . Durch Verzicht auf die with-Anweisung ändern sich PASCAL-Programme lediglich syntaktisch . Die Kontrollstrukturen von PASCAL (if .. then .. else , case , while , repeat) sowie Rekursion machen Sprunganweisungen, die in FORTRAN nötig sind, in vielen Fällen überflüssig. Das PASQUALE-System , selbst in PASCAL geschrieben, enthält bei 17.000 Quellzeilen Code eine einzige Sprunganweisung (vgl. Abschnitt 5). Sie wird ausgeführt, wenn im Eingabeprogramm eine Schranke für die Fehlerzahl überschritten ist.

Zurück zu unserem Beispiel (Bild 1) und seiner Bearbeitung mit dem PASQUALE-
-System . Die Steuerung von Weiche und Signalen erfolge durch ein PASCAL-Programm. Bei Aufruf des Programms sei bekannt, ob die beiden Strecken frei sind.
Das Programm soll aufgrund dieser Informationen bestimmen, wie Weiche und Signale für einen von links kommenden Zug gestellt werden.

Das kann etwa nach folgendem Algorithmus geschehen . Ist mindestens eine der
beiden Strecken frei, so wird zunächst geprüft, ob Strecke 1 frei ist. Ist das
der Fall , wird Signal 2 auf Rot gestellt , die Weiche auf Gerade und Signal 3
auf Grün . Wenn nicht, ist Strecke 2 frei : Signal 1 auf Rot, Weiche auf Kurve,
Signal 3 auf Grün. Ist keine der beiden Strecken frei, werden alle drei Signale
auf Rot gestellt . Dieser Algorithmus lässt sich direkt in ein PASCAL-Programm
umsetzten :

```
    program BAHN ;
    type W = ( GERADE, KURVE ) ;
        STRECKE = ( FREI, BELEGT ) ;
        SIGNAL = ( ROT, GRUEN ) ;
    var  WEICHE : W ;
        STRECKE1, STRECKE2 : STRECKE ;
        SIGNAL1, SIGNAL2, SIGNAL3  : SIGNAL ;
    (*# exit   ( ( WEICHE = GERADE ) impl ( SIGNAL2 = ROT ) )
                and
              ( ( WEICHE = KURVE ) impl ( SIGNAL1 = ROT ) )   #*)
    begin
    if ( STRECKE1 = FREI ) or ( STRECKE2 = FREI )
    then
        begin
        if STRECKE1 = FREI
        then
            begin SIGNAL2 := ROT ; WEICHE := GERADE ; SIGNAL3 := GRUEN end
        else
            begin SIGNAL1 := ROT ; WEICHE := KURVE ; SIGNAL3 := GRUEN end
    else
        begin SIGNAL1 := ROT ; SIGNAL2 := ROT ; SIGNAL3 := ROT end
    end .
```

Wie in Abschnitt 1 ausgeführt, soll nach Ablauf dieses Programms die Sicherheitsanforderung 'keine Flankenfahrten' gelten . Nach der PASQUALE-L-Syntax ist
der Zustand nach Ablauf eines Programms mit dem Schlüsselwort exit formal zu
spezifizieren . Die Spezifikation hat , als (*# Formalkommentar #*) , zwischen
Deklarationsteil und Anweisungsteil zu stehen.

Das obige annotierte, d.h. mit Formalkommentaren versehene, PASCAL-Programm ist
die Eingabe an das PASQUALE-System. Nach lexikalischer und syntaktischer Analyse und Übersetzung der Quelle in den Zwischensprachenbaum PASQUALE-Z erfolgt
als Ausgabe eine Auflistung der Quelle, ggf. mit Fehlermeldungen . Syntaktisch
korrekte Programme werden an den Verification Condition Generator des Systems
übergeben. In unserem Beispiel wird durch Anwendung der Verifikationsregeln die
folgende Verifikationsbedingung erzeugt und nach Rückübersetzung in Text ebenfalls ausgegeben :

```
(((STRECKE1 = FREI) or (STRECKE2 = FREI))
 impl (STRECKE1 = FREI
        impl (GERADE = GERADE impl (ROT = ROT))
            and (GERADE = KURVE impl (SIGNAL1 = ROT))
       )
      and (not(STRECKE1 = FREI)
            impl (KURVE = GERADE impl (SIGNAL2 = ROT))
                and (KURVE = KURVE impl (ROT = ROT))
           )
  )
 and (not((STRECKE1 = FREI) or (STRECKE2 = FREI))
       impl (WEICHE = GERADE impl (ROT = ROT))
           and (WEICHE = KURVE impl (ROT = ROT))
     )
```

Trotz der Länge der Verifikationsbedingung werden zum Beweis nur wenige Regeln
aus der Aussagenlogik benötigt. Die Regeln sind alle im Modul SIMPLIF (einfacher automatischer Beweiser) des PASQUALE-Sytems implementiert, so dass wir
als letzte Ausgabe 'true' (wahr) erhalten, d. h. die Verifikationsbedingung
ist bewiesen . Damit gilt nach der axiomatischen Definition von PASCAL /5/ :
Das Steuerprogramm genügt der Sicherheitsanforderung 'keine Flankenfahrten'.

3. Spezifikation und Verifikation von Prozeduren

In PASQUALE ist die Unterscheidung zwischen Funktionen (zur Berechnung von
Werten) und Prozeduren (zur Änderung von Zuständen) wesentlich strenger als
in PASCAL.

PASQUALE - Funktionen verhalten sich wie mathematische Abbildungen, sie berech-
nen Werte in Abhängigkeit von explizit in der Parameterliste angegebenen Parametern , die Verwendung von Globalvariablen als implizite Parameter ist nicht
erlaubt . Der Funktionswert ist die einzige Ausgangsgrösse , Änderungen von
Variablenparametern und Globalvariablen (Nebenwirkungen des Funktionsaufrufs)
sind nicht gestattet.

Prozeduren verändern Zustände , indem sie Variablenparametern und Globalvariablen (implizite Variablenparameter) neue Werte zuweisen . Prozeduren dürfen
also Nebenwirkungen haben, ebenso sind implizite Parameter erlaubt . Sowohl Nebenwirkungen als auch implizite Parameter müssen aber spezifiziert werden.   ·

Zur Spezifikation und Verifikation von Prozeduren folgen wir einem Ansatz von
Hoare und Wirth /5/, den wir mit Hilfe einer Transformationsregel nach /3/ realisieren.

In der axiomatischen Definition von PASCAL /5/ wird die durch einen Prozeduraufruf bewirkte Zustandsänderung mit Hilfe einer Funktion beschrieben und mit
dem folgenden Beispiel erläutert.

```
procedure P ( var A : integer ; B : integer ) ;
begin
B := 2 * B ;
if A >= B then A := B
end ;
```

Die Prozedur P verändert ihren Variablen-Parameter A in Abhängigkeit der Werte
von A und dem Wertparameter B bei Prozeduraufruf, P wirkt also wie die Wertzuweisung A := F(A, B) mit zunächst nicht bekannter Funktion F. Einem Aufruf von P mit den Aktualparametern X und Y entspricht dann die Wertzuweisung
X := F(X, Y) . Hierfür ist die Verifikationsregel bekannt , das Hoaresche
'axiom of assignment' :

$$R \, ^{X}_{F(X,Y)} \, \{ \, P(\, X, \, Y \,) \, \} \, R$$

Jedes freie Auftreten von X in der Nachbedingung R wird durch F(X,Y) ersetzt.

Wir sehen an dem Beispiel die beiden Wirkungen eines Prozeduraufrufs, nämlich
Berechnung eines Wertes, der von Parametern abhängt, genauer den Werten der Parameter X und Y bei Prozeduraufruf, und Zuweisung dieses Wertes an die Variable
X, die dem formalen Variablenparameter A entspricht. In PASQUALE wird das , in
einer PASCAL-ähnlichen Syntax, formal spezifiziert als

```
sfunction F ( X, Y : integer ) : integer ;
procedure P ( var A : integer ; B : integer )
    actslike A := F( A, B ) ;
```

Durch Anwendung der Transformationsregel für Prozeduren (s.u.) entsteht aus
Spezifikation und Deklaration der Prozedur P automatisch

```
procedure P ( var A : integer ; B : integer ) ;
    sfunction F ( X, Y : integer ) : integer ;
    var A, B : integer ;
    begin
    (A, B) := (X, Y) ;
        begin
        B := 2 * B ;
        if A >= B then A := B
        end ;
     F(X,Y) := A
    end ;
begin A := F( A, B ) end ;
```

'Berechnung eines Wertes F(A, B)' und 'Zuweisung dieses Wertes an den Variablenparameter A' sind so sauber voneinander getrennt.

Im allgemeinen Fall (/3/, /6/) habe die Prozedur P einen Variablenparameter U
vom Typ T1 und einen Wertparameter V vom Typ T2 . Sie ändere ausserdem die Glo-
balvariable X vom Typ T3 (impliziter Variablenparameter) und benutze die Glo-
balvariable Y vom Typ T4 (impliziter Wertparameter). In PASQUALE wird das wie
folgt spezifiziert.

```
sfunction P ( UO : T1 ; VO : T2 ; XO : T3 ; YO : T4 )
   : record UO : T1 ; XO : T3 end ;
procedure P ( var U : T1 ; V : T2 )
   actslike ( U, X ) := P( U, V, X, Y ).( UO, XO ) ;
```

d.h. an U wird die Komponente P(U, V, X, Y).UO zugewiesen und an X die Komponente P(U, V, X, Y).XO .

Die Prozedur P mit Anweisungsteil S sei deklariert als

```
procedure P ( var U : T1 ; V : T2 ) ;
begin S end ;
```

und wird, in einer an PASCAL angelehnten Notation, transformiert zu

```
procedure P ( var U : T1 ; V : T2 ) ;
   sfunction P ( UO : T1 ; VO : T2 ; XO : T3 ; YO : T4 )
      : record UO : T1 ; XO : T3 end ;
   var U : T1 ; V : T2 ; X : T3 ; Y : T4 ;
   begin
   (U, V, X, Y) := (UO, VO, XO, YO) ;
   begin S end ;
   P(UO, VO, XO, YO).(UO, XO) := (U, X)
   end ;
begin ( U, X ) := P( U, V, X, Y ).( UO, XO ) end ;
```

Einem Prozedur-Aufruf P(I, K) entspricht dann die kollaterale Wertzuweisung

$$(I, X) := P(I, K, X, Y).(UO, XO) ,$$

womit wir bei gegebener Nachbedingung Q die folgende Verifikationsregel haben :

$$Q \, ^{(I, X)}_{P(I,K,X,Y).(UO,XO)} \quad \{ \ P(I, K) \ \} \ Q$$

Die Schreibweise bedeutet 'gleichzeitiges' Ersetzen von I durch die Komponente P(I ,K ,X ,Y).UO und von X durch P(I, K, X, Y).XO in der Nachbedingung Q . I und X dürfen dabei nicht dieselbe Variable bezeichnen.

Die Transformationsregel für Prozeduren und die Ersetzung von Prozeduraufrufen durch die entsprechende Wertzuweisung ist im Modul SYNTAX des PASQUALE-Systems implementiert. Beides erfolgt auf der Ebene der Zwischensprache PASQUALE-Z, so dass die Quelle unverändert und damit korrektes PASCAL bleibt.

Als Beispiel für die Spezifikation von Prozeduren und die Verifikation von Prozeduraufrufen betrachten wir zwei Prozeduren zum Multiplizieren und Invertieren von Matrizen :

```
sfunction MULT ( X, Y, Z : MATRIX ) : MATRIX ;
procedure MULT ( var A, B, R : MATRIX )
   actslike R := MULT( A, B, R ) ;
sfunction INVERT ( X, Y : MATRIX ) : MATRIX ;
procedure INVERT ( var A, R : MATRIX )
   actslike R := INVERT( A, R ) ;
```

Nach der Anweisungsfolge

```
INVERT( X, Y ) ; (* Y := INVERT( X, Y ) *)
MULT( X, Y, Z )  (* Z := MULT( X, Y, Z ) *)
```

soll die Nachbedingung Z = E   gelten , wobei E die Einheitsmatrix bezeichne.

Durch Anwendung der Verifikationsregeln erhalten wir die Verifikationsbedingung

$$MULT(X, INVERT(X, Y), Z) = E ,$$

oder, in der gewohnten Schreibweise , $X * X^{-1} = E$. Unter der Voraussetzung , dass die Prozeduren MULT und INVERT korrekt implementiert sind, ist die Verifikationsbedingung wahr.

4. Modulkonzept und abstrakte Datentypen

PASCAL nach /9/ kennt kein Modulkonzept, auch der Vorschlag für einen PASCAL-
-Standard /2/ sieht kein Modulkonzept vor. Das fehlende Modulkonzept war einer der Gründe für die Entwicklung der PASCAL-Nachfolger MODULA und MODULA-2 /12/.

Das Modulkonzept von VAX-PASCAL /11/ bietet eine Möglichkeit zur Aufteilung einer PASCAL-Quelle in ein Hauptprogramm und mehrere Module , die unabhängig übersetzbar sind. Hauptprogramm und Module müssen die gleichen externen Dateien deklarieren , die gleichen Konstanten und Typen definieren sowie die gleichen Variablen deklarieren . Um das zu gewährleisten , werden die Deklarationen und Definitionen in eine Deklarationsdatei geschrieben, die von den einzelnen Übersetzungseinheiten (Programm bzw. Modul) mit einem '%INCLUDE'-Kommando kopiert wird . Das Hauptprogramm (Schlüsselwort 'program') enthält einen Anweisungsteil, wie ein PASCAL-Programm nach /9/ , während in den Modulen (Schlüsselwort 'module') lediglich Funktionen und Prozeduren deklariert werden. Durch Binden des Hauptprogramms mit den Modulen entsteht lauffähiger Code.

Eine in einem Modul deklarierte Prozedur

```
      procedure P ( var X : T1 ; Y : T2 ) ;
          . . .
      begin . . . end ;
```
kann in jedem anderen Modul und im Hauptprogramm aufgerufen werden. Die Prozedur muss nur im dortigen Deklarationsteil als

```
      procedure P ( var X : T1 ; Y : T2 ) ; extern ;
```
deklariert werden.

Der VAX-PASCAL-Compiler (Version 1.x) prüft Aufrufe von P mit Aktualparametern auf Konsistenz mit dieser extern-Deklaration . Der Linker überprüft lediglich, ob der Name P in einem anderen Modul deklariert wurde . Die Konsistenz der Parameterlisten von Deklaration und extern-Deklaration wird nicht überprüft. Das Modulkonzept von VAX-PASCAL reduziert sich somit zu einer Möglichkeit zur unabhängigen Übersetzung von zu Modulen zusammengefassten Funktionen und Prozeduren.

PASQUALE benutzt dieses Modulkonzept lediglich zur physikalischen Aufteilung eines PASCAL-Programms nach /9/ in mehrere unabhängig übersetzbare Einheiten, die in verschiedenen Dateien abgelegt sind. Diese maschinenabhängige Bequemlichkeit ist uns aber nicht so wichtig wie die dadurch gebotene Möglichkeit zur Strukturierung von Programmen durch Modularisierung, d.h. durch Zusammenfassung von logisch zusammengehörenden Routinen zu Modulen. Das Modulkonzept von PASQUALE beinhaltet weit mehr als das Modulkonzept von VAX-PASCAL , nämlich Deklaration der Modulstruktur eines Programms durch Benutzungsrelationen, Überprüfung der Einhaltung dieser Modulstruktur , Spezifikation der Schnittstellen von Modulen, Führen einer Schnittstellenbibliothek sowie die Deklaration interner Daten von Modulen.

Wie in VAX-PASCAL erfolgt in PASQUALE die Deklaration bzw Definition von externen Dateien, Konstanten, Typen und Variablen in einer Deklarationsdatei, die sich die einzelnen Übersetzungseinheiten mit einem '%INCLUDE'-Kommando kopieren. In der Deklarationsdatei hat auch die Deklaration der Modulstruktur des Programms zu erfolgen . In der Modulstruktur wird angegeben, welche Module eine Übersetzungseinheit benutzt (Schlüsselwort 'use') und welche Funktionen und Prozeduren ein Modul in seiner Schnittstelle anderen Übersetzungseinheiten zur Verfügung stellt (Schlüsselwort 'export').

```
Beispiel :      (*# program P use M1, M2 ;
                    module M1 use M3 export F1, F2 ;
( Bild 3 )          module M2 export G1, G2, G3 ;
                    module M3 export H1 ;
                #*)
```

Im Beispiel benutzt ein Programm P die beiden Module M1 und M2, d.h. im Anweisungsteil von P durten die von M1 und M2 exportierten Funktionen und Prozeduren (F1, F2 bzw G1, G2, G3) aufgerufen werden . Ein Aufruf von H1 aus dem Modul M3 im Hauptprogramm P, der nach der deklarierten Modulstruktur nicht erlaubt ist, führt zu einer Fehlermeldung des PASQUALE-Vorübersetzers.

In einem PASCAL-Programm nach /9/ könnte das Beispiel so implementiert werden :

```
                program P ;
                  procedure F1 ;
                    function H1 ;
                    begin ... end ;
                  begin ... end ;
                  procedure F2 ;
                    function H1 ;
                    begin ... end ;
                  begin ... end ;
                  function G1 ;
                  begin ... end ;
                  function G2 ;
                  begin ... end ;
                  function G3 ;
                  begin ... end ;
                begin ... end .
```

Die oben durch die Benutzungsrelationen angegebene Struktur des Programms kann
nur noch bedingt überprüft werden. Eine Möglichkeit zur Abkapselung von H1 besteht darin, die Funktion sowohl in F1 als auch in F2 lokal zu deklarieren. Gegenseitige Aufrufe von F1 und F2 bzw G1, G2 und G3 lassen sich nur durch Pro-
grammierdisziplin verhindern.

Ein PASQUALE-Modul hat die Form

```
            module M
            %INCLUDE 'DECLPART. DCL'
            (*# Schnittstellenspezifikation ;
                Implementierungsspezifikation  #*)
            'Deklaration von Funktionen und Prozeduren'
            end .
```

Nach dem Schlüsselwort 'module' und dem Modulnamen wird die Deklarationsdatei
kopiert . Es folgt die zweistufige Modulspezifikation, nämlich Schnittstellenspezifikation und Implementierungsspezifikation.

In der Schnittstellenspezifikation werden zunächst die vom Modul exportierten
Funktionen und Prozeduren mit Parameterliste und ggf. Ergebnistyp aufgeführt.
Der PASQUALE-Vorübersetzer überprüft , ob genau die Funktionen und Prozeduren
angegeben sind , die laut Modulstruktur vom betreffenden Modul exportiert werden . Es folgt eine Beschreibung der einzelnen Routinen und ihres Zusammenwir-
kens in Form von Axiomen. Der gesamte Text der Schnittstellenspezifikation wird
vom Vorübersetzer in die Schnittstellenbibliothek kopiert.

In der Implementierungsspezifikation werden die einzelnen Routinen des Moduls
mit Eingangs- und Ausgangszusicherungen nach der Hoareschen Assertion-Technik
(/4/, /5/, /8/) spezifiziert.

Nach der Spezifikation des Moduls folgt die Deklaration seiner Routinen als
PASCAL - Funktionen und - Prozeduren gemäss /9/. Der PASQUALE-Vorübersetzer
prüft , ob Parameterlisten und Ergebnistyp der einzelnen Routinen mit der
Schnittstellenspezifikation übereinstimmen . Der Text des Moduls schliesst mit
'end . ' .

Ein PASQUALE - Modul kann zwei Arten von internen Daten haben :

```
            type R = record S : integer ; T : boolean end
                      (*# local to M #*) ;
                  A = array [ 1 .. 10 ] of integer
                      (*# private to M #*) ;
            var X : integer (*# local to M #*) ;
```

Wir unterscheiden zwischen lokalen Typen und Variablen eines Moduls und privaten Typen . Lokale Typen und Variable, gekennzeichnet durch 'local to M' , sind
nur in den Routinen des betreffenden Moduls sichtbar, von anderen Übersetzungs-

einheiten aus kann auf sie nicht zugegriffen werden. Bei privaten Typen ist der
Name allgemein bekannt, während die Struktur verborgen bleibt. Im Beispiel

```
        type A = array [ 1 .. 10 ] of integer
             (*# private to M #*) ;
```

kann nur von Routinen des Moduls M auf einzelne Komponenten von Variablen des
Typs A zugegriffen werden. In anderen Übersetzungseinheiten dürfen zwar Variable und Parameter des Typs A deklariert werden, ihre Bearbeitung ist aber nur
mit den vom Modul M exportierten Routinen möglich.

Textlich erfolgt die Deklaration von lokalen Typen und Variablen sowie privaten
Typen als Formalkommentar in der allen zusammengehörenden Übersetzungseinheiten
zugänglichen Deklarationsdatei . Der Vorübersetzer des PASQUALE-Systems überprüft jedoch die durch 'local' bzw. 'private' eingeschränkten Zugriffsrechte.

Die Absicht, einen Modul M zu benutzen, d.h. die von ihm exportierten Funktionen und Prozeduren aufzurufen, muss durch

```
             (*# use M ; #*)
```

angezeigt werden . Der Vorübersetzer prüft , ob die Benutzung von M nach der
Modulstruktur zulässig ist, und kopiert dann aus der Schnittstellenbibliothek
den Text der Schnittstellenspezifikation von M in die benutzende Übersetzungseinheit. Zusätzlich müssen die von M exportierten Funktionen und Prozeduren in
der aufrufenden Einheit als 'extern' deklariert werden . Das ist einmal nötig,
damit der PASQUALE-Modul ein übersetzbarer VAX-PASCAL-Modul bleibt, zum anderen
überprüft der Vorübersetzer die Konsistenz von Parameterlisten und ggf. Ergebnistyp zwischen der als extern deklarierten Routine und ihrer Spezifikation in
der Schnittstellenbibliothek . Da auch die Konsistenz zwischen Schnittstellenspezifikation und Deklaration im exportierenden Modul überprüft wird, ist gewährleistet, dass eine Routine im benutzenden Modul so aufgerufen wird, wie sie
im exportierenden Modul spezifiziert ist. Fehler, die sonst erst zur Laufzeit
auftreten, werden so bereits beim Übersetzen bemerkt.

Unter einem abstrakten Datentyp verstehen wir die Deklaration einer Datenstruktur zusammen mit ihren Bearbeitungsfunktionen als eine Einheit . Beispielsweise
kann eine Baumstruktur in PASCAL als array [1 .. MAX] of integer implementiert werden. Die einzelnen Komponenten des Feldes sind dann, je nach Stellung,
Schlüssel für die in der Wurzel des Baumes oder eines Unterbaumes abgelegte Information, Verweise auf Unterbäume oder bedeutungslos , dann nämlich, wenn zur
Darstellung des Baumes nicht das ganze Feld benötigt wird. Bearbeitungsfunktionen für eine Baumstruktur sind beispielsweise Funktionen, die den Schlüssel der
Wurzel eines Baumes oder den Zeiger auf einen bestimmten Unterbaum liefern.

Das PASQUALE-System erlaubt die Implementierung von abstrakten Datentypen in
Modulen /7/. Bei der Implementierung des abstrakten Datentyps 'Baum' in einem
Modul TREEMOD werden die Bearbeitungsfunktionen deklariert und in der Schnitt-
stelle des Moduls nach aussen zur Verfügung gestellt. Der Baum wird als

      type TREE = array [1 .. MAX] of integer (*# private to TREEMOD #*) ;

deklariert . Zugriffe auf den Baum sind dann nur noch mit den Bearbeitungsfunktionen aus TREEMOD möglich.

Die eingeschränkten Zugriffsrechte auf den Baum bringen zwei Vorteile . Einmal
wird Schreibarbeit gespart , wenn der Aufbau eines Unterbaums durch den Aufruf
einer Routine erfolgt, und nicht durch explizites Belegen von einzelnen Komponenten eines Feldes . Zum anderen bringt das explizite Belegen die Gefahr von
Fehlern mit sich, wobei die Schreibfehler eher harmlos sind . Viel gefährlicher
sind die Fehler, die durch die Ausnutzung der Darstellung des Baumes als Feld
entstehen können . Beispielsweise mag es aus der Sicht eines Bearbeiters vor-
teilhaft scheinen, einzelne, von ihm nicht benötigte Komponenten des Feldes zum
Abspeichern von irgendwelchen Zwischenwerten zu benutzen. Ein anderer Bearbeiter greift später auf den Baum zu und findet die von ihm benötigten Informationen überschrieben.

5. Das PASQUALE-System

Abschliessend wollen wir das Verifikationssystem PASQUALE kurz vorstellen. Das
System umfasst etwa 17.000 Quellzeilen PASCAL-Code und wurde von drei Personen
geschrieben . Bild 4 zeigt die Grundstruktur des Systems, die der eines Über-
setzers ähnelt.

PASQUALE-L-Programme werden im Modul LEXAN (Scanner) lexikalisch analysiert und
als Symbolstrom an den Modul SYNTAX (Parser) weitergegeben. SYNTAX führt syntaktische Analyse, Typprüfungen etc. durch und übersetzt den Symbolstrom in die
baumförmige Zwischensprache PASQUALE-Z. LEXAN und SYNTAX bilden zusammen den
Vorübersetzer des PASQUALE-Systems.

Das Hauptprogramm PSQMAIN übergibt die zwischensprachliche Darstellung an VCGEN
(Verification Condition GENerator), der mit Hilfe des Hoareschen Kalküls (/4/,
/5/, /8/) daraus Verifikationsbedingungen erzeugt. Die Verifikationsbedingungen sind in der Zwischensprache PASQUALE-Z dargestellt.

Im Modul SIMPLIF sind einige einfache Regeln zum automatischen Beweis von Verifikationsbedingungen implementiert (Aussagenlogik , Arithmetik , Information über die Datentypen von PASCAL). SIMPLIF arbeitet ebenfalls auf der Zwischensprache PASQUALE-Z.

Der Modul EDITOR übersetzt die Verifikationsbedingungen aus der Zwischensprache zurück in Text (PASCAL-Syntax) . PROTOKOLL stellt Routinen für Fehlermeldungen, Testausdrucke etc. zur Verfügung.

Die baumförmige Zwischensprache PASQUALE-Z ist als
```
        type PLEX = array [1 .. PLEXMAX] of integer
                    (*# private to PLEXHANDL #*) ;
```
realisiert. PLEX ist ein abstrakter Datentyp , dessen Bearbeitungsroutinen im Modul PLEXHANDL implementiert sind . Insgesamt vier Module (SYNTAX, VCGEN, SIMPLIF, EDITOR) benutzen und verändern dieselbe Variable vom Typ PLEX mit den Bearbeitungsroutinen aus PLEXHANDL.

Literaturverzeichnis

1. AdaTEC (Ed.): Reference Manual for the Ada Programming Language -Draft-. United States Department of Defense, July 1982
2. British Standards Institution : Specification for Computer Programming Language Pascal. BS 6192 : 1982
3. The CIP Language Group : Report on A Wide Spectrum Language for Program Specification and Development. Technische Universität München, Institut für Informatik. TUM-18104, May 1981
4. Hoare,C.A.R.: An Axiomatic Basis for Computer Programming. Communications of the ACM, Vol 12 No 10 (1969), 576 - 583
5. Hoare,C.A.R. and Wirth,N.: An Axiomatic Definition of the Programming Language PASCAL. acta informatica 2, 335 - 355 (1973)
6. Hohlfeld,B.: Zur Verifikation von Funktionen und Prozeduren in PASCAL. AEG-TELEFUNKEN, Forschungsinstitut Ulm, Technischer Bericht Nr. 12.010/82
7. Hohlfeld,B.: Implementierung von abstrakten Datentypen in PASCAL-Programmen. AEG-TELEFUNKEN, Forschungsinstitut Ulm, Technischer Bericht Nr. 12.026/83
8. Hohlfeld,B.: Verifikationsregeln für eine PASCAL-Untermenge mit Modulkonzept. AEG-TELEFUNKEN, Forschungsinstitut Ulm, Technischer Bericht Nr. 12.050/83
9. Jensen,K. and Wirth,N.: PASCAL: User manual and report. Springer, New York 1975
10. Stanford PASCAL Verifier - User Manual . Computer Science Departement Stanford University 1979
11. VAX-11 PASCAL V1.2 : Language Reference Manual . digital equipment corporation, Maynard, Massachusetts 1979
12. Wirth,N.: Programming in MODULA-2. Springer-Verlag, Berlin 1982
13. Wolter (ed) : Höhere Programmiersprachen für Industrieroboter. Kernforschungszentrum Karlsruhe, KFK - PFT 51

Abbildungen

Bild 1   Sicherheitsanforderung für ein Steuerprogramm : Keine Flankenfahrten

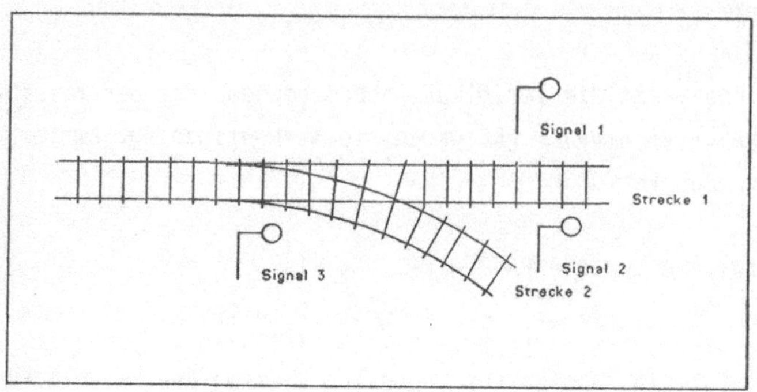

Bild 2

Bild 3

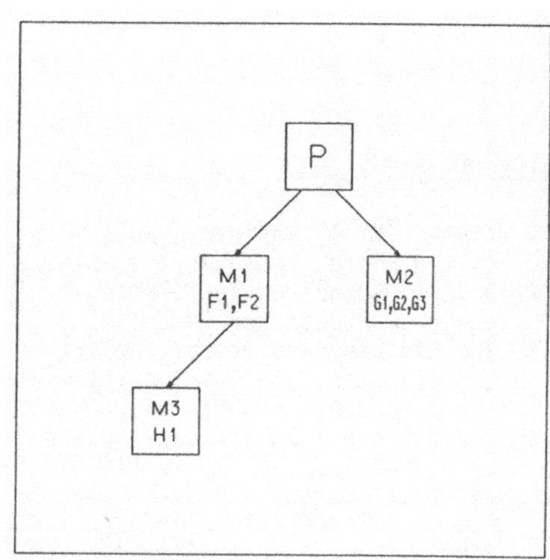

Bild 4   Verifikationssystem PASQUALE

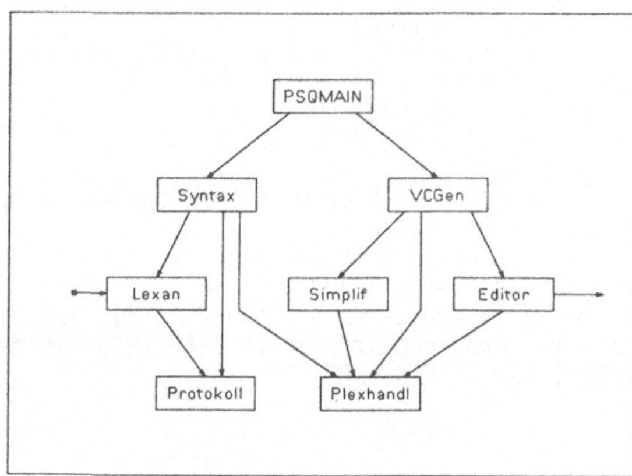

Transformational Derivation of Parsing Algorithms Executable on Parallel Architectures[1]

H.Partsch

Institut für Informatik
Technische Universität München

Abstract

Comparatively few work has been published on how to construct correct parsing algorithms that are profitably executable on parallel architectures. We advocate transformational programming as a suitable methodology for the derivation of such "parallel algorithms" and illustrate our ideas by means of a comprehensive case study: Starting from a formal specification - actually the usual problem definition from Formal Language Theory - we derive by simple correctness-preserving transformations a version of the Cocke-Kasami-Younger parsing algorithm that is suited for execution on a vector machine.

1. Introduction

The idea of speeding up a computation by doing certain parts of it in parallel seems to be rather old - e.g. [Kuck et al. 72] even attribute it to Charles Babbage, 140 years ago. In the last decade, due to the advent of appropriate hardware, a vast amount of research in this area has been done (cf. [Andrews, Schneider 83] for an overview), quite a lot of it on the specific problem of how to construct appropriate software for these new architectures.

Apart from approaches aiming at parallel execution of sequential programs by providing supplementary information for the underlying operating system (cf. e.g. [Gonzalez, Ramamoorthy 72]), most of the work concentrated on detecting possibilities for parallel execution on the source level (and providing linguistic means to explicitly express it there). The investigations focussed on massaging arithmetic expressions (e.g. [Baer, Bovet 68], [Baer 73], or [Muller, Preparata 76]), on rearranging blocks of statements (cf. e.g. [Bernstein 66]), on restructuring loops (cf. [Lamport 74,75,79]), or also on several of these aspects (e.g. [Kuck et al. 72], [Kuck 75, 76]). Although most of this research was done for FORTRAN as source language, some

---

1) This research was carried out within the Sonderforschungsbereich 49, Programmiertechnik, Munich.

of the results actually are to some extent language independent and thus well-suited as a basis for further investigations with less restrictive source languages.

Parallel to these approaches which focussed on principles of parallel programming also a lot of work has been done that was oriented towards particular application software. However, comparatively few work has been published on the specific problem domain of parsing and compiling algorithms. The respective papers mainly dealt with lexical analysis ([Lincoln 7o], [Zosel 73], [Donegan, Katzke 75]), symbol table manipulation ([Ellis 71]), certain parts of parsing, e.g. parsing of arithmetic expressions and statements ([Zosel 73], [Ellis 71], [Fischer 80]), or code generation ([Krohn 75]). Measured with the yardstick of modern programming methodology, all these approaches appear rather ad hoc and some of them even unsystematic. A conceptually different approach can be found in [Baer, Ellis 77]. There, by modelling a classical sequential compiler by Extended Petri Nets, it was tried to extract the necessary information for restructuring the petri net in order to allow parallel execution. Although the general idea there looks somewhat more systematic the technical treatment itself leaves a lot of open questions. What is most striking, however, is the fact that nearly none of the results of the above-mentioned principal investigations had any impact on the particular problem of parallel parsing and compiling.

Parallel in time but conceptually rather independent of this research on parallel programming, a lot of work on programming methodology - aiming at mastering the complexity of software - has been done (for accounts on the state of the art see e.g. [Gries 78], [Bauer, Broy 79]). In particular, transformational programming, i.e. program development by transformations, became a steadily growing field of interest.

Program development by transformations (for an introduction see e.g. [Bauer, Wössner 82]) is the idea of developing from a formal specification by stepwisely applying correctness-preserving transformation rules programs that meet certain (a priori given) criteria (e.g. efficiency, certain basic instruction sets, available data structures, etc.). Although most of the work actually done focussed on sequential programs for the von Neumann-type architecture, it seems to be not only a straightforward logical consequence but also one of the great advantages of this approach to use the method of program transformations also for developing parallel programs (cf. e.g. [Loveman 76], [Pepper 81]), e.g. for array or vector machines.

In [Partsch 83a] we have demonstrated how to employ the idea of transformational programming in the development of classical sequential parsing and recognition algorithms, by deriving a whole family of individual algorithms from one formal specification. In the present paper we are going to focus on parallel parsing, i.e. on the problem of developing parsing algorithms suited for execution on parallel machines, by using the same basic ideas.

2. Developing parallel algorithms by transformations

There is an obvious way to combine ideas on transformational program development and approaches to parallel programs: A formal problem specification is first transformed into a (sequential) iterative solution (e.g. using the techniques described in [Bauer, Wössner 82]); then applying suitable transformations for parallelizing sequential programs (which simply can be obtained by adapting and extending some of the above-mentioned principal ideas, e.g. [Bernstein 66], [Kuck 75a,b], [Lamport 74,75,79]), will finally result in a parallel program. This is exactly the way how [Loveman 76] incorporated Lamport's ideas into a transformational environment.

However, a closer look at such a development will indicate that this way of proceeding is somewhat unnatural: Usually, a transformational derivation from a formal specification passes an applicative program as an intermediate version. Such an applicative program - apart from "natural sequentialization" (cf. [Bauer, Wössner 82]) resulting from function application - does not yet enforce any particular order of computation - in particular, if it is also non-deterministic. Strict sequentiality is but introduced by an unreflected transition to the imperative level (usually including removal of non-determinism). Thus, on the imperative level one is faced with the problem of partially re-eliminating (this just previously introduced) sequentiality by suitable transformations for parallelization.

In contrast to that we suggest a more straightforward way (that avoids this obvious detour). Its basic idea (cf. also [Pepper 82] is to maintain (as far as possible) parallel executability when removing non-determinism and/or switching from applicative to imperative formulations.

Another characteristic aspect of our proposal is that we do not presuppose a particular hardware or specific language constructs for expressing parallelism. Similarly to the ideas in [Lengauer 82], [Lengauer, Hehner 82] we favour viewing parallelism as an additional property of the execution of a program[2] , rather than a semantic property of the program itself. Within our transformational approach this means that the goal of our development is not a program containing particular constructs for expressing parallelism, but rather a conventional program that allows parallel execution. This view has the additional advantage that we do not need any new transformation rules[3] .

---

[2] In [Lengauer 82], [Lengauer, Hehner 82] these properties are expressed by assertions, reflecting the fact that they deal with imperative programs.

[3] These become only necessary, if a particular notation is aimed at.

3. Transformational development of a parallel parsing algorithm

We will demonstrate our ideas by developing a "parallel" version of the well-known Cocke-Kasami-Younger parsing algorithm (cf. [Aho, Ullman 72]), i.e. a version that is suited for execution on a vector machine. Since the development will be done by correctness-preserving transformations, the resulting program will be correct by construction.

Our final algorithm also will be new, since, to our knowledge, it has not yet been published elsewhere. Thus, as a by-product, our development will also contradict the wide-spread prejudice that transformational programming may help in understanding known algorithms, but does not support the invention of new algorithms.

The Cocke-Kasami-Younger algorithm, as does Earley's algorithm (cf. also [Aho, Ullman 72]), allows to recognize an arbitrary (even ambiguous) context-free grammar in cubic time. Its basic idea is to keep track of all possible derivations (ending in a given input string) by means of a suitably organized matrix. Unlike Earley's algorithm, though, its practical use is limited to specific applications. It is, however, conceptually significantly simpler than Earley's algorithm, and thus better suited for demonstration purposes. Note, though, that a transformational development of a parallel version of Earley's algorithm[4] could be done with exactly the same development strategy.

3.1. Preliminaries

In order to provide the reader with the necessary background to follow our derivation we first will introduce some notation[5].

As usual (cf. [Aho, Ullman 72]), a context-free grammar G=(V,T,S,P) consists of

- a (finite) set V of symbols (denoted by **char**)
- a set T⊆V of terminal symbols (denoted by **term**)
- a distinguished element ("axiom") S∈V\T, and
- a (finite) set P of pairs ("productions") p∈(V\T)xV* .

The set V\T of nonterminal symbols will be denoted by **nonterm**.

For arbitrary strings x,y∈V* we have the relation ("derivable in one step")

$$x \rightarrow_P y =_{def} \exists\ l,r \in V^*, (a,b) \in P: x=lar \wedge y=lbr\ .$$

To express the reflexive transitive closure of the $\rightarrow$ relation, we use the "top-down" variant (cf. [Partsch 83a])

$$x \rightarrow_P^* y =_{def} (x=y) \vee (x \rightarrow_P y) \vee (\exists\ z \in V^*: x \rightarrow_P z \wedge z \rightarrow_P^* y)\ .$$

---

[4] A transformational development of the (sequential) Earley algorithm can be found in [Partsch 83b]

[5] However in a slightly informal way in order not to deviate the reader's attention from our main concerns.

The elements of V* are considered as (indexed) <u>sequences</u> over V (for a formal definition compare the type FLEX in [Bauer, Wössner 82]), denoted by **sequ char.** For V* we assume the operations

<>	denoting the empty sequence
¦.¦	denoting the length of a sequence
&	denoting concatenation (& will be supressed, if there are no ambiguities)

Widening operations (converting characters into one-element sequences) are not explicitly denoted; thus & also captures the operations of attaching a single character to a sequence.

Based on the (hidden) partially defined operations
  <u>**top**</u> (<u>**bottom**</u>)   denoting the first (last) element
  <u>**rest**</u> (<u>**upper**</u>)   denoting the remainder after removing the first (last) element
we use furthermore indexing and trimming, defined by

$$\textbf{funct}(\textbf{sequ m } s, \textbf{nat } i: 1 \le i \le |s|)m \cdot [\cdot],$$
$$\textbf{funct}(\textbf{sequ m } s, \textbf{nat } n,m: 0 \le n \le m \le |s|)\textbf{sequ m } \cdot [\cdot \ldots \cdot]$$
$$\forall \ \textbf{sequ m } s,t, \ \textbf{nat } i,n,m: 1 \le i < |s| \ \wedge \ 0 \le n \le m \le |t|:$$
$$s[i] =_{def} \textbf{if } i=1 \textbf{ then } \underline{\textbf{top}} \text{ s } \textbf{else } (\underline{\textbf{rest}} \text{ s})[i-1]$$
$$t[n..m] =_{def} \textbf{if } m<|t| \textbf{ then } (\underline{\textbf{upper}} \text{ t})[n..m]$$
$$\textbf{elif } n>0 \textbf{ then } (\underline{\textbf{rest}} \text{ t})[n-1..m-1]$$
$$\textbf{else } t \qquad\qquad \textbf{fi } .$$

Defining the trimming operation in this particular way, has the technical advantage that the empty sequence is included without a more complicated domain restriction. Note also that this particular definition implies that
$$\forall \ \textbf{sequ m } t, \ \textbf{nat } n: 0 \le n < |t|: t[n..n+1] = t[n+1], \text{ and } a[n..n]=<>.$$

Further primitive data structures will be:

<u>Sets</u> with the usual operations such as

{}	set former (with or without restricting predicate)
∈	element relation
⊆	subset relation

and

<u>tuple structures</u> (e.g. pairs or four-tuples), with (..) for the tuple constructor and individual identifiers for the respective selectors.

All these data structures are assumed to be defined algebraically ("abstract data types")[6] such that the characteristic axioms as e.g.
$$\forall \ s,x: \textbf{top}(x \& s) = x$$
are available for program transformations. Furthermore it is assumed that these data types may appear hierarchically structured (cf. [Wirsing et al. 80]), e.g. pairs of sequences, etc.

For formulating programs we use the ALGOL-variant of CIP-L (cf. [Bauer et al. 81]) which should be self-explanatory. As additional abbreviations, $\wedge$ and $\vee$ for sequential conjunction and disjunction, resp., will be used.

As to the transformations, we assume the reader to be familiar with the basic rules

---

[6] In [Laut 81] it has been shown how to represent also productions and grammars as (monomorphic) abstract types.

given in [Burstall, Darlington 77]. In particular, "unfold", i.e. the replacement of a call by its appropriately substituted body, and "fold", the inverse of unfold, will be used without further explanation.

3.2. Formal specification

Our overall intention is to deal with the parsing problem for context-free grammars. Since, however, any solution to the (simpler) recognition problem can be extended[7] in a straightforward way to solve the parsing problem, too, we restrict ourselves to the former one.

Formally, the recognition problem is specified by

$$\textbf{funct } RP \equiv (\textbf{sequ term } w)\textbf{bool}: S \xrightarrow{*}_{P} w \ .$$

Strictly speaking, the context-free grammar $G=(V,T,S,P)$ is a further parameter. However, since it is a constant parameter, it is not explicitly listed.

The particular algorithm we are aiming at additionally expects a grammar in Chomsky Normal Form[8] :

A grammar is said to be in <u>Chomsky Normal Form</u>, iff every $p \epsilon P$ is of one of the forms
(a) (A,BC) $A,B,C \epsilon V \backslash T$
(b) (A,a) $A \epsilon V \backslash T$, $a \epsilon T$
(c) $(S,<>)$ provided S does not occur in the righthand side of any other production.

The latter requirement in particular means that the problems of recognizing the empty word and a non-empty word can be clearly separated, i.e.

$$\textbf{funct } RP \equiv (\textbf{sequ term } w)\textbf{bool}: (w=<> \ \wedge \ (S,<>)\epsilon P) \ \vee \ RP'(w)$$

where

$$\textbf{funct } RP' \equiv (\textbf{sequ term } w: w \neq <>)\textbf{bool}: S \xrightarrow{*}_{P'} w$$
$$\text{with } P' =_{def} P \backslash \{(S,<>)\}.$$

Hence, in the sequel we will concentrate on RP'.

3.3. Detailed development

The main strategy we will use in development is the unfold/fold method (cf. [Burstall, Darlington 77]). In order to make our initial specification amenable to this method,

---

[7] See [Partsch 83a] for a discussion of this aspect from the viewpoint of transformational program development.

[8] As is known, this is not a restriction of the generality of the algorithm, since every context-free grammar can be converted into Chomsky Normal Form (cf. [Aho, Ullman 72]).

as a first step we apply an <u>embedding technique</u> (cf. [Schmitz 82] for an extensive discussion on that topic), i.e. we start from

    funct RP' ≡ (**sequ term** w: w≠<>)**bool**: CKY(S,w)

where

    funct CKY ≡ (**nonterm** u, **sequ term** v: v≠<>)**bool**:
        u $\longrightarrow^{*}_{P'}$ v .

3.3.1. Deriving a recursive solution

Our first intermediate development goal is a recursive solution to the above stated problem.

Simple unfolding of $\longrightarrow^{*}_{P'}$ (as defined above) leads to

    funct CKY ≡ (**nonterm** u, **sequ term** v: v≠<>)**bool**:
        (u=v) $\lor$ (u$\longrightarrow$p'v) $\lor$ ($\exists$ **sequ char** w: u$\longrightarrow$p'w $\land$ w$\longrightarrow^{*}_{P'}$v) .

Since u is a nonterminal character and v a (nonempty) sequence of terminals, (u=v) is constantly false. Furthermore, by definition of $\longrightarrow$p',

    $\forall$ v: (u$\longrightarrow$p'v $\Leftrightarrow$ (u,v)∈P)

holds which in turn implies that v must be a single terminal character. Additionally, we can restrict the quantification to (nonempty) sequences of nonterminals of length 2 due to Chomsky Normal Form[9] . Hence we have

    funct CKY ≡ (**nonterm** u, **sequ term** v: v≠<>)**bool**:
        ((u,v)∈P' $\land$ |v|=1) $\lor$
        $\exists$ **nonterm** w_1,w_2: (u,w_1w_2)∈P' $\land$ $w_1w_2\longrightarrow^{*}_{P'}$v .

Now we use a characteristic property of context-free grammars (cf. [Harrison 78], for a proof of the general case) which for grammars in Chomsky Normal Form reads[10] :

    $\forall$ **nonterm** w_1,w_2:
  $w_1w_2\longrightarrow^{*}_{P'}$v $\Leftrightarrow$ $\exists$ **sequ term** v_1,v_2: v_1≠<> $\land$ v_2≠<> $\land$ v_1v_2=v $\land$
                            $w_1\longrightarrow^{*}_{P'}v_1$ $\land$ $w_2\longrightarrow^{*}_{P'}v_2$.

Thus we obtain

---

[9] By this step the existential quantification is restricted to a bounded domain and hence together with (u,w_1w_2)∈P' could be operationally realized.

[10] Here, a similar remark on operationalization of the existential quantifier holds.

$$\textbf{funct } CKY \equiv (\textbf{nonterm } u, \textbf{ sequ term } v: v \neq <>)\textbf{bool}:$$
$$((u,v)\epsilon P' \ \wedge \ |v|=1) \ \vee$$
$$\exists \ \textbf{nonterm } w_1,w_2: (u,w_1w_2)\epsilon P' \ \wedge$$
$$\exists \ \textbf{sequ term } v_1,v_2: v_1 \neq <> \ \wedge \ v_2 \neq <> \ \wedge \ v_1v_2=v \ \wedge$$
$$w_1 \xrightarrow{*}_{P'} v_1 \ \wedge \ w_2 \xrightarrow{*}_{P'} v_2$$

and by folding CKY

$$\textbf{funct } CKY \equiv (\textbf{nonterm } u, \textbf{ sequ term } v: v \neq <>)\textbf{bool}:$$
$$((u,v)\epsilon P' \ \wedge \ |v|=1) \ \vee$$
$$\exists \ \textbf{nonterm } w_1,w_2: (u,w_1w_2)\epsilon P' \ \wedge$$
$$\exists \ \textbf{sequ term } v_1,v_2: v_1 \neq <> \ \wedge \ v_2 \neq <> \ \wedge \ v_1v_2=v \ \wedge$$
$$CKY(w_1,v_1) \ \wedge \ CKY(w_2,v_2) \ .$$

In order to ensure the correctness of the folding transformation we have to prove termination of CKY (cf. [Kott 82]). However, this is trivial here, since the length of the second parameter is a suitable termination function.

3.3.2. Tuning the recursive solution

Since CKY is to be considered local with respect to RP', it is easily to be seen that

$$\exists \ \textbf{nat } i,j: 0 \leq i<j \leq |w|: v=w[i..j]$$

is an additional input assertion for CKY (to be proved by computational induction). Hence,

$$(*) \quad \exists \ \textbf{nat } i,j: 0 \leq i<j \leq |w|: v=w[i..j] \ \Rightarrow$$
$$(\exists \ \textbf{sequ term } v_1,v_2: v_1 \neq <> \ \wedge \ v_2 \neq <> \ \wedge \ v_1v_2=v$$
$$\Leftrightarrow \quad \exists \ \textbf{nat } k: i<k<j \ \wedge \ v_1=v[i..k] \ \wedge \ v_2=v[k..j])$$

holds in the body of CKY.

This means that we can substitute the second parameter by the (supressed) global parameter w and a pair of indices i,j. Formally we define

$$\textbf{funct } CKY1 \equiv (\textbf{nonterm } u, \textbf{nat } i,j: 0 \leq i<j \leq |w|)\textbf{bool}:$$
$$CKY(u,w[i..j])$$

from which by unfolding CKY, simplification using (*) and subsequent folding (which is harmless here) we obtain

$$\textbf{funct } CKY1 \equiv (\textbf{nonterm } u, \textbf{nat } i,j: 0 \leq i<j \leq |w|)\textbf{bool}:$$
$$((u,w[i..j])\epsilon P' \ \wedge \ |w[i..j]|=1) \ \vee$$
$$\exists \ \textbf{nonterm } w_1,w_2: (u,w_1w_2)\epsilon P' \ \wedge$$
$$\exists \ \textbf{nat } k: i<k<j \ \wedge \ CKY1(w_1,i,k) \ \wedge \ CKY1(w_2,k,j) \ .$$

Since $w=w[0..|w|]$, we have $CKY(S,w)=CKY1(S,0,|w|)$ such that our complete intermediate version reads (after additionally simplifying the first disjunct according to the axioms of sequences)

> **funct** RP' ≡ (**sequ term** w: w≠<>) **bool**: CKY1(S,0,|w|),
> **funct** CKY1 ≡ (**nonterm** u,**nat** i,j: 0 ≤ i<j ≤ |w|)**bool**:
>   ((u,w[j])∈P' ∧ j=i+1) ∨
>   ∃ **nonterm** w_1,w_2: (u,w_1w_2)∈P' ∧
>   ∃ **nat** k: i<k<j ∧ CKY1(w_1,i,k) ∧ CKY1(w_2,k,j) .

With an operational view of the existential quantifiers, this is exactly an applicative counterpart of the well-known Cocke-Kasami-Younger algorithm (cf. e.g. [Aho, Ullman 72]).

3.3.3. Recursion removal

Our next steps aim at removing recursion. Since we ultimately aim at applying a tabulation technique (cf. [Broy, Pepper 82]) we have to transform CKY1 into a form with one argument of sort **nat**. As a preparatory step this requires to get rid of (implicit) non-determinism by simply considering the set of all possible executions.

Using the well-known property of predicates P

$$P(x,y) \iff x \in \{z: P(z,y)\}$$

we first pass to (using CKY1(S,0,|w|) = S ∈ CKY2(0,|w|))

> **funct** RP' ≡ (**sequ term** w: w≠<>) **bool**: S ∈ CKY2(0,|w|),
> **funct** CKY2 ≡ (**nat** i,j: 0 ≤ i<j ≤ |w|)**set nonterm**:
>   {**nonterm** u: CKY1(u,i,j)=true} .

Next, in order to disentangle the parameters i and j, we use a simple index translation for CKY2 (for the correctness cf. [Berghammer 83])

$$CKY3(i,j) = CKY2(i,i+j) \quad \text{(and thus, conversely, } CKY2(i,j) = CKY3(i,j-i))$$

where

> **funct** CKY3 ≡ (**nat** i,j: 0 ≤ i ≤ |w|-j ∧ 1 ≤ j ≤ |w|)**set nonterm**:
>   CKY2(i,i+j) .

Note that this index translation does not affect the initial call of CKY2; hence, RP' simply transforms to
> **funct** RP' ≡ (**sequ term** w: w≠<>)**bool**: S ∈ CKY3(0,|w|) .

Then we discriminate the cases j=1 and j>1 which leads to

> **funct** CKY3 ≡ (**nat** i,j: 0 ≤ i ≤ |w|-j ∧ 1 ≤ j ≤ |w|)**set nonterm**:
>   **if** j=1 **then** CKY2(i,i+1) **else** CKY2(i,i+j) **fi** .

Now by unfolding CKY2 and CKY1 we get

> **funct** CKY3 $\equiv$ (**nat** i,j: $0 \le i \le |w|-j \;\wedge\; 1 \le j \le |w|$)**set nonterm**:
>   **if** $j=1$ **then**
>   {**nonterm** u: $((u,w[i+1]) \epsilon P' \;\wedge\; i+1=i+1) \;\vee\;$
> $\exists$ **nonterm** w_1,w_2: $(u,w_1w_2) \epsilon P' \;\wedge\;$
> $\exists$ **nat** k: $i<k<i+1 \;\wedge\; CKY1(w_1,i,k) \;\wedge\; CKY1(w_2,k,i+1)$}
>   **else**
>   {**nonterm** u:
> $((u,w[i+j]) \epsilon P' \;\wedge\; i+j=i+1) \;\vee\;$
> $\exists$ **nonterm** w_1,w_2: $(u,w_1w_2) \epsilon P' \;\wedge\;$
> $\exists$ **nat** k: $i<k<i+j \;\wedge\; CKY1(w_1,i,k) \;\wedge\; CKY1(w_2,k,i+j)$} **fi**

which simplifies (using $\neg\exists$ **nat** k: $i<k<i+1$ and $\neg((i+j=i+1) \;\wedge\; j>1)$) to

> **funct** CKY3 $\equiv$ (**nat** i,j: $0 \le i \le |w|-j \;\wedge\; 1 \le j \le |w|$)**set nonterm**:
>   **if** $j=1$ **then** {**nonterm** u: $(u,w[i+1]) \epsilon P'$}
>   **else**
>   {**nonterm** u: $\exists$ **nonterm** w_1,w_2: $(u,w_1w_2) \epsilon P' \;\wedge\;$
> $\exists$ **nat** k: $i<k<i+j \;\wedge\; CKY1(w_1,i,k) \;\wedge\; CKY1(w_2,k,i+j)$} **fi** .

By applying another index translation that transforms

> $\exists$ **nat** k: $i<k<i+j \;\wedge\; CKY1(w_1,i,k) \;\wedge\; CKY1(w_2,k,i+j)$

into

> $\exists$ **nat** k: $1 \le k \le j-1 \;\wedge\; CKY1(w_1,i,k+i) \;\wedge\; CKY1(w_2,k+i,i+j)$

and folding both CKY2 and CKY3[11]) we obtain

> **funct** CKY3 $\equiv$ (**nat** i,j: $0 \le i \le |w|-j \;\wedge\; 1 \le j \le |w|$)**set nonterm**:
>   **if** $j=1$ **then** {**nonterm** u: $(u,w[i+1]) \epsilon P'$}
>   **else**
>   {**nonterm** u: $\exists$ **nonterm** w_1,w_2: $(u,w_1w_2) \epsilon P' \;\wedge\;$
> $\exists$ **nat** k: $1 \le k \le j-1 \;\wedge\; w_1 \epsilon CKY3(i,k) \;\wedge\; w_2 \epsilon CKY3(i+k,j-k)$} **fi** .

Now, by embedding the last call $CKY3(i+k,j-k)$ into a suitable function SHIFT, defined by

$$SHIFT(CKY3(i,j-k),k) = CKY3(i+k,j-k)$$

we have developed a version the body of which keeps the parameter i constant.

In order to render the tabulation transformation applicable we apply the well-known mathematical property

$$A \times B \to C \;\Leftrightarrow\; B \times A \to C \;\Leftrightarrow\; A \to (B \to C),$$

---

11)Again, these foldings are harmless.

i.e. we pass to a new version CKY4 that is intended to fulfil

   CKY4(j)(i) = CKY3(i,j)

and thus reads

funct CKY4 ≡ (**nat** j: $1 \le j \le |w|$)**funct**(**nat** i: $0 \le i \le |w|$ -j)**set nonterm**:
  if j=1 **then**
   (**nat** i: $0 \le i \le |w|$ -1)**set nonterm**:
   {**nonterm** u: $(u,w[i+1]) \in P'$ }
    else
   (**nat** i: $0 \le i \le |w|$ -j)**set nonterm**:
   {**nonterm** u: $\exists$ **nonterm** w_1, w_2: $(u, w_1 w_2) \in P' \wedge$
    $\exists$ **nat** k: $1 \le k \le j-1 \wedge w_1 \in CKY3(i,k) \wedge w_2 \in SHIFT(CKY3(i,j-k),k)$} **fi** .

Now, finally the transformations TABULATE (i.e. eliminating recursion by tabulating
the values of "previous" calls)[12]

 funct f ≡ (**nat** n) r: E(n)

$$\text{————————} \Big\langle \forall \ \textbf{nat} \ i: \text{DEFINED}(f(i+1)) \Rightarrow \text{DEFINED}(f(i))$$

 funct f ≡ (**nat** n) r:
  begin
  [0..n] **array var r** a;
  for i **from** 0 **to** n **do**
   { $\forall$ **nat** j: $j<i \Rightarrow a[j]=f(j)$ }
   a[i] := E(i) { $\forall$ **nat** j: $j<i+1 \Rightarrow a[j]=f(j)$ } **od**;
  a[n]
 end

and FLATTEN (i.e. unrolling a loop and treating certain cases separately)

 for i **from** a **to** b **do** S {P(i)} **od**

$$\text{————————————}$$

 if $a \le b$ **then nat** i ≡ a; S **fi**;
 for i **from** a+1 **to** b **do** {P(i-1)} S {P(i)} **od**

from [Broy, Pepper 82] are applicable[13] and yield (after simplification acording to
the generated assertions)

---

12){..} denote assertions that may be used for later simplifications.

13)Actually, we use a variant of TABULATE which is restricted to positive natural numbers.

```
funct CKY4 ≡ (nat j: 1 ≤ j ≤ |w|)funct(nat i: 0 ≤ i ≤ |w|-j)set nonterm:
     begin
     array[1..j] var funct(nat)set nonterm a;
     a[1]:=(nat i: 0 ≤ i ≤ |w|-1)set nonterm:
          {nonterm u: (u,w[i+1])∈P'}
     for j' from 2 to j do
        a[j']:=(nat i: 0 ≤ i ≤ |w|-j')set nonterm:
               {nonterm u: ∃ nonterm w₁,w₂: (u,w₁w₂)∈P' ∧
                   ∃ nat k: 1 ≤ k ≤ j'-1 ∧ w₁∈a[k](i) ∧ w₂∈SHIFT(a[j'-k](i),k)} od;
     a[j]
     end .
```

Functions on bounded intervals of natural numbers are just denotations for vectors (and thus we have essentially reached our intended goal). Consequently, variables for such functions can be represented by (conventional) arrays. For expressing the independence of the function bodies from the respective arguments i we use an intuitive notation (cf. [Lengauer, Hehner 82] or [Lamport 75])[14]

$$\langle \forall\ i:\ 0 \le i \le |w|-1:\ S(i)\rangle$$

(which means execution of S for all values of the indicated domain of i.)

Additionally, the set within the loop can be computed sequentially[15] and we thus get

```
funct CKY4 ≡ (nat j: 1 ≤ j ≤ |w|)array set nonterm:
     begin
     array [1..|w|] array [0..|w|-1] set nonterm a;
     < ∀ i: 0 ≤ i ≤ |w|-1:
         a[1][i]:={nonterm u: (u,w[i+1])∈P'}>;
     for j' from 2 to |w| do
        < ∀ i: 0 ≤ i ≤ |w|-j':
        a[j'][i]:=∅;
        for k from 1 to j'-1 do
           a[j'][i] := a[j'][i] ∪ {nonterm u: ∃ nonterm w₁,w₂: (u,w₁w₂∈P') ∧
                                  w₁∈a[k][i] ∧ w₂∈SHIFT(a[j'-k][i],k)} od> od;
     a[j]
     end .
```

____

[14] Note that the transition to arrays instead of variable functions is just intended to help the readers intuition. The other transfromations are independent of this transition.

[15] By substituting the set by a call h(∅,1) of the auxiliary function
h(M,1) =_{def} M ∪ {nonterm u: ∃ nonterm w₁,w₂: (u,w₁w₂)∈P' ∧
          ∃ nat k: 1 ≤ k ≤ j'-1 ∧ w₁∈a[k](i) ∧ w₂∈SHIFT(a[j'-k](i),k)} fi od
the formal transformational derivation of the sequential computation is a simple exercise using the unfold/fold strategy.

Unfolding CKY4 in RP' (and renaming j' into j) yields our final result

```
funct RP' ≡ (sequ term w: w≠<>)bool:
      begin
      array [1..|w|] array [0..|w|-1] set nonterm a;
      < ∀ i: 0 ≤ i ≤ |w|-1:
          a[1][i]:={nonterm u: (u,w[i+1])∊P'}>;
      for j from 2 to |w| do
        < ∀ i: 0 ≤ i ≤ |w|-j:
        a[j][i]:=∅;
        for k from 1 to j-1 do
           a[j][i] := a[j][i] ∪ {nonterm u: ∃ nonterm w1,w2: (u,w1w2∊P' ∧
                                   w1∊a[k][i] ∧ w2∊SHIFT(a[j-k][i],k)} od> od;
      S ∊ a[|w|][0]
      end .
```

It is obvious that this program is well suited for execution on a typical vector machine: It operates on vectors (the a[j]), and all operations (on these vectors) are either typical vector operations (such as SHIFT) or operations that are independent of particular components.

3.4.   Final remarks on the example

When switching from sequential to parallel computation one usually expects a gain in speed (whereas space complexity will remain the same). Thus, we will briefly comment on the time complexity of our final algorithm.

Obviously, any of the a[j][i] contains at most $N=|V \setminus T|$ elements (which is a constant for a fixed grammar G). Accordingly, constructing elements of a[j][i] from a[k][i] and a[j][k] by mutual comparison needs at most N^2 comparisons and N assignments (and again is of constant time complexity with respect to the length n of the input string w). For dealing with vector a[j], all pairs of vectors a[j'] and a[j-j'], with $1 \le j' \le j-1$ have to be considered, i.e. 2(j-1) vectors. Summing up for all j with $1 \le j \le n$ then yields the whole number of operations. Thus, assuming a sufficient number of processors (i.e. at least n) we have n cycles and an overall time complexity of $O(n^2)$. Compared to the complexity $O(n^3)$ of the sequential algorithm (cf. [Aho, Ullman 72]) this is a decrease of one order of magnitude.

Even if the number of processors is less than n, which is likely to be the case, there is a saving in speed, since each of the vectors a[j] can be broken into pieces of appropriate length where the components of the pieces can be computed in parallel whereas the pieces have to be treated sequentially (cf. the technique of "strip mining" in [Lamport 75])[16] . Due to the specific form of the vectors a[j], e.g. for n/2 processors this leads to 3n/2 cycles.

Of course, also further optimizations could be thought of. For instance, one could exploit the fact that the matrix a actually is a left-upper triangular matrix and thus periodically (i.e. whenever the "last" piece of a vector is considered) some of the processors are inactive and could be used to compute the first elements of the "next vector" (provided the computation of the respective components of the "current vector" is already finished). However, optimizations of this kind are not our concern here, since they are not independent of particular hardware organizations (e.g. how the "pipe-lining" is organized). But it should be noted, that, given a particular hardware, these steps, too, could be done by appropriate transformations.

4. Concluding remarks

In our paper we have tried to demonstrate that developing parallel programs in a transformational way is less a question of appropriate rules but rather a question of appropriate objectives in selecting applicable transformations. In particular, the transformations for removing non-determinism play a central role in this approach to parallel programs.

Of course, this approach is generally applicable and not restricted to the particular example. A similar treatment for the Aitken-Neville algorithm can be found in [Pepper 82].

In [Partsch 83a] we have shown how to derive from a formal specification of the recognition problem a variety of non-deterministic algorithms (which are the conceptual basis of all known parsing techniques). It is a consequent next step to examine these non-deterministic algorithms for further development similar to our Cocke-Kasami-Younger example, i.e. in particular how to remove non-determinism while maintaining possibilities for parallel execution, in order to come up with further, formally verified parallel parsing algorithms.

Our previous sample development was exclusively oriented towards execution on vector or array machines. In addition to expecting comparable results for other parsing techniques (also focussing on array or vector machines), we are also convinced that similar techniques might successfully be used for other kinds of architectures (cf. e.g. [McGraw 80], [Schwartz 80], or [Treleaven et al. 82]). Experiments, aiming at parsing algorithms formulated in data flow languages are on the way.

---

16)Of course, this includes as a borderline case an architecture with a single processor.

Acknowledgement: I would like to thank H. Wössner for critical remarks on an earlier version of this paper.

References

[Aho, Ullman 72]
Aho, A.V., Ullman, J.D.: The theory of parsing, translation, and compiling. Volume I: Parsing. Englewood Cliffs, N.J.: Prentice-Hall 1972

[Andrews, Schneider 83]
Andrews, G.R., Schneider, F.B.: Concepts and notations for concurrent programming. Computing Surveys 15:1, 3-43 (1983)

[Baer 73]
Baer, J.L.: Theoretical spects of multiprogramming. Computing Surveys 5, 31-80 (1973)

[Baer, Bovet 68]
Baer, J.L., Bovet, D.P.: Compilation of arithmetic expressions for parallel computations. Proc. IFIP Congress 1968, pp. 340-346

[Baer, Ellis 77]
Baer, J.L., Ellis, C.S.: Model, design, and evaluation of a compiler for a parallel processing environment. IEEE Transactions on Software Engineering, Vol. SE-3, No. 6, 394-405 (1977)

[Bauer, Broy 79]
Bauer, F.L., Broy, M.: Program construction. Lecture Notes in Computer Science **69**. Berlin-Heidelberg-New York: Springer 1979

[Bauer, Wössner 82]
Bauer, F.L., Wössner, H.: Algorithmic language and program development. Berlin-Heidelberg-New York: Springer 1982

[Bauer et al. 81]
Bauer, F.L., Broy, M., Dosch, W., Geiselbrechtinger, F., Hesse, W., Gnatz, R., Krieg-Brückner, B., Laut, A., Matzner, T., Möller, B., Partsch, H., Pepper, P., Samelson, K., Wirsing, M., Wössner, H.: Report on a wide spectrum language for program specification and development. Institut für Informatik der TU München, TUM-I8104, 1981

[Berghammer 83]
Berghammer, R.: Zur formalen Entwicklung graphentheoretischer Algorithmen durch Transformation. Institut für Informatik der TU München, Dissertation, to appear 1983

[Bernstein 66]
Bernstein, A.J.: Analysis of programs for parallel processing. IEEE Transactions on Electronic Computers, Vol. EC-**15**, No. 5, 757-763 (19660

[Broy, Pepper 81]
Broy, M., Pepper, P.: Program development as a formal activity. IEEE Transactions on Software Engineering SE-7, 10-22 (1982)

[Burstall, Darlington 77]
Burstall, R.M., Darlington, J.: A transformation system for developing recursive programs. Journal ACM 24:1, 44-67 (1977)

[Donegan, Katzke 75]
Donegan, M.K., Katzke, S.W.: Lexical analysis and parsing techniques for vector machines. Proc. Conf. on Programming Languages and Compilers for Parallel and Vector Machines. SIGPLAN Notices **10**:3, 138-145 (1975)

[Ellis 71]
Ellis, C.A.: Parallel compiling techniques. Proc. ACM 26th National Conference, 508-519 (1971)

[Fischer 80]
Fischer, C.N.: On parsing and compiling arithmetic expressions on vector computers. ACM TOPLAS 2:2, 203-224 (1980)

[Gonzalez, Ramamoorthy 71]
  Gonzalez, M.J., Ramamoorthy, C.V.: Program suitability for parallel processing. IEEE Transactions on Computers Vol. C-20, No. 6, 647-654 (1971)
[Gries 78]
  Gries, D.(ed.): Programming methodology: a collection of articles by members of IFIP WG 2.3. Berlin-Heidelberg-New York: Springer 1978
[Harrison 78]
  Harrison, M.A.: Introduction to formal language theory. Reading, Ma.: Addison-Wesley 1978
[Kott 82]
  Kott, L.: Unfold/fold program transformations. INRIA Centre de Rennes, Rapport de Recherche N^O 155 (1982)
[Krohn 75]
  Krohn, H.: A parallel approach to code generation for FORTRAN like compilers. Proc. Conf. on Prohgramming Languages and Compilers for Parallel and Vector Machines. SIGPLAN Notices 10:3, 146-149 (1975)
[Kuck 75]
  Kuck, D.J.: Parallel processor architecture - a survey. Proc. 1975 Sagamore Conf. on Parallel Processing, Sagamore Lake, NY 1975, pp. 15-39
[Kuck 76]
  Kuck, D.J.: Parallel processing of ordinary programs. In: Advances in Computers Vol. 15, New York: Academic Press 1976, pp. 119-179
[Kuck et al. 72]
  Kuck, D.J., Muraoka, Y., Chen, S.-C.: On the number of operations simultaneously executable in FORTRAN-like programs and their resulting speedup. IEEE Transactions on Computers, Vol. C-21, No. 12, 1293-1310 (1972)
[Lamport 74]
  Lamport, L.: The parallel execution of DO loops. Comm. ACM 17:2, 83-93 (1974)
[Lamport 75]
  Lamport. L.: Parallel execution on array and vector computers. 1975 Sagamore Conference on Parallel Processing, Sagamore Lake 1975
[Lamport 79]
  Lamport, L.: The coordinate method for the parallel execution of iterative loops. SRI International, Report 1979
[Laut 82]
  Laut, A.: Von abstrakter Syntax zu verketteten Bäumen - Entwicklung einer Datenstruktur für die Programm-Manipulation. Institut für Informatik der TU München, TUM-I8114, 1981
[Lengauer 82]
  Lengauer, C.: A methodology for programming with concurrency: the formalism. Science of Computer Programming 2:1, 19-52 (1982)
[Lengauer, Hehner 82]
  Lengauer, C., Hehner, E.R.C.: A methodology for programming with concurrency: an informal presentation. Science of Computer Programming 2:1, 1-18 (1982)
[Lincoln 70]
  Lincoln, N.: Parallel programming techniques for compilers. SIGPLAN Notices 5:10, 18-31 (1970)
[Loveman 76]
  Loveman, D.B.: Program improvement by source to source transformation. Proc. 2nd ACM Symp. on Principles of Programming Languages, Atlanta, Georgia, Jan. 19-21, 1976, pp. 140-152
[McGraw 80]
  McGraw, J.R.: Data flow computing - software development. IEEE Transactions on Computers, Vol. C-29, No. 12, 1095-1103 (1980)
[Muller, Preparata 76]
  Muller, D.E.:, Preparata, F.P.: Restructuring of arithmetic expressions for parallel evaluation. Journal ACM 23:3, 534-543 (1976)

[Partsch 83a]
   Partsch, H.: A transformational approach to parsing and recognition. Institut für Informatik der TU München Technical Report 1983
[Partsch 83b]
   Partsch, H.: Structuring transformational developments: a case study based on Earley's recognizer. To appear in Science of Computer Programming, 1984
[Pepper 82]
   Pepper, P.: Transformational development of algorithms for vector and array machines. Unpublished manuscript 1982
[Schmitz 78]
   Schmitz, L.: An exercise in program synthesis: algorithms for computing the transitive closure of a relation. Science of Computer Programming 1:3, 235-254 (1982)
[Schwartz 80]
   Schwartz, J.T.: Ultracomputers. ACM TOPLAS 2:4, 484-521 (1980)
[Treleaven et al. 82]
   Treleaven, P.C., Brownbridge, D.R., Hopkins, R.P.: Data-driven and demand-driven computer architecture. Computing Surveys 14:1, 93-143 (1982)
[Wirsing et al. 80]
   Wirsing, M., Pepper, P., Partsch, H., Dosch, W., Broy, M.: On hierarchies of abstract data types. Institut für Informatik der TU München, TUM-I8007, 1980. Also: Acta Informatica 20, 1-33 (1983)
[Zosel 73]
   Zosel, M.: A parallel approach to compilation. Proc. ACM Symp. on Principles of Programming Languages, Boston, Ma., 1973, pp. 59-70

Th. Letschert
Technical University (TH) Darmstadt

Abstract

We discuss polymorphism, overloading and coercions. A simple applicative language with these features and the data type constructors function, record, list and sum are defined. Then we introduce a formal system of deduction. It is used to fix the notion of type inference. Certain properties of the system, which are caused by the intention to base an efficient typing algorithm on it, are discussed. These properties, which are merely restrictions, then lead to considerable simplifications of the deduction system. Finally we define an algorithm which, given a term, computes a set of types for this term. This set of types is the smallest one containing a representative of every legal type t of a term, where t represents t` if t is a subtype of t`.

Introduction

A language is called strongly typed if all type information can be determined at compile time. Strong typing has several advantages, but it also has some drawbacks: Procedures which differ only in types have to be rewritten for each version. To remedey this flaw while maintaining the advantages of strong typing, a programming environment should allow the user to write type-free programs which are then typed by the system. Types are inferred rather than checked by such a system.

As identifiers do not have to be declared and the language probably contains operators defined on arguments of different types, an expression usually has more than one type. According to the kind of operators which cause this multitude of types assignable to expressions, we distinguish:

- Polymorphism, caused by polymorphic operators.

  A polymorphic operator corresponds to a type constructor and is defined on infinitely many types. E.g. the head operator, which takes the first element of a list, is defined on any list. Types of polymorphic operators can always be described using type variables. The head operator for example has type t-list $\rightarrow$ t for every type t.

- Overloading, caused by overloaded operators.

  An operator defined on a set of types is called overloaded if the set is finite and its elements are not related in such a parametric way as in the case of polymorphism. The typical example is "+", used to denote several kinds of addition.

Polymorphism and overloading of basic operators naturally extend to expressions:

$\lambda x \cdot x+x : (\text{int} \longrightarrow \text{int})\ \&\ (\text{real} \longrightarrow \text{real})\quad -1-$

$\lambda x \cdot \text{head}(x) : \prod t.\ t\text{-list} \longrightarrow t \qquad -2-$

-1- If + is an operator of type int $\times$ int $\longrightarrow$ int and real $\times$ real $\longrightarrow$ real then $\lambda x.x+x$ has type int $\longrightarrow$ int and real $\longrightarrow$ real. To denote this we write $\lambda x.x+x :$ (int $\longrightarrow$ int) & (real $\longrightarrow$ real). (Read & as and.)

-2- The expression has type t-list $\longrightarrow$ t for every type t, so we write $\lambda x.\text{head}(x) : \prod t.$ t-list $\longrightarrow$ t. (Read $\prod t$ as for every type t)

A further issue to be discussed in connection with types is coercion (or conversion), i.e. the process whereby a value of one type is converted into a value of another type. Probably the most widespread example of coercions is that of transforming integer to real values.

The interaction between overloading and coercions should be well designed to avoid anomalies like expressions, the value of which depends on an arbitrary choice of some order of conversions.

The Terms and their Types

We introduce a purely functional language with polymorphic and overloaded operators, type coercions and the type constructors function, list, record and sum. The (abstract) syntax of the language Is based on
- a set O of basic constants and overloaded operators, and
- a set P of polymorphic operators.

We specify neither P nor O. Of course P should contain operators for construction and (or) selection from lists, records and sums. To assure a reasonable interaction with coercions, we assume that the types of arguments of an overloaded function have to be sufficient to identify each of its instances, and that constants are not overloaded.

1. Definition

Let C (=P $\cup$ O), V and Id be finite sets (of constants and operators, variables and identifiers). Let c range over C, x over V, id over Id, and M,N over term. The set of terms is generated by the following grammar:

$M ::= c\ |\ x$
$\quad |\ <M>\ |\ \underline{rec}(id_1 : M_1 \ldots id_n : M_n)$
$\quad |\ \underline{sum}(id : M)$

$$| \lambda x.M$$
$$| \underline{case} \; x \; \underline{is}(id_1:M_1 \ldots id_n:M_n)$$
$$| M(N)$$
$$| \underline{let} \; x=M \; \underline{in} \; N$$

The list $<M>$ has type t-list if M is of type t. Records in the term language are like records in Pascal, except that there are no variants and that records can be denoted directly by expressions. If M_i has type t_i, $i = 1 \ldots n$, then

$$\underline{rec}(id_1:M_1 \ldots id_n:M_n)$$

is of type

$$rect(id_1:t_1 \ldots id_n:t_n).$$

Two record types are equal if the components types are equal and tagged with equal identifiers. The order in which the pairs identifier – term and identifier – type appear is immaterial.

An object denoted by the term M can be injected into a sum (disjoint union) type by writing $\underline{sum}(id:M)$. If M is of type t, then $\underline{sum}(id:M)$ is of type sumt(id:t). The case expression

$$\underline{case} \; x \; \underline{is}(id_1:M_1, \ldots id_n:M_n)$$

denotes a function which takes a value, checks whether it is a sum tagged with id_i, $i = 1 \ldots n$, binds x to the tagged value and then the result is the value of M_i. Example:

$$(\underline{case} \; x \; \underline{is}(i:x+1, \; r:trunc(x)) \; \underline{sum}(r:1.1) = 1$$

All other terms are as usual.

2. <u>Definition</u> (Types)

Let T be an unspecified set (of type variables), and a ranging over T. B is an unspecified finite set (of basic types), b ranges over B and t over the set of types.

$$t ::= b \mid a$$
$$| \; t\text{-list}$$
$$| \; rect(id_1:t_1, \ldots id_n:t_n)$$
$$| \; sumt(id_1:t_1, \ldots id_n:t_n)$$
$$| \; t_1 \rightarrow t_2$$
$$| \; t_1 \& \ldots t_n$$
$$| \Pi a.t$$

To introduce conversions between types, we suppose the set B to be equipped with a partial ordering $<_B$. $b_1 <_B b_2$ is to say, that there is a conversion function from values of type b_1 to values of type b_2. This also means that a term of type b_1 is allowed in any position that asks for a b_2 term. We suppose B's conversions and the overloaded functional constants behave well with respect to each other, i.e. the value of an expression does not depend on the relative order in which conversions are performed. A thorough treatment of what well behavior of conversions and overloading (`genericity` called there) means can be found in [7]. The subtype relation is an extension of the ordering on B to the whole set of types.

3. <u>Definition</u> (Polymorphic Type, Generic Instance)

A polymorphic type is a type of the form $\Pi a.t$. A (generic) instance of a polymorphic type $\Pi a.t$ is a type $\Pi a_1 \dots a_n.t[t'/a]$, $0 < n$, where t' is neither polymorphic nor overloaded, and $a_1 \dots a_n$ do not appear free in t (but possibly in t').

4. <u>Definition</u> (Subtype Relation)

$<$ is the least partial ordering such that:

$$\text{if } b_1 <_B b_2 \text{ then } b_1 < b_2$$
$$\text{if } t_1 < t_2 \text{ then } t_1\text{-list} < t_2\text{-list} \text{ and}$$
$$rect(id:t_1) < rect(id:t_2)$$
$$sumt(id:t_1) < sumt(id:t_2)$$
$$t \to t_1 < t \to t_2$$
$$t_2 \to t < t_1 \to t$$
$$t_1 \& \dots t_n < t_i \quad i = 1 .. n$$
$$\Pi a.t < t' \quad \text{if } t' \text{ is a generic instance of } t$$

$$sumt(id_{11}:t_{11}, \dots id_{1n}:t_{1n})$$
$$< sumt(id_{21}:t_{21}, \dots id_{2m}:t_{2m})$$
$$iff \; \{id_{11}, \dots id_{1n}\} \subseteq \{id_{21}, \dots id_{2m}\}$$
$$\text{and if } id_{2i} = id_{1j} \text{ then } t_{1j} < t_{2i}$$

$$rect(id_{11}:t_{11}, \dots id_{1n}:t_{1n})$$
$$< rect(id_{21}:t_{21}, \dots id_{2m}:t_{2m})$$
$$iff \; \{id_{21}, \dots id_{2m}\} \subseteq \{id_{11}, \dots id_{1n}\}$$
$$\text{and if } id_{1i} = id_{2j} \text{ then } t_{1i} < t_{2j}$$

The subtype relation on records, sums and functions is the same as in [8], motivation and justification can be found there.

An operator or function with type $t_1 \& t_2$ is overloaded with meanings of type t_1 and t_2, and thus it can serve as an operator of any of the two types, just as an integer value may serve as a real value. A similiar argumentation applies to polymorphic types. If M has type $\Pi a.t$, then it has type t' for every instantiation of this polymorphic type.

A Deduction System for Types

We introduce a deduction system for deriving sentences like $A \vdash M:t$, which are statements about the types of terms. A is a type assignment which associates types to variables, and the sentence above states that if the variables occurring free in M are assigned types according to A, then it can be deduced that M has type t.

5. _Definition_ (Type Assignment, Simple Type)

  (i) A type assignment is a mapping from variables to types.

  (ii) A type is called simple if it is neither polymorphic nor overloaded.

     In the following s will range over simple types.

6. _Definition_ (Type Deduction)

 Let M be a term, t a type, and A a type assignment.

 M has type t under assumption A :

  $A \vdash M:t$

 if $A \vdash M:t$ can be deduced by the following axioms and rules of inference.

(i) _Axioms_

  (a1) $A \vdash c:t$ for any operator or constant of type t

  (a2) $A \vdash x:t$ for any assignment A and variable x with $A(x)=t$

(ii) _Rules_

$$(r1) \quad \frac{A \vdash M:t}{A \vdash \langle M \rangle : t\text{-list}}$$

$$(r2) \quad \frac{A \vdash M_1:t_1 \; \ldots \; A \vdash M_n:t_n}{A \vdash \underline{rec}(id_1:M_1, \ldots id_n:M_n): rect(id_1:t_1, \ldots id_n:t_n)}$$

$$(r3) \quad \frac{A \vdash M:t}{A \vdash \underline{sum}(id:M) : sumt(id:t)}$$

$$(r4) \quad \frac{A+[x \rightarrow s_1] \vdash M:t_1 \; \ldots \; A+[x \rightarrow s_n] \vdash M:t_n}{A \vdash \lambda x.M : (s_1 \rightarrow t_1) \; \& \; \ldots \; (s_n \rightarrow t_n)}$$

$$(r5) \quad \frac{A+[x \rightarrow s_1] \vdash M_1:t \; \ldots \; A+[x \rightarrow s_n] \vdash M_n:t}{\underline{case} \; x \; \underline{is}(id_1:M_1, \ldots id_n:M_n) : sumt(id_1:s_1, \ldots id_n:s_n) \rightarrow t}$$

$$(\text{r6}) \quad \frac{A \vdash M:(t_1 \rightarrow t_2) \quad A \vdash N:t_1}{A \vdash M(N) : t_2}$$

$$(\text{r7}) \quad \frac{A \vdash M:t_1 \quad A+[x \rightarrow t_1] \vdash N:t_2}{A \vdash \underline{let}\ x=M\ \underline{in}\ N : t_2}$$

$$(\text{r8}) \quad \frac{A \vdash M:t_1}{A \vdash M:t_2} \quad t_1 < t_2$$

$$(\text{r9}) \quad \frac{A \vdash M:t}{A \vdash M:\Pi a.t} \quad a \text{ not free in } A$$

7. Example

1. $[x \rightarrow a] \vdash x:a$ (a2)

2. $[x \rightarrow a \rightarrow a] \vdash x:(a \rightarrow a)$ (a2)

3. $\vdash \lambda x.x\ :(a \rightarrow a)\&((a \rightarrow a) \rightarrow (a \rightarrow a))$ (r4) from 1.,2.

4. $[I \rightarrow (a \rightarrow a)\& ((a \rightarrow a) \rightarrow (a \rightarrow a))]$ (a2)

   $\vdash I : (a \rightarrow a)\&((a \rightarrow a) \rightarrow (a \rightarrow a))$

5. $[I \rightarrow (a \rightarrow a)\& ((a \rightarrow a) \rightarrow (a \rightarrow a))]$ (r8) from 4.

   $\vdash I : (a \rightarrow a) \rightarrow (a \rightarrow a)$

6. $[I \rightarrow (a \rightarrow a)\& ((a \rightarrow a) \rightarrow (a \rightarrow a))]$ (r8) from 4.

   $\vdash I : a \rightarrow a$

7. $[I \rightarrow (a \rightarrow a)\& ((a \rightarrow a) \rightarrow (a \rightarrow a))]$ (r6) from

   $\vdash I(I) : a \rightarrow a$ 5.,6.

8. $\vdash \underline{let}\ I = \lambda x.x\ \underline{in}\ I(I) : a \rightarrow a$ (r7) from 7.,3.

9. $\vdash \underline{let}\ I = \lambda x.x\ \underline{in}\ I(I) : \Pi a.a \rightarrow a$ (r9) from 8.

8. Lemma

(i)   If $A \vdash M:t$ then t is a legal type.

(ii) If $A \vdash M:t$ and x not free in M then $A_{\text{dom}(A)\ -\{x\}} \vdash M:t$

(iii) The relation $<$, the set of axioms, and the rules are recursive.

<u>Proof</u>

(i) and (ii) by induction on the deduction tree.

(iii) $<_B$ is assumed to be recursive, use induction on the structure of t_1 to decide wether $t_1 < t_2$, the axioms are obviously recursive, and so the rules are recursive too.

Thus we can check deduction trees. Of course Lemma 8 does not state or imply that $A \vdash M{:}t$ is recursive.

The "Let Anomaly"

Because of the restriction on (r4) and (r5) to abstract only simply typed variables, self-application of variables can not be typed, unless the variable is bound by <u>let</u> to a term which can be applied to itself (and can be typed), e.g. $\lambda x.x$. So there are terms that can be typed as subterms of let terms, but not in general. This special treatment of <u>let</u> has been introduced by Milner in [6]. In our case it is due to the above mentioned restrictions, which do not appear in the rule for let abstractions.

9. <u>Observation</u>

(i) $(\lambda y.y)(\lambda y.y)$ can be typed.

(ii) $(\lambda x.xx)(\lambda y.y)$ can not be typed.

(iii) <u>let</u> $x = \lambda y.y$ <u>in</u> $x(x)$ can be typed.

(iv) Let v,w be two constants of different types $t_v \; t_w$

$\quad \lambda f. \dots f(v) \dots f(w) \dots$

can not be typed unless

either $t_v < t_w$

or $\quad t_w < t_v$

(v) <u>let</u> $f = \lambda x.x$

$\quad$ <u>in</u> $\dots f(v) \dots f(w) \dots$

can be typed.

The restriction of the abstraction mechanism, except let abstraction, is motivated by the intended type deduction <u>algorithm</u>: When an algorithm starts typing the body of an abstraction, it does not know anything about the type of the variables occurring free within it. In order to avoid total ignorance it assumes that the same simple type – within the range of conversions – should be assigned to each occurrence of a variable within its scope.

Without such a restriction there are no limits (of overloading or polymorphism) of types of variables. Whenever typing fails, the algorithm would have to try again with a still more general type of variables. (Try to type $(\lambda x.xx)(\lambda x.xx)$ with an unrestricted rule for lambda abstraction!)

In case of a let binding

    <u>let</u> f = M <u>in</u> N

the situation is a different one. The (hypothetical) algorithm can type M first, leading to a type $t_1 \& \dots t_n$ ($\Pi a.t$), and this type now gives a "limit" within which the (simple) types of occurences of f may range.

10. <u>Lemma</u>

  Iff $A \vdash \underline{let}\ x{=}M\ \underline{in}\ N : t$

    then $A \vdash N[^{M}\!/_{x}] : t$

<u>Proof</u>

  A deduction tree for each of the two sentences can be constructed from one for the other.

Referring to this lemma we will simplify discussion by omitting <u>let</u> terms from the set of terms. So from now on let terms be non – <u>let</u>- terms, and remove (r7) from the set of derivation rules.

<u>Polymorphism and Overloading</u>

One might suspect, that polymorphic types do not increase the power of the typing system, i.e. if $A \vdash M: a.t$ then $A \vdash M: t_1 \& \dots t_n$ where t_i is a generic instance of $\Pi a.t$. This is not true :

  $\vdash (\lambda f.f)(\lambda x.x) : \Pi a.a{\rightarrow}a$, but

  $\vdash (\lambda f.f)(\lambda x.x) : (int \rightarrow int)\& (real \rightarrow real)$

    does not hold.

It would be true if we had included the additional rule (r&)

  $A \vdash M{:}t_1\ A \vdash M{:}t_2$

   $A \vdash M{:}(t_1 \& t_2)$

So our system is weaker than one with only overloaded types and the rule (r&). However the additional sentences that could be proved in such a system are inessential: $\Pi a.t$ is a "better" (i.e. more general) type than $(int \rightarrow int)\& (real \rightarrow real)$. The restricted use of polymorphism and overloading we adopted, following the line of [6], and the exclusion of <u>let</u>-terms entails that a polymorphic type is always as good as any of its overloaded "approximations".

11. Lemma

If A contains only simple types and if $A \vdash M{:}s$ then this sentence can be deduced without using polymorphism or overloading, i.e. with (a1) modified to (a1$_r$) $A \vdash c{:}s$, where s is a simple instance of the type of the constant c, and (r4) modified to (r4$_r$):

$A+[x{\rightarrow}s] \vdash M{:}t$

$A \vdash \lambda x.M : s{\rightarrow}t,$

and (r9) omitted.

Proof

By induction on the deduction for $A \vdash M{:}s$. Note, that we have no _let_-terms at present.

Lemma 11 does not entail that there is always only one type that can be assigned to a term given a certain type assignment.

Principal Types and Typing

From now on take type deduction as in lemma 11. We want to find all types that can be assigned to a term. As we have seen this set gives enough information about the types of a term.

12. Definition (Pair, Complete Set of Pairs)

(i) A pair $\langle A,s \rangle$ consisting of a typeassignment with only simple types, and a simple type is called a pair. A pair $\langle a,s \rangle$ is called correct for M, if $A \vdash M{:}s$. Let $\langle A,a \rangle$ and $\langle B,b \rangle$ be pairs, we write $\langle A,a \rangle < \langle B,b \rangle$ if $a < b$ and $B < A$. Where $B < A$ is defined as if $B(x) = t$ then either $A(x)$ is undefined, or $t < A(x)$.

(ii) A set of pairs C, with $p \in C$ correct for M, is called complete (for M) iff if $A \vdash M{:}s$ then $\langle B,b \rangle \in C \ \langle B,b \rangle < \langle A,s \rangle$.

Complete set of pairs for a term M contain all type information about M – modulo conversations.

13. Lemma

If $A_1 \vdash M{:}s_1$ and $\langle A_1,s_1 \rangle < \langle A,s \rangle$

then $A \vdash M{:}s.$

<u>Proof</u>

It is obvious how to construct a deduction for $A \vdash M{:}s$, using an appropriate number of instances of (r8), from the assumed deduction for $A_1 \vdash M{:}s_1$ Note the antimonotony of the ordering of pairs in their first component.)

We should like to find the least complete set of pairs for a term M, because it would convey non-redundant type information for M.

14. <u>Definition</u> (Principle Pair Set)

The principle pair set for a term M :

pps(M)

is defined inductively as :

pps(c) = { $\langle [],s \rangle$ | s is a simple instance of the type of c }

pps(x) = { $\langle [x \rightarrow s],s \rangle$ | s is a simple type }

$\text{pps}(MN) = \{ \langle A, t_2 \rangle \mid A = \max(\{ B \mid \exists t_1, t_{11}, A_M, A_N.$

$$B < A_M, \; B < A_N,$$
$$\langle A_M, t_1 \rightarrow t_2 \rangle \in \text{pps}(M)$$
$$\langle A_N, t_1 \rangle \in \text{pps}(N)$$
$$t_{11} < t_1 \qquad\qquad \} \,)\}$$

$\text{pps}(\lambda x.M) = \{ \langle A, t_1 \rightarrow t_2 \rangle \mid \langle A + [x \rightarrow t_1], t_2 \rangle \in \text{pps}(M)$

$$\text{or } \langle A, t_2 \rangle \in \text{pps}(M) \text{ and } A(x) \text{ undefined} \}$$

$\text{pps}(\langle M \rangle) = \{ \langle A, t\text{-list} \rangle \mid \langle A, t \rangle \in \text{pps}(M) \}$

$\text{pps}(\underline{\text{sum}}(id{:}M)) = \{ \langle A, \text{sumt}(id{:}t) \rangle \mid \langle A, t \rangle \in \text{pps}(M) \}$

$\text{pps}(\underline{\text{rec}}(id_1{:}M_1 \ldots id_n{:}M_n)) =$

$$\{ \langle A, \text{rect}(id_1{:}t_1 \ldots id_n{:}t_n) \rangle$$
$$\mid A = \max (\{ B \mid \exists A_i, i=1 .. n .$$
$$\langle A_i, t_i \rangle \in \text{pps}(M_i),$$
$$B < A_i \qquad\qquad \} \,)\}$$

$\text{pps}(\underline{\text{case}} \; x \; \underline{\text{is}}(id_1{:}M_1, \ldots id_n{:}M_n)) =$

$$\{ \langle A, \text{sumt}(id_1{:}t_1, \ldots id_n{:}t_n) \rightarrow t \rangle$$
$$\mid A = \max (\{ B \mid \exists A_i, t. \; \langle A_i + [x \rightarrow t_i] \rangle \in \text{pps}(M_i),$$
$$B < A_i \; i = 1..n \qquad \} \,)\}$$

15. <u>Example</u>

We show the construction of pps((x+0.5)+(x+1)). To improve readability we use infix notation for the functional constant +.

Take: i,r as abbreviations for integer and real,

$\qquad + : (i \rightarrow i \rightarrow i) \ \& \ (r \rightarrow r \rightarrow r)$

1. $pps(x) = \{<x\rightarrow s],s> \mid s \text{ is a simple type }\}$

2. $pps(+) = \{<[],i\rightarrow i\rightarrow i>,<[],r\rightarrow r\rightarrow r>\}$

3. $pps(+(x)) = \{<[x\rightarrow i],i\rightarrow i>,<[x\rightarrow r],r\rightarrow r>\}$

4. $pps(0.5) = \{<[],r>\}$

5. $pps(x+0.5) = \{<[x\rightarrow r],r>\}$

6. $pps(x+1) = \{<[x\rightarrow i],i>,<[x\rightarrow r],r>\}$

7. $pps(+(x+0.5)) = \{<[x\rightarrow r],r\rightarrow r>\}$

8. $pps((x+0.5)+(x+1)) = \{<[x\rightarrow r],r>\}$

In the same way you may compute:

9. $pps((x+0.5)+(x\underline{div}1)) = \{<[x\rightarrow i],r>\}$

$\qquad$ if $\underline{div} : (i \rightarrow i \rightarrow i)$

16. <u>Lemma</u>

If $<A,t> \in pps(M)$ then there is no A_1 different from A with $A_1 < A$ and $<A_1,t> \in pps(M)$.

<u>Proof</u> By induction on the definition of pps.

17. <u>Theorem</u>

$pps(M)$ is the least complete set of pairs for M.

<u>Proof</u>

$\qquad$ a) By induction on M show that if $<A,t> \in pps(M)$ then $A \vdash M:t$.

$\qquad$ b) By induction on the (modified) deduction system show that if $A \vdash M:t$ then there is a A_1 and t_1 with $<A_1,t_1> \in pps(M)$ and $<A_1,t_1> < <A,t>$.

$\qquad$ c) Use lemma 16 to show that $pps(M)$ is the least complete set of pairs for M.

In a typing discipline with pure polymorphism, without conversions and overloading, the set $pps(M)$ would contain only elements that could be produced from a single one by the operation of substitution. This special element then carries all type information and is usually called the principle type of a term. In our case such a simple representation of $pps(M)$ is obviously not possible.

Relation to other Work

Milner, in [6], presented the first typing algorithm for a language with pure polymorphism. Several years later, in [1], a deduction system is shown, on which this algorithm could be based. The typing algorithm, and hence the deduction system treat <u>let</u> and lambda binding in different ways, just as we do. The algorithm marks variables in the type-assignment that are bound by let, the deduction system distinguishes types and type-schemes. Type-schemes correspond to our polymorphic types, and types to our simple types. Conversions and overloading are not treated.

In [2] type inference rules for the pure lambda calculus, i.e. a language without constants and datatype constructors, is presented. The system is not restricted to polymorphism, it allows arbitrary overloadings (rule (r&) included), though their notation is different from ours. We shortly mentioned, that overloadings even with unrestricted abstraction rules are not enough to type every term. This problem is solved by introducing a new type "any-type". Now a term has a least type "any-type". In such a system the relation $A \vdash M{:}t$ is not recursive, so it can not be used as a basis for a typing algorithm.

McQueen and Sethi, in [5], introduced the notation for polymorphism, $\Pi a.t$, that we used here. They are not concerned with type checking, and so do not have to pose any restrictions on the deduction system they present.

The type deduction algorithm of Henhapl et al. [3] is not explicitly based on a deduction system, but from the algorithm a system can be extracted which is similiar to ours in dealing with restricted abstraction rules. (They type "incomplete expressions", i.e. expressions without declarations, corresponding to our bodies of lambda abstractions.) Polymorphism and overloading is included, but coercions are not. The system does not enable the user to escape from the restricted abstraction using (some kind of) <u>let</u> – term; i.e. they do not allow a special treatment in the case where declarations are present.

Comparison with other deduction systems gives evidence that we have chosen a type discipline which is as flexible as possible while still permitting efficient type checking.

Conclusion

The typing algorithm that could be based on the definition of pps should replace sets of pairs by representations. Usually (e.g. in [6]) types with variables are taken as representations of the set of types that can be derived by uniformly replacing variables by types. Matching of type sets can then be done using the unification algorithm. In our case unification has to be replaced by a more general matching procedure.

Also note that the definition of pps has a structure different from Milners ([6]) algorithm w. pps works strictly "bottom - up", i.e. if M is a term with subterms M_1 and M_2, then it finds independent $<A_1,t_1>$ and $<A_2,t_2>$ with $A_i \vdash M_i:t_i$ i = 1,2. Algorithm w instead starts with a type assignment A and finds substitution S which modifies A in such a way that $S(A) \vdash M:t$ for some t. Typing of subexpressions is not independent, but performed sequentially. In [4] we treat an implementation of pps.

References

[1] L.Damas, R.Milner
Principal Type-Schemes for Functional Languages
Proc. 9th Annual Principles of Programming Languages
Symposium (POPL) 1982 pp. 207 - 212

[2] M.Coppo, M.Deziani-Ciancaglini, B.Venneri
Functional Characters of Solvable Terms
Zeitschr. f. mathem. Logik und Grundl. der Mathematik
27, pp 45 - 58 (1981)

[3] W.Henhapl, G.Snelting
Context Relations - A Concept for Incremental Context
Analysis in Program Fragments
these proceedings

[4] T. Letschert
Type Inference in the Presence of Polymorphism,
Overloading and Coercions
Part I TH Darmstadt, FB Informatik, Report PU1R7-83 (1983)
Part II in preparation

[5] D.B.McQueen, R.Sethi
A Semantic Model of Types for Applicative Languages
ACM Symp. on Lisp and Functional Programming 1982
pp 243 -252

[6] R.Milner
A Theory of Type Polymorphism in Programming
Languages
Journal of Comp. and System Science 17,
pp 348 - 375 (1978)

[7] J.C.Reynolds
Using Category Theory to Design Implicit Conversions
and Generic Operators
Lecture Notes in Computer Science 94, pp 211 - 258
(1980)

[8] J.C. Reynolds
The Essence of Algol
in: International Symposium on Algorithmic Languages
edited by deBakker and vanVliet, North-Holland Pub. Comp.
(1981), pp 245 - 372

Ein konstruktives Typsystem für funktionale Programmiersprachen *

Fritz Müller

Fachbereich 10 - Informatik
Universität des Saarlandes
D-6600 Saarbrücken 11

Abstract

We develop the concept of a constructive type system for functional
programming languages. As with Martin-Löf's Intuitionistic Theory of
Types, the underlying principle says: A type is defined by the rules
for constructing its elements. We describe these constructions as processes modelled by Concrete Data Structures (Kahn/Plotkin).
A hierarchy of type universes is introduced. In addition to simple
types it contains higher order objects composed of types and operators
acting on these objects. These language constructs support the formulation of abstract programming schemes as type procedures.

1. Einführung

In dieser Arbeit entwickle ich das Konzept eines konstruktiven Typsystems für funktionale Programmiersprachen. Beispiele für bereits implementierte einfachere Typsysteme bieten die Sprachen ML [GMW 79] und
HOPE [BMS 80]. Die Betrachtungen lassen sich zum großen Teil auch auf
andere Sprachklassen übertragen.

Typsysteme teilen die Datenelemente der Programmiersprache in bestimmte Typen ein, es wird nur ein typ-disziplinierter Gebrauch der
Operatoren (z.B. Addition, Zuweisung oder benutzerdefinierte Funktionen) zugelassen: Die Typen der Argumente des Operators sind statisch
festgelegt, das Resultat hat unter dieser Vorbedingung einen garan-
tierten Typ, der Operator erhält also einen bestimmten funktionalen
Typ. Das bedeutet aber, daß durch ein Typsystem der Programmierer ge-
zwungen wird, die programmierte Aufgabe zu einem gewissen Teil zu spezifizieren und daß die Korrektheit des Programms bezüglich dieser
Teilspezifikation automatisch überprüft werden kann.

Beispiel: Die Aufgabe besteht darin, Listen natürlicher Zahlen nach

---

* Diese Arbeit wurde gefördert durch Mittel des Bundesministers für
Forschung und Technologie und der Deutschen Forschungsgemeinschaft.

aufsteigender Reihenfolge zu sortieren. Die Typ-Spezifikation des Programms lautet in einer passenden Programmiersprache als Funktionstyp:

Liste natürlicher Zahlen → Liste natürlicher Zahlen.

Das ist aber nicht die vollständige Spezifikation der Aufgabe, diese wäre:

a: Liste nat. Z. → (b: Liste nat. Z., b aufsteigend,

b Permutation von a).

(Hier ist der Resultattyp abhängig vom Argument a!) In einem erweiterten Typsystem wie dem Kalkül der intuitionistischen Typtheorie [MAR 73, MAR 79, NOR 83] läßt sich auch dieser Typ angeben, man erhält so eine einheitliche Spezifikations- und Programmiersprache. In ihr werden Typen mit logischen Aussagen und Spezifikationen identifiziert, der Beispieltyp mit der Aussage:

∀ a ∈ Liste nat. Z.   ∃ b ∈ Liste nat. Z. (b aufsteigend und

b Permutation von a).

Zusammen mit der Absicherung gegen Typfehler fördert ein Typsystem eine übersichtlich strukturierte Programmiermethodik, die (Teil-) Spezifikation durch Typen ist ein Teil der Programmdokumentation. Es stellt Sprachmittel zur direkten Programmierung abstrakter Datenstrukturen zur Verfügung, während eine ungetypte Programmiersprache entsprechende Repräsentationen und Codierungen erfordert.

Aller Vorteile eines Typsystems zum Trotz schwören aber viele LISP-Programmierer auf die Freiheiten, die ihnen das ungetypte Programmieren in dieser Sprache bietet. Der Grund hierfür liegt wohl auch darin, daß sich in den Typsystemen bisher implementierter Programmiersprachen viele Programmierkonzepte, vor allem höherer Ordnung, nicht beschreiben lassen. Zunächst ist zu fordern, daß das Typsystem übliche Grundtypen enthält und unter Anwendung der Typkonstruktoren × (kartesisches Produkt, Record-Bildung), + (disjunkte Vereinigung), → (Funktionstyp) und unter rekursiven Typgleichungen abgeschlossen ist. (Es soll also auch Funktionstypen beliebiger höherer Ordnung enthalten.)
Als nächstes sollen Operatoren implizite oder explizite Typ-Parameter erhalten können (Typ-Polymorphie). Weiterhin soll das Typsystem parametrisierte Datentypen enthalten, d.h. vom Benutzer definierte neue Typoperatoren wie z.B. einen Typoperator "List", der einen Typ als Argument erhält und dazu den Typ der Listen von Argument-Elementen als Resultat erzeugt. ML und HOPE bieten auch noch diese Sprachkonstrukte.

Wir wollen nun die Funktion sort zum Sortieren von Listen nach dem Typ der Listenelemente parametrisieren, ihr Typ wäre dann:

sort ∈ t: <u>type</u> → (List(t) → List(t)).

Hier zeichnet sich wieder eine notwendige Erweiterung des klassischen

Funktionsbegriffs ab: Der Resultattyp von sort ist nicht statisch vor-
bestimmt, sondern selbst abhängig vom Argument t.

Der obige Typ hat noch einen Mangel: Der Parameter ist nicht bloß
als Menge von Elementen zu verstehen, sondern mit ihm ist eine Ordnungsrelation verbunden, die die Grundlage des Sortieralgorithmus darstellt. Eine Lösung wäre, diese Ordnungsrelation als zweiten Parameter
einzuführen:

sort $\in$ t: <u>type</u> $\to$ [(t × t $\to$ Bool) $\to$ (List(t) $\to$ List(t))].

Eine andere Lösung unterstützt die Programmierung abstrakter Datentypen und faßt den Typ der Grundmenge mit der Ordnungsrelation zu einem Datentyp "Ordnung" zusammen. So würde die Deklaration von sort in
CLU [LSA 77] so aussehen:

```
sort = proc [t: type] (l: list[t]) returns list[t]
       where t has ≤: proctype(t,t) returns (bool) <body>.
```

Hinter der Methodik von CLU (und auch von ML) steht die Anschauung,
daß die Operationen mit dem betreffenden Datentyp starr verbunden
sind, ausgedrückt durch eigene Sprachkonstrukte wie "where". Dies wird
aber dann unzureichend, wenn die Zusammensetzung von Typ-Argumenten
variabel gehalten werden soll (z.B. t mit verschiedenen Ordnungsrela-
tionen), vor allem wenn Operatoren höherer Ordnung solche zusammengesetzten (Typ-) Objekte als Resultat bilden sollen.

Diese Aufgaben lassen sich aber lösen, wenn man in einem allgemeine-
ren Typsystem <u>mit Typen (getypt) rechnen</u> kann wie mit einfachen Objekten auch: Die Typen der ersten Stufe (erzeugt aus Grundtypen, ×, +, $\to$
und Rekursion) werden zu dem Typ <u>type</u> der zweiten Stufe (zu einer <u>Art</u>)
zusammengefaßt. Aus <u>type</u> und den Typen erster Stufe als Grundarten erzeugt man mit denselben Konstruktionsmitteln neue Arten (Typen zweiter
Stufe), darunter z.B. die Art der Ordnungen. Ordnungen sind Paare der
Form (t: <u>type</u>, ≤: t×t$\to$Bool).

Dieses Typsystem verkörpert den Systemen der intuitionistischen Typtheorie und der PL/CV3-Typtheorie [CON 81, CON 82] eigene "konstruktive" Prinzipien, wurde jedoch unabhängig von jenen Systemen unter dem
Gesichtspunkt nützlicher Konstrukte für funktionale Programmiersprachen entwickelt. Eine Neuerung besteht in der Darstellung der Kon-
struktionsverfahren für Elemente von Typen durch konkrete Datenstrukturen [KP 78]. Dadurch wird es möglich, Datenelemente nicht nur in
fester sequentieller Reihenfolge, sondern auch durch parallele Prozesse aufzubauen.

Im folgenden werden zwar entsprechende Verweise gemacht, jedoch ist
die Kenntnis der konstruktiven Systeme und der konkreten Datenstruktu-

ren nicht vorausgesetzt.

Kapitel 2 erläutert die Definition der konkreten Datenstrukturen,
Kapitel 3 beschreibt den Aufbau der Typen erster Stufe,
Kapitel 4 zeigt die Übertragung der Konstrukte auf höhere Stufen der
Typhierarchie und gibt Beispiele für Programmieranwendungen. Ein Bei-
spiel für eine umfangreichere Anwendung enthält der Bericht [MUE 83].

2. Konkrete Datenstrukturen

Als Grundlage der Typkonstruktionen in 3.3 ist hier die Definition
der konkreten Datenstrukturen (concrete data structures) aus [BER 81,
BC 82] wiedergegeben:

Eine **konkrete Datenstruktur** (**CDS**) $M = (C,V,E,\vdash)$ besteht aus einer
abzählbaren Menge C von **Zellen** (cells), einer abzählbaren Menge V von
Werten (values), einer Menge $E \subseteq C \times V$ von **Ereignissen** (events) und einer **Zugriffsrelation** (enabling relation) $\vdash \subseteq F(E) \times C$, wobei $F(E)$ die
Menge der endlichen Teilmengen von E ist.

Eine CDS modelliert den materiellen Aufbau von Datenstrukturen in
Raum und Zeit: Man kann die Zellen C deuten als Speicherzellen eines
Computers (d.h. Orte im Raum), die Menge E der Ereignisse legt fest,
mit welchen Werten aus V jede Zelle belegt werden kann. Ein Ereignis
$e=(c,v)$ findet statt, wenn (zu einem Zeitpunkt) die Zelle c mit dem
Wert v besetzt wird.

Zwischen Ereignissen können kausale Abhängigkeiten bestehen, wodurch
ihre zeitliche Reihenfolge festgelegt wird. Diese Abhängigkeiten werden durch die Zugriffsrelation $\vdash$ ausgedrückt:
Die **Regel** $e_1, e_2, \ldots, e_n \vdash c$ bedeutet, daß die Zelle c nur dann besetzt
werden kann (d.h. ein Ereignis (c,v) kann stattfinden), wenn vorher
alle Ereignisse der **Voraussetzung** $\{e_1, e_2, \ldots, e_n\}$ stattgefunden haben.

Sei $c' < c$ für $c,c' \in C$, falls es eine Regel $e_1, \ldots, e_n \vdash c$ gibt mit
$e_i = (c',v)$ für ein i. Man fordert von der CDS, daß $<$ keine unendliche
absteigende Kette hat.

Ein **Zustand** s der CDS M ist eine Menge von Ereignissen, so daß in s
jede Zelle mit höchstens einem Wert besetzt ist und jedes Ereignis aus
s eine Voraussetzung hat, die selber in s enthalten ist. Ein Zustand
gibt also einen Zwischenzustand an, der während eines Prozesses zur
Besetzung der Zellen mit Werten auftritt. Ein solcher Prozeß beginnt
mit der Besetzung von Zellen mit leerer Voraussetzung (**initiale Zellen**
$\vdash c$) und verwendet vorher besetzte Zellen, um auf weitere Zellen zugreifen zu können.

<u>Beispiele für konkrete Datenstrukturen</u>:

<u>primitiver Grundtyp Void</u>:
Besteht aus einer einzigen Zelle c, dem Wert () (=Nulltupel) und dem
Ereignis (c,()) mit ⊢c.
Die Zustände sind also $\emptyset$ und {(c,())}.

<u>primitiver Grundtyp Bool</u>:
Eine Zelle c, Werte O und 1, Ereignisse (c,O), (c,1) mit ⊢c.
Die Zustände sind: $\emptyset$, {(c,O)} und {(c,1)}.

<u>CDS für eine ungetypte freie Termalgebra</u>:
Gegeben ist eine Menge von Operatorsymbolen der Form f_n, wobei n die
Stelligkeit angibt. Die freie Termalgebra über die f_n läßt sich durch
folgende CDS darstellen (Terme sind Bäume mit den f_n als Knotenmarkie-
rungen):
$C = \mathbb{N}^*$, endliche Folgen natürlicher Zahlen,
$V = $ Menge der f_n, $E = C \times V$,
⊢ ε, die leere Folge ist initiale Zelle,
$(c,f_n) \vdash c \cdot i$ für $1 \le i \le n$, • ist die Konkatenation.
Durch den Operator f_n in der Zelle c werden die ersten n Söhne von c
erreichbar.

Eine CDS beschreibt nicht nur den Prozeß des Aufbaus, also der Erzeugung einer Datenstruktur, sondern auch den Prozeß des <u>Erkennens</u> der
Datenstruktur. Ist z.B. ein Element der Termalgebra gegeben, so kann
man auf den Wert einer bestimmten Zelle nur zugreifen, wenn man vorher
(schrittweise) alle Vorgängerknoten besucht hat. Nach diesem Schema
müssen auch alle Algorithmen zur Verarbeitung konkreter Datenstrukturen arbeiten.

Durch die starre Zuordnung von Ereignissen zu bestimmten Zellen ist
es mit CDS nicht möglich, eine eindeutige Darstellung für Elemente
z.B. des Datentyps "Menge" anzugeben. Dies kann nur über die Abstraktion der Quotientenbildung geschehen, indem z.B. Mengen als Äquiva-
lenzklassen von Listen dargestellt werden. Eine solche Quotientenbildung sollte Bestandteil einer Programmiersprache sein, wird hier aber
nicht ausgeführt.

<u>3. Typaufbau erster Stufe</u>

<u>3.1.</u> In diesem Kapitel wird die Konstruktion der Typen erster Stufe
beschrieben, hier in 3. kurz Typen genannt ("small types" in
[MAR 73]). Zunächst ist die Frage zu klären: Was sind Typen? Hier wird

die konstruktive Anschauung aus [MAR 73] übernommen:

<u>Jedes Objekt</u> (d.h. jede Konstruktion) <u>ist Element eines Typs</u>, es ist immer zusammen mit seinem Typ gegeben.

<u>Ein Typ wird durch Regeln definiert, die angeben, wie seine Elemente konstruiert sind.</u>

Ein Typ wird also nicht als abstrakte Gesamtheit von Objekten verstanden, auch ist nicht erforderlich, die Gesamtheit der Objekte des Typs oder auch ein einzelnes Objekt effektiv zu erzeugen. Es wird nur gefordert, entsprechend den Konstruktionsregeln entscheiden zu können, ob ein gegebenes Objekt (Konstruktion) Element des Typs ist, geschrieben $a \in T$.

Dieses Konzept hat als Grundlage die erlaubten Mittel für Konstruktionen (z.B. Paarbildung), die in 3.2 durch die konventionellen Typkonstruktoren ähnlich [MAR 73, MAR 79] gegeben werden. In 3.3 mache ich mit der Anwendung konkreter Datenstrukturen den Versuch, diese Konstruktionen zu verallgemeinern und ihnen eine an realen Prozessen orientierte Deutung zu geben.

3.2. <u>Typaufbau durch Typkonstruktoren</u> × <u>und</u> →

Die primitiven Grundtypen sind Void mit dem Element () und Bool mit den Elementen 0 und 1. Zu jedem Typ gibt es den üblichen if-then-else-Operator, ein besonderer if-then-else-Operator ist auf Typen (statt einfache Elemente) anwendbar. Alle Typen werden erzeugt aus Void und Bool durch Anwendung der Typkonstruktoren × und → und rekursiver Typgleichungen.

<u>Typkonstruktor</u> × <u>(abhängiges Produkt)</u>

In der Literatur trägt × die Bezeichnung disjunkte Vereinigung einer Familie von Typen (Σ), wird hier aber zur Verwendung in einer Programmiersprache umbenannt.

× ist selber von einem Typ zweiter Stufe, der hier zunächst nur intuitiv verstanden werden kann:

× $\in$ A:<u>type</u> → [(A → <u>type</u>) → <u>type</u>], (die Klammern [] werden künftig weggelassen).

Dabei bezeichnet <u>type</u> den Typ aller Typen erster Stufe. × kann als Funktion aufgefaßt werden, deren Resultattyp vom Argument abhängt. Das erste Argument ist ein Typ A, das zweite eine Funktion, die jedem Element von A einen Typ zuordnet. (Solche Typfunktionen können zunächst durch Lambda-Ausdrücke dargestellt werden.) Zu den Argumenten A $\in$ <u>type</u> und B $\in$ A→<u>type</u> erzeugt × als Resultat den Typ A×B. Ist B keine Typ-funktion, sondern ein Ausdruck mit einer freien Variable a vom Typ A, so kann a auch durch folgenden Ausdruck gebunden werden: a:A × B, gleichbedeutend mit A × λa.B.

A×B wird natürlich durch eine Konstruktionsregel für seine Elemente definiert: Ist a$\in$A und b$\in$B(a), so ist P_{AB}ab $\in$ A×B. Dabei ist P_{AB} der Paarkonstruktor für A×B [CON 82],

P_{AB} $\in$ a:A → B(a) → A×B.

Mit A×B sind auch zwei Selektoren verbunden:

first_{AB} $\in$ A×B → A, $\text{first}_{AB}(P_{AB}\text{ab})$ = a,

second_{AB} $\in$ c:(A×B) → B(first_{AB}(c)), $\text{second}_{AB}(P_{AB}\text{ab})$ = b.

Ist B eine konstante Funktion, so entsteht der Spezialfall des gewöhnlichen _kartesischen Produkts_ A×B (Recordtyp), hier kann B auch einfach als konstanter Typ geschrieben werden.

Beispiel für eine entsprechende Typdefinition:

Aufsatz = aufsatz(a:Autor × t:Titel).

Dabei sind Autor und Titel vorher definierte Typen. Der Typ Aufsatz arbeitet mit dem neu eingeführten Paarkonstruktor aufsatz (statt P) und ist daher verschieden von Autor × Titel. Die Selektoren erhalten hier die Namen a bzw. t; sie werden auch verwendet als Namen der entsprechenden Komponenten in Anwendungen des Konstruktors aufsatz der Form aufsatz(a=..., t=...).

Die übliche _disjunkte_ (diskriminierende) _Vereinigung_ zweier Typen ist ein Spezialfall eines echt abhängigen Produkts:

A + B = b:Bool × if b=0 then A else B.

Die Elemente von A+B sind Paare der Form P_{A+B}bx mit b$\in$Bool und x$\in$A für b=0, x$\in$B für b=1.

Die Verwendung des Paarkonstruktors und der Selektoren für + ist aber in der Programmierung meist unbequem, daher sollen Elemente von A bzw. B auch direkt die entsprechenden Elemente von A+B bezeichnen, falls ihre Zugehörigkeit zu A bzw. B eindeutig entscheidbar ist.

Beispiel:

Aufsatz-Liste = nil(Void) + cons(head:Aufsatz × tail:Aufsatz-Liste).

Dies ist eine rekursive Typgleichung unter Verwendung der Typkonstruktoren + und ×, ihr minimaler Fixpunkt ist der Typ aller endlichen Listen von Aufsätzen (in der Sprechweise der denotationalen Semantik). nil(Void) ist dabei der Typ mit dem einzigen Element nil, er entsteht durch Anwendung des (neu eingeführten) Konstruktors nil auf das Element () von Void. Es ist eindeutig entscheidbar, zu welchem der Typ-

Argumente von + ein Objekt gehört, daher können Elemente von Aufsatz-Liste auch direkt durch nil oder durch Objekte der Form cons(x,y) bezeichnet werden.

Typkonstruktor → (abhängiger Funktionstyp)

→ wird in der Literatur als kartesisches Produkt einer Familie von Typen bezeichnet (Π).
→ ist vom selben Typ zweiter Stufe wie ×:
→ ∈ A:<u>type</u> → (A → <u>type</u>) → <u>type</u>. (Die → im Typausdruck sind aus der zweiten Stufe, verschieden von →!)
Zu den Argumenten A∈type und B∈A→type erzeugt → als Resultat den Typ A→B. Seine Elemente haben die Wirkung von Funktionen (Operatoren), die jedem a∈A ein b∈B(a) zuordnen, Beispiele waren bereits P_{AB}, first und second.
Ist B ein Ausdruck mit einer freien Variable a vom Typ A, so kann man wieder a:A → B statt A → λa.B schreiben.

Die Funktionen des Typs A→B können auf verschiedene Art konstruiert werden, ein abschließendes Rezept kann hier nicht gegeben werden.
[MAR 73] konstruiert Funktionen als Lambda-Ausdrücke: Sei b ein Ausdruck mit einer freien Variablen x, so daß unter der Voraussetzung x∈A immer b∈B(x) ist. Dann ist die Abstraktion λx.b Element von A→B.
[CON 81, CON 82] konstruiert Funktionen mit den Kombinatoren S und K, diese Methode ist der Verwendung von Paarkonstruktoren bei A×B ähnlicher.
Ein f ∈ A→B kann auf ein a∈A angewandt werden: f(a) ∈ B(a). Übliche Array-Typen sind Spezialfälle von A→B mit konstantem B. Darüber hinaus können Arrays mit "gemischten" Komponententypen durch nichtkonstantes B dargestellt werden.

3.3. Typaufbau durch konkrete Datenstrukturen

Der Paarkonstruktor P_{AB} nimmt seine Argumente nur in fester Reihenfolge an, denn das erste Argument bestimmt den Typ B(a) des zweiten. Oder andersherum: Aus der Kenntnis des zweiten Arguments folgt die Kenntnis des ersten. Dies zeigt schon, daß ein Konstruktor (und allgemein jeder Operator) den Charakter eines Prozesses hat, der klassische Funktionsbegriff ist entsprechend zu erweitern. Die betrachteten Ereignisse des Prozesses sind in diesem Fall Argument-Übergaben, sie sind durch die logischen Typ-Abhängigkeiten <u>kausal</u> geordnet. P_{AB} hat aber den Mangel, die Reihenfolge der Argumente auch bei konstantem B

festzulegen, obwohl dann keine Abhängigkeiten bestehen. Es lassen sich
auch komplexere Typen denken, z.B. ein dreifaches Produkt
$a:A \times b:B \times C[a,b]$, in dem nur eine Abhängigkeit des dritten Arguments
vom ersten und **zweiten** besteht. Dann können das erste und zweite Argument zuerst _parallel_ (d.h. in beliebiger Reihenfolge oder gleichzeitig) übergeben werden, danach das dritte.

Um solche kausalen Abhängigkeiten beim Aufbau von Datenstrukturen
auszudrücken, bieten sich CDS an. Die Konstruktion der Elemente eines
Typs soll also durch eine CDS beschrieben werden. Dazu wird hier (als
erster Ansatz) eine besondere Art der Typbeschreibung entwickelt:

Eine _getypte CDS_ besteht aus einer endlichen Folge von _Komponenten_.
Eine Komponente ist aufgebaut aus:

náme: der Name n der Komponente;

celltype: der Typ A der Zellen, das ist selbst wieder eine getypte CDS
oder der Name einer solchen (Rekursion möglich), zusammen
mit Zugriffsbedingungen in Abhängigkeit von anderen Komponenten;

valuetype: eine Funktion $F \in A \to$ _type_, welche die Typen für Werte der
einzelnen Zellen angibt.

Aus der getypten CDS läßt sich eine eigentliche CDS $M=(C,V,E,\vdash)$
herleiten. Dabei bestimmt eine Komponente die Teilmenge C' der Zellen
n.a für $a \in A$, sowie die Teilmenge $n.a:C' \times F(a)$ von E und den Teil der
Zugriffsrelation $\vdash$ für die Zellen C'.

Beispiel: getypte CDS für $A \to B$ mit gegebenem $A \in$ _type_ und $B \in A \to$ _type_,
hat nur eine Komponente:
    name: c; _celltype_: A; _valuetype_: B .

Die erzeugte CDS sieht arrayartig aus: Die Zellen c.a mit $a \in A$ haben
(ohne Zugriffsbedingungen) Werte aus B(a). Eine andere Darstellung von
Funktionen (genauer: sequentiellen Algorithmen auf CDS) durch CDS ist
in [BC 82] angegeben.

Beispiel: getypte CDS für $A \times B$:
1. Komponente:
    name: first; _celltype_: Void; _valuetype_: A (konstant)
2. Komponente:
    name: second; _celltype_: (name: first/access); _valuetype_: B .

Die Typbeschreibung von _celltype_ der 2. Komponente enthält eine Zu-
griffsbedingung. Allgemein kann eine Typbeschreibung (_name_: c/access)
innerhalb einer _celltype_-Typbeschreibung vorkommen und bedeutet dann

den Wertetyp der Zelle mit Namen c in einer der anderen Komponenten. Der Zugriff auf die betreffenden Zellen (hier die Zellen second.a der 2. Komponente) ist nur erlaubt, wenn c den entsprechenden Wert des Zellennamens (hier a) trägt.

<u>Beispiel</u>: getypte CDS für a:A × b:B × C[a,b]:

1. Komponente:
   <u>name</u>: first;   <u>celltype</u>: Void;   <u>valuetype</u>: A   (konstant)
2. Komponente:
   <u>name</u>: second;   <u>celltype</u>: Void;   <u>valuetype</u>: B   (konstant)
3. Komponente:
   <u>name</u>: third;   <u>celltype</u>: (<u>name</u>: first/access; <u>name</u>: second/access);
   <u>valuetype</u>: $\lambda(a,b).C$.

<u>celltype</u> der 3. Komponente gibt hier den Typ A×B an (B unabhängig) mit entsprechenden Zugriffsbedingungen von den Komponenten first und second.

In einer Programmiersprache wird man die einfachere Schreibweise des abhängigen Mehrfachprodukts mit × gegenüber der getypten CDS bevorzugen, aus den Typ-Abhängigkeiten der Parameter läßt sich eine entsprechende getypte CDS erzeugen. Man kann auch hier spezielle Konstruktoren definieren, die sich als Prozeß gemäß der CDS verhalten, z.B. tripel(a:A × b:B × c:C[a,b]).

<u>4. Typen höherer Stufe und Universen</u>

<u>4.1.</u> Entsprechend dem Prinzip aus 3.1 "Jedes Objekt ist Element eines Typs" haben auch die Typen erster Stufe einen Typ, man faßt sie zu dem Typ <u>type</u> der zweiten Stufe zusammen. Ein Typ zweiter Stufe wird eine <u>Art</u> genannt ("large type" in [MAR 73], in [MCC 79] wird der Typ eines Typs "kind" genannt). Auch das zweite Prinzip aus 3.1 ist erfüllt: Die Art <u>type</u> wird durch Konstruktionsregeln für ihre Elemente (die Typen erster Stufe) definiert. Diese Konstruktionsregeln können auf zwei Arten gegeben werden: durch die Typkonstruktoren in 3.2 und durch getypte CDS in 3.3.

Analog zur Notation von [MAR 73] ist <u>type</u> das erste Glied V_1 einer unendlichen Kette von <u>Universen</u> $V_1 \in V_2 \in V_3 \in \ldots$ Die ersten drei Universen nenne ich <u>type</u> $\in$ <u>kind</u> $\in$ <u>kindtype</u>, höhere Universen werden (bisher) in der Programmierung nicht verwendet. Die Elemente des dritten Universums <u>kindtype</u> nenne ich <u>Arttypen</u>.

Das Universum <u>kind</u> der Arten wird analog zu <u>type</u> konstruiert, nur sind jetzt die <u>primitiven Grundarten</u> <u>type</u> sowie alle Elemente $t \in$<u>type</u>. (Alle Typen aus <u>type</u> sind also auch Arten, diese etwas unschöne Lösung entspricht [MAR 79]. [CON 81] verwendet statt dessen einen expliziten up-Konstruktor, der Typen und ihre Elemente auf die Ebene der Arten "liftet", dies erfordert aber mehr Schreibarbeit.)

Es gibt <u>Artkonstruktoren</u> $\times_2$, $\to_2 \in$ A:<u>kind</u> $\to_3$ (A $\to_3$ <u>kind</u>) $\to_3$ <u>kind</u>, $+_2$ abgeleitet aus $\times_2$, welche analog den entsprechenden Typkonstruktoren arbeiten. (Dabei ist $\to_3$ der Funktionstypkonstruktor 3. Stufe, der ähnlich wie $\to_2$ bei der Deklaration von $\to$ im Vorgriff benutzt wurde.) Die Arten entstehen aus den primitiven Grundarten durch Anwendung von $\times_2$, $\to_2$ und Rekursion. Auch die Konstruktion durch getypte CDS und durch abhängige Mehrfachprodukte läßt sich übertragen.

Allgemein wird ein Universum V_{n+1} ($n \geq 1$) aufgebaut aus den primitiven Grundtypen V_n und $t \in V_n$ unter Anwendung der Typkonstruktoren $\times_{n+1}$, $\to_{n+1}$ und Rekursion.

4.2. Die folgenden <u>Beispiele</u> sollen zeigen, daß das soeben beschriebene Typsystem die Anforderungen des Kap. 1 an das "getypte Rechnen mit Typen" erfüllt. Sie führen zur Programmierung eines abstrakten Programmschemas durch einen Operator zweiter Stufe, dessen Argumenttyp durch eine rekursiv definierte Art gegeben ist. Solche rekursiven Arten lassen sich nur in einem Typsystem definieren, welches neben dem Universum <u>type</u> auch ein vollständig ausgeprägtes Universum <u>kind</u> formalisiert.

ORDER = order (set: <u>type</u> $\times_2$
                rel: (set $\times$ set $\to$ Bool))
    $\in$ <u>kind</u>.

Die Elemente der Art ORDER werden mit dem Konstruktor order konstruiert, welcher nacheinander als Argumente einen Typ set und dann eine beliebige Relation aus set $\times$ set $\to$ Bool annimmt. (Der Relationentyp wird hier als Art behandelt, siehe den Typ von $\times_2$.) set und rel sind Selektoren, set ist zusätzlich die gebundene Variable im abhängigen Produkt. Man beachte, daß Ordnungen (d.h. Elemente der Art ORDER) keine Typen sind und (dementsprechend) keine Elemente haben.

Ein bekannter rekursiver Typoperator:

List: $\underline{type} \rightarrow_2 \underline{type}$,   (wobei $\underline{type} \rightarrow_2 \underline{type} \in \underline{kind}$)

List(t) = nil(Void) + cons(head:t × tail:List(t)).

Hier werden die Konstruktoren nil, cons und die Selektoren head, tail
polymorph verwendet, d.h. ohne Bezeichnung des speziellen Elementtyps.

 Man kann auch die Art von Listen von Elementen einer Art bilden,
durch den entsprechenden rekursiven Artoperator:

Typelist: $\underline{kind} \rightarrow_3 \underline{kind}$,   (wobei $\underline{kind} \rightarrow_3 \underline{kind} \in \underline{kindtype}$)

Typelist(a) = nil(Void) $+_2$ cons(head:a $\times_2$ tail:Typelist(a)).

(Hierbei wird der Typ nil(Void) auf die Stufe der Arten "geliftet".)

 Nun soll folgende Aufgabe programmiert werden: Gegeben sei eine
Grundmenge und eine Liste von vollständig geordneten Attributmengen
mit jeweils einer Projektion von der Grundmenge in die Attributmenge.
(Z.B.: Die Grundmenge ist Aufsatz aus Kap. 3, die Attributmengen Autor
und Titel (mit den Projektionen a bzw. t) sind jeweils mit der alpha-
betischen Ordnung versehen.)
Eine solche Struktur wird beschrieben durch die (mit Hilfe von
Typelist definierte) Art KOMPLEXORDER:

KOMPLEXORDER =
  komplexorder (kset: $\underline{type}$ $\times_2$

                alist: Typelist(attribute: ORDER $\times_2$
                              projection:(kset $\rightarrow$ set(attribute)))).

Die Aufgabe besteht darin, einen Operator zweiter Stufe "Buildorder"
zu programmieren, der eine Komplexordnung (ein Element der Art
KOMPLEXORDER) in die durch die Attributordnungen erzeugte Ordnung auf
der Grundmenge kset überführt. Dabei soll an erster Stelle nach der
ersten Attributordnung der alist geordnet werden. (Die entstehende
Ordnung ist i.a. nicht antisymmetrisch. Im Beispiel: Die Aufsätze
sollen an erster Stelle nach Autoren, an zweiter Stelle nach Titeln
geordnet sein.)
Buildorder arbeitet rekursiv über der Komponente alist.

```
Buildorder: KOMPLEXORDER →₂ ORDER

Buildorder(ko) =
order (set = kset(ko),
        rel = if alist(ko) = nil
              then λ(x,y).1   {Relation rel konstant erfüllt}
              else
                 let ordatt  = rel(attribute(head(alist(ko)))),
                     proj     =    projection(head(alist(ko))),
                     ordhead = λ(x,y).ordatt(proj(x),proj(y))
                                  ∈ set × set → Bool,
                     ordtail = rel(Buildorder
                                      (komplexorder(kset(ko),
                                                     tail(alist(ko)))))
                 in
                 λ(x,y).if ordhead(x,y) and ordhead(y,x)
                        then ordtail(x,y)
                            {x=y bez. der höherwertigen Relation
                             ordhead: der Rest ordtail bestimmt die
                             Reihenfolge von x,y in rel}
                        else ordhead(x,y) )
                            {x≠y bez. ordhead:
                             nur ordhead bestimmt die Reihenfolge}.
```

5. Ausblick

Die Darstellung der Typkonstruktion durch konkrete Datenstrukturen
weist auf einen fundamentalen Zusammenhang zwischen intuitionistischer
Logik und parallelen Prozessen (in der Form von Ereignisstrukturen
oder Petri-Netzen) hin. Die Untersuchung dieses Zusammenhangs wurde
auch bereits in [MB 81] begonnen und sollte fortgeführt werden. (In
diesem Zusammenhang müßte die mathematische Semantik der hier vorgestellten Typen genauer definiert und untersucht werden.)
Aus einer entsprechenden einheitlichen Theorie könnte ein praktisches
Programmiersystem mit einer Spezifikations- und Programmiersprache
hervorgehen, welche mit wenigen einfachen, aber mächtigen Sprachkon-
strukten die Aufgaben einer Programmierlogik, einer logischen und
funktionalen Programmiersprache sowie einer Sprache zur Beschreibung
paralleler Prozesse erfüllt.

Anmerkungen: Ich danke Claus-Werner Lermen, Dieter Maurer, Beatrix
Weisgerber und Reinhard Wilhelm für die Diskussionen über diese
Arbeit.

Literatur:

[BC 82]   Berry,G.;Curien,P.L.: Sequential algorithms on concrete data
          structures. Theoretical Computer Science 2o(1982)265-321
[BER 81] Berry,G.: Programming with concrete data structures and se-
          quential algorithms. Proc. of the 1981 Conf. on Functional
          Programming Languages and Computer Architecture, ACM,
          Wentworth-by-the-Sea 1981, pp. 49-57
[BMS 8o] Burstall,R.M.; MacQueen,D.B.; Sannella,D.T.: HOPE: An experi-
          mental applicative language. Conference Record of the 198o
          LISP Conference, Stanford 198o, pp. 136-143
[CON 81] Constable,R.L.; Zlatin,D.R.: The type theory of PL/CV3.
          Logics of Programs (D. Kozen ed.), LNCS 131, pp. 72-93.
          Berlin-Heidelberg-New York: Springer 1981
[CON 82] Constable,R.L.: Intensional analysis of functions and types.
          Report CSR-118-82, Dept. of Comp. Sci., Univ. Edinburgh 1982
[GMW 79] Gordon,M.; Milner,R.; Wadsworth,C.: Edinburgh LCF.
          LNCS 78. Berlin-Heidelberg-New York: Springer 1979
[KP 78]   Kahn,G.; Plotkin,G.: Structures de données concrètes.
          Rapport IRIA-LABORIA 336, 1978
[LSA 77] Liskov,B.; Snyder,A.; Atkinson,R.; Schaffert,C.: Abstraction
          mechanisms in CLU. Comm. of the ACM 2o,8(Aug. 1977)564-576
[MAR 73] Martin-Löf,P.: An intuitionistic theory of types: predicative
          part. Logic Colloquium '73 (H.E. Rose, J.C. Sheperdson eds.),
          pp. 73-118. Amsterdam: North-Holland 1975
[MAR 79] Martin-Löf,P.: Constructive mathematics and computer program-
          ming. Logic, Methodology and Philosophy of Science VI (1979)
          (L.J. Cohen etal eds.), pp. 153-175. Amsterdam: North-Holland
          1982
[MB 81]   Mauri,G.; Brambilla,M.: On the logic of concurrency and con-
          flict. Second European Workshop on Application and Theory of
          Petri Nets 1981 (C. Girault, W. Reisig eds.), Informatik-
          Fachberichte 52, pp. 258-268. Berlin-Heidelberg-New York:
          Springer 1982
[MCC 79] McCracken,N.J.: An investigation of a programming language
          with a polymorphic type structure. Dissertation, School of
          Computer and Information Science, Syracuse University 1979
[MUE 83] Müller,F.: Funktionale Programmiersprache mit konstruktivem
          Typsystem - Beispiel Datenbankprogrammierung. Bericht Fachbe-
          reich 10 - Informatik, Universität des Saarlandes,
          Saarbrücken 1983
[NOR 83] Nordström,B.: Types and specifications. Information Process-
          ing 83 (IFIP) (R.E.A. Mason ed.), pp. 915-92o. Amsterdam:
          North-Holland 1983

Portable adaptierbare Compiler*

Richard Ammer
Peter Meinen
Gerhard Rehmann

Softlab GmbH, München

Zusammenfassung:

Für das Entwicklungssystem CAMIC wurde eine Familie von Cross-Compilern für Mikroprozessoren entwickelt. Wichtigste Anforderung war die effiziente Adaptierbarkeit an neue Prozessoren. Der Vortrag gibt einen Überblick über die Konzepte und einen Erfahrungsbericht unserer Vorgehensweise bei Entwurf und Realisierung. Im besonderen wird auf die universelle Zwischensprache und ihr Speichermodell, die Baumtransformatoren, die universellen Optimierer und das symbolische Debugging eingegangen.

1. Der Rahmen für das Projekt

Keine existierende Programmiersprache ist heute für alle Anwendungen, gerade im Bereich der Mikroprozessoranwendungen, durchgängig geeignet. Neuere Entwicklungen von Breitbandsprachen und Transformationssystemen sind vielversprechend, auch über die reine Implementierung hinaus die Formalisierung des Entwurfs zu unterstützen, haben aber derzeit - vor allem in der apparativen Unterstützung - noch keine Praxisreife.

Ein Mikrocomputer-Entwicklungssystem muß deshalb ein Spektrum von Sprachen anbieten, das die programmiertechnischen Möglichkeiten des Prozessors auf der einen Seite und die Anforderungen der Anwendung auf der anderen Seite berücksichtigt:

- PASCAL als breit akzeptierte und (weitgehend) standardisierte höhere Sprache, insbesondere für die neueren leistungsfähigen 16-Bit-Prozessoren,

- C als "die" portable standardisierte maschinennahe Sprache
  und

---

* Das Projekt wurde teilweise mit Mitteln des Bundesministeriums für Forschung und Technologie gefördert.

- "Spartanische" Sprachen für Anwendungsfälle, in denen C und PASCAL nicht in Frage
  kommen, insbesondere für die Single-Chip-Prozessoren.

Im Vortrag geben wir einen Überblick, wie wir für unser universelles Mikroprozessor-
Entwicklungssystem CAMIC Cross-Compiler für PASCAL und C entwickelten: Anforderungen
und Randbedingungen, Konzept und Realisierung werden vorgestellt.

2. CAMIC

CAMIC (Computer Aided Microprocessing) ist ein Entwicklungssystem neuer Art, das die
Methoden des Software-Engineering, die sich in den vergangenen Jahren in großen Ent-
wicklungsvorhaben bewährt haben, auch für Mikroprozessor-Anwendungen verfügbar
macht: die Unterstützung aller Projektphasen und die zentrale Haltung aller Daten
(Entwicklungsdokumentation, Programme, Testdaten usw.) eines Projektes auf einem
leistungsfähigen Rechnersystem sind seine wesentlichen Merkmale. Eingebettet in
diesen methodischen Rahmen sind zahlreiche Werkzeuge für einzelne Entwicklungs-
schritte. Eine wesentliche Werkzeuggruppe für die Implementierungsphase sind die
Cross-Compiler für PASCAL und C. Basissystem von CAMIC ist UNIX.

3. Randbedingungen

Während der Entwicklung des CAMIC-Systems mußten wir feststellen, daß der zunächst
verfolgte Weg, vorhandene fertige Cross-Software-Produkte in CAMIC zu integrieren,
wenig erfolgreich war - aus technischen Gründen, weil wir höhere Ansprüche hatten,
oder weil die Palette unterstützter Prozessoren und/oder Sprachen bei jeweils einem
Hersteller zu schmal war. Hinzu kam noch die Anforderung, schnell auf Kundenwünsche
reagieren zu können, z. B. einen Codegenerator für einen x-beliebigen Prozessor mit
einer Lieferzeit von wenigen Monaten bereitzustellen. Dies machte es notwendig,
gerade auf dem Sektor der Cross-Software die Kompetenz im Hause zu behalten.

Für die Entwicklung des gesamten Cross-Compiler-Paketes stand etwa ein Jahr zur Verfügung. In dieser Zeit wurden Cross-Compiler für 8086, M68000, Z8001, Z8002 und Z80
entwickelt; danach folgte der Cross-Compiler für M6809.

4. Anforderungen

Aus der Aufgabenstellung ergaben sich eine Reihe von Anforderungen an das Cross-Com-
piler-Paket:

a) Effiziente Adaptierbarkeit an neue Zielprozessoren: neue Codegeneratoren sollen mit kalkulierbarem Aufwand in relativ kurzer Zeit realisiert werden können.

b) Effiziente Codeerzeugung für eine möglicherweise komplexe Adreßraum-Architektur: Mikroprozessor-Systeme haben häufig unzusammenhängende Adreßräume mit speziellen Adressierungsbedingungen, wie Interruptvektoren, Overlays, E/A-Adressen; die Zeit- und Platzeffizienz spielt eine besondere Rolle.

c) Unterstützung des quellsprachbezogenen Debuggings, auch unter Verwendung extern angekoppelter Geräte: der Anwender kann am CAMIC-Terminal mit einem In-Circuit-Emulator symbolisch debuggen.

d) Einfache Bedienbarkeit nach dem Konzept der "Wissensbasiertheit".

e) Portabilität des Compilers auf verschiedene Basismaschinen (schon während der Entwicklung zeigte sich, daß die ursprünglich als Basis ausgewählte PDP11 nur geringe Bedeutung haben würde; inzwischen laufen die Compiler auch auf VAX, CADMUS (M68000) und Perkin-Elmer 32xx).

f) Unterstützung eines auf der Datenabstraktion basierenden Konzepts der Modularisierung.

g) Adaptierbarkeit an weitere Sprachen: die aus der Marktsituation heraus getroffene Entscheidung für PASCAL und C darf der Einbindung neuer Parser nicht entgegenstehen (z. B. für Modula oder Ada).

Aus der knappen Terminsituation ergab sich noch die weitere Anforderung, Vorhandenes möglichst gut auszunutzen. Zusammen mit g) ergab sich zusätzlich die Forderung der

h) Einbindbarkeit vorhandener Parser.

5. Das Gesamtkonzept

Da wir in bezug auf die Modularisierung eigene Ideen hatten (konzeptionell an Ada angelehnt), wurde dafür ein eigenständiger "Strukturierungscompiler" geschrieben. Dieser wertet die "sichtbaren" Teile (=Schnittstelle) eines Moduls aus und erzeugt daraus Listen exportierter Objekte. Die Listen importierter Objekte von anderen Modulen werden entsprechend ausgewertet. Diese "Strukturierungs-Information" wird ähnlich wie der Objektcode in Bibliotheken verwaltet.

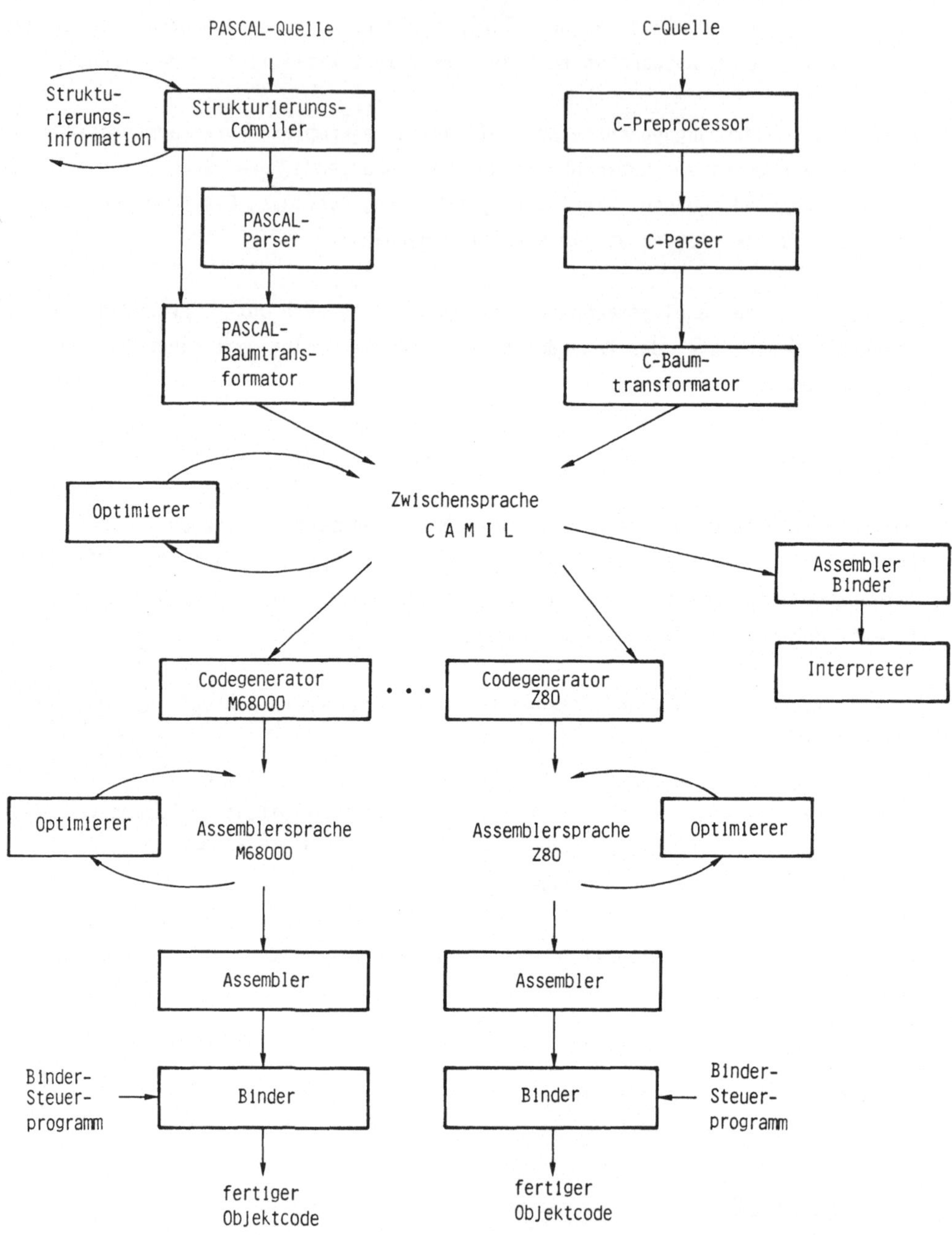

Abb. 1: CAMIC - Compiler - Gesamtkonzept

Die Strukturierung, d. h. die Modularisierung, geschieht also außerhalb des Parsers.
Modularisierung wie auch der Parser sind getrennt verwendbar, d. h. es ließe sich
auch ein anderes Modularisierungskonzept oder ein anderes PASCAL einfach integrieren.

Als Parser wurden in praktisch unveränderter Form fertige Produkte genommen: der
bestmöglichen Portabilität auf verschiedene Basismaschinen wegen die im PDP-11-UNIX
verfügbaren C- und PASCAL-Parser: der C-Parser von D. M. Ritchie (1) und der PASCAL-
Parser ´pi´ aus Berkeley (Thompson, Graham, Joy, Haley) (2). Durch ihre weite Ver-
breitung definieren beide einen de-facto Standard. Der ´pi´ zeichnet sich zudem
durch eine ausgezeichnete Syntaxfehlerbehandlung aus.

Die benutzten C- und Pascal-Parser erzeugen sehr unterschiedliche Zwischencodes, die
durch Baumtransformatoren in die CAMIC-Zwischensprache "CAMIL" umgewandelt werden.

Auf der Zwischensprache setzten nun die Codegeneratoren auf, die ein Programm in
Assemblersprache produzieren. Daran schließen sich die in CAMIC vorhandenen Cross-
Assembler und -Binder an. Letztere besorgen die Anordnung im Adreßraum und den end-
gültigen Aufbau der für das Debugging benutzten Symboltabelle. Der Bindevorgang wird
durch eine spezielle "Binde-Steuersprache" gesteuert, die das Demultiplexing der
übersetzten Moduln in Codeteile mit verschiedenen Adressierungsbedingungen (in CAMIC
"Attribute" genannt) und das Aufteilen auf Segmente angibt.

Die Hauptlast der Optimierung tragen Peephole-Optimierer, die sowohl auf der
Zwischensprache als auch auf dem erzeugten Zielprozessor-Assembler arbeiten. Hierfür wurde eine adaptierbare Lösung gefunden.

6. Die Zwischensprache CAMIL

Da die Implementierer neuer Codegeneratoren stets auf der Zwischensprache aufsetzen,
wurde ihr in der Entwurfsphase ganz besondere Bedeutung zugemessen. Nach eingehender
Begutachtung vieler existierender Compiler-Zwischensprachen wurde beschlossen, eine
eigene Sprache zu definieren. Beispielgebend dafür waren im besonderen

- die sehr hohe, abstrakte Zwischensprache des C-Compilers in UNIX V.7 (1),

- die in der PASCAL-Welt verbreiteten relativ niedrigen Zwischensprachen, z. B. die
  vom Berkeley-pi (3) oder die des Micro Concurrent Pascal mCP von Enertec (4),

- die portable, für mehrere Sprachen einsetzbare EM aus Amsterdam (5) (die jedoch das symbolische Debugging nicht ausreichend unterstützt).

Die neu definierte Zwischensprache CAMIL ist

- niedrig genug, um einfach Codegeneratoren zu schreiben und um sie zu interpretieren,

- trotzdem aber ausdrucksstark (und auch redundant) genug, um effizient in den Maschinencode der gängigen Prozessoren übersetzt zu werden,

- linear und als Baum interpretierbar,

- für das quellsprachbezogene Debugging geeignet,

- interpretierbar und bindefähig.

Die letzte Eigenschaft der Zwischensprache schafft die Möglichkeit, Programme getrennt zu übersetzen, sie zu binden und dann zu interpretieren (siehe Abb. 1). Die Bindefähigkeit wurde durch die Einbettung der CAMIL-Syntax in die Rahmensyntax der (adaptierbaren) CAMIC-Assembler erreicht.

Einen Überblick über die Sprachelemente gibt der Anhang A. CAMIL enthält 116 Operatoren, die zum Teil redundant sind. Von diesen sind 50 typisiert. Diese Typen entsprechen den elementaren Typen der Quellsprachen; in CAMIL wird ihnen jedoch keine semantische Bedeutung zugemessen. Es handelt sich also lediglich um Aufzählungstypen, deren Vorrat beliebig erweiterbar ist. Die derzeit für C und PASCAL vorgesehenen 13 Typen sind:

char / unsigned char	mit der Länge 1 Byte
short / unsigned short	mit der Länge 2 Byte
int / unsigned int	mit einer Länge, die zwischen der von short und der von long liegt, je nach Zweckmäßigkeit auf dem jeweiligen Prozessor
long / unsigned long	als Grundtypen aller ganzzahligen Typen

float / double   für Gleitpunktzahlen zweier ver-
                                  schiedener Längen

extended   für IEEE-Gleitpunktarithmetik

pointer   für Pointer (Adressen)

bool   für logische Werte

CAMIL kann man sich als die Maschinensprache einer hypothetischen Keller-Maschine
vorstellen: alle Operationen erwarten ihre Daten im Keller und hinterlassen ihre
Ergebnisse ebenfalls dort. Weiter wird der Keller verwendet, um die dynamische und
statische Verkettung festzuhalten und Prozedurparameter zu übergeben.

Die typisierten CAMIL-Operationen erwarten Operanden vom gleichen Typ im Keller.
Zur Typkonversion steht ein universeller Konvertieroperator zur Verfügung.

Es gibt keine In-Line-Funktionen für Ein-Ausgabe, Speicherverwaltung (Heap) und ähn-
liches. Diese Dienste werden als Aufrufe an das Laufzeitsystem abgebildet.

7. Das Speichermodell von CAMIL

Die Definition eines Speichermodells wurde in die CAMIL-Sprachdefinition aufgenom-
men,

- um eine konzeptionell klare Grundlage für das Verständnis zu haben,

- um dem Implementierer von Codegeneratoren eine möglichst genaue Anleitung zu
  geben und

- um die Implementierung portabler Laufzeitsysteme und portabler Test- und Debug-
  werkzeuge zu unterstützen.

Der CAMIL zugrundeliegende Speicher ist byteorientiert, d. h. die kleinste adres-
sierbare Einheit ist das Byte. Die Größe der Bytes ist dabei ohne Bedeutung. Auf-
einanderfolgende Bytes haben die Adreßdifferenz Eins. Bytes können zielmaschinen-
abhängig zu Worten zusammengefaßt sein; dies ist jedoch für CAMIL ohne Bedeutung,
mit einer Ausnahme: es kann für einen Zielprozessor festgelegt sein, daß nicht jede
beliebige Anzahl von Bytes als Operanden von Keller-Operationen verwendet werden
kann.

Adressen (im Speicher) haben eine beliebige, aber für einen speziellen Zielprozessor nach oben beschränkte Größe, die die Zahl der Bytes festlegt, die zum Abspeichern einer Adresse benötigt werden.

Getrennte Adreßräume für Befehle und Daten sind gestattet. Befehlsbereich und Datenbereich müssen jeder für sich jedoch homogen sein.

Weitere Adreßräume können existieren, werden jedoch von CAMIL nicht berührt, z. B. der Heap (der mittels Laufzeitroutinen bedient wird) und allgemein verwendbare Register.

Der Datenadreßraum ist aufgeteilt in zwei getrennte Bereiche:

- globale Daten und
- Keller (Stack) für lokale Daten.

Diese beiden Bereiche müssen Bestandteil desselben Adreßraums sein, da alle Daten mit Pointern desselben Typs adressiert werden.
Der globale Datenbereich wird durch Ablageanweisungen in Objekte zerteilt und zum Teil vorbesetzt. Aufteilung und Vorbesetzung sind rein statisch und erfolgen spätestens beim Binden. Objekte im globalen Bereich werden in CAMIL durch Namen angesprochen.

Der Keller besteht aus sog. "Stack Frames", die die lokalen Daten und einige organisatorische Information aller an einer momentanen Aufrufverschachtelung beteiligten Blöcke enthalten. Der obere Teil eines Stack Frames enthält den Operandenkeller für die Stackoperationen.

Die CAMIL-Definition geht von (der Fiktion von) folgenden zwei Spezialregistern aus:

- SP (stack pointer) und
- LB (local base).

Die Adresse der obersten Zelle des Operandenkellers steht im Register SP, die Anfangsadresse des obersten Stack Frames im Register LB. Objekte im Stack werden adressiert entweder über ihre Distanz (Offset) vom Anfang des Stack Frames, zu dem sie gehören, oder relativ zu SP. Im CAMIL werden diese Offsets durch absolute Zahlen gegeben. Die Parser enthalten dafür eine Parametrisierung mit den Typlängen.

Stack Frames werden erzeugt beim Aufruf von Prozeduren und Funktionen; sie werden
entfernt bei der Rückkehr aus diesen. Die Stack Frames auf dem Stack sind durch je
eine statische und dynamische Verweiskette miteinander verbunden, d. h. jeder Block
enthält je einen Verweis auf seinen statischen und seinen dynamischen Vorgänger.
Einen besonderen "Display-Vector" gibt es nicht. Funktions- und Prozeduraufrufe mit
variabler Parameterzahl werden nicht ausgeschlossen.

8. Baumtransformatoren

Wie erwähnt, wurden in CAMIC bereits vorhandene Parser eingesetzt, die selber sehr
unterschiedliche Zwischencodes produzieren:

- Der C-Parser erzeugt einen recht "hohen" abstrakten Syntaxbaum mit maximal zwei-
  stelligen Operatoren. Die lineare Aufschreibung dieses Zwischencodes wäre nicht
  interpretierbar. Erklärbar aus der Geschichte von C, werden neuere Eigenschaften
  durch monadische Präfix-Operatoren ausgedrückt, z. B.

  -- ASSIGN (linke Seite, rechte Seite)
     für normale Zuweisungen und

  -- STRASSIGN (ASSIGN (linke Seite, rechte Seite))
     für Struktur-Zuweisungen.

  Programmverzweigungen werden durch numerierte Marken ausgedrückt.

- Der Pascal-Parser erzeugt einen ziemlich niedrigen (aber unmittelbar interpre-
  tierbaren) Code. Operatoren können eine variable Stelligkeit haben. Programmverzweigungen werden durch absolute, d. h. Zwischencode-relative Adressen dargestellt.

Für beide Parser wurden Baumtransformatoren geschrieben, die i. w. den vom Parser
aufgebauten Syntaxbaum in einem CAMIL-Baum umwandeln und in linearer Form ausgeben.
Implementierungsmäßig bestehen sie also aus einem baumaufbauenden und einem baumab-
bauenden Teil.

Schon während der Cross-Compiler-Entwicklung hat sich die Entscheidung für den Einsatz von Baumtransformatoren voll bewährt: Änderungen an der Zwischensprache CAMIL
konnten problemlos berücksichtigt werden.

Auch bieten die Baumtransformatoren eine gute Basis für gewisse Optimierungen, z. B. für die Pascal-Anweisung

$$i: = i \; op \; expr$$

die zunächst einmal in

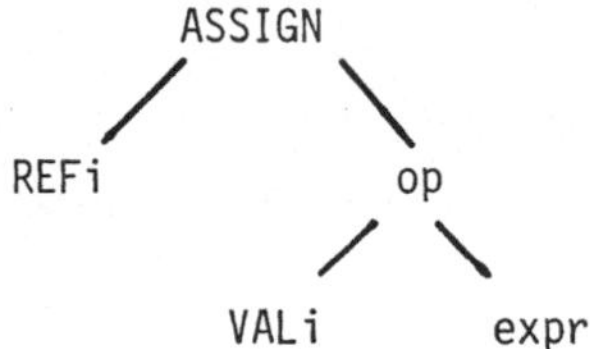

umgewandelt wird, aus dem schließlich

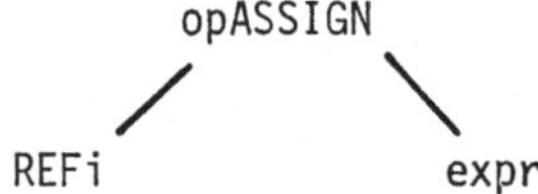

wird. Diese (an sich redundanten) opASSIGNs wurden in CAMIL vorgesehen, um dem Code-generator die Arbeit leicht zu machen, Inkrement- oder Addiere-im-Speicher-Befehle des Zielprozessors zu verwenden.

Über abgeleitete Attribute wird z. B. der Einsatz des bestmöglichen Typs für Zwischenresultate in Formeln gesteuert. Gerade bei den "schwächeren" Mikroprozessoren trägt es sehr zur Effizienz bei, nicht mit unnütz langen Größen zu rechnen.

9. Optimierung

Die Hauptlast der Code-Optimierung tragen Peephole-Optimierer, sowohl auf der CAMIL-Ebene wie im erzeugten Assemblercode. Einem Vorschlag von Lamb (6) folgend, wird dafür ein universeller Optimierer eingesetzt, der auf jeweils speziellen Sätzen von Rewrite-Rules arbeitet. Diese sind in Assembler-ähnlicher Notation gehalten. Sie sind dadurch in der Praxis leicht änderbar, auch experimentell; sie sind dem Anwender zur Anpassung an seine Bedürfnisse zugänglich.

Beispiel (8086):   &0, &1, ... bezeichnen syntaktische Variable

```
Regel 1:                          Regel 4:
    mov &0,BP                         push &0
    add &0,&1                         pop &1
    mov AX,[&0]                       ->
    push AX                           mov &1,&0
    ->
    push WORD PTR [BP][&1]        Regel 5:
                                     mov &0,&0
Regel 2:                             ->
    push &0
    mov &1,&2                     Regel 6:
    pop &3                            mov &1,&2
    ->                               and &0,&1
    mov &3,&0                         ->
    mov &1,&2                         and &0,&2

Regel 3:                          Regel 7:
    mov DI,SP                         mov DI,SP
    mov DI,[DI][2]                    mov DI,[DI]
    pop AX                            mov [DI],&1
    ->                               add SP,2
    pop AX                            ->
    mov DI,SP                         pop DI
    mov DI,[DI]                       mov [DI],&1


Eingabe:
    mov SI,BP
    add SI,-08H
    mov AX,[SI]
    push AX
    mov SI,BP                     Ausgabe:
    add SI,-0AH                       mov AX,WORD PTR [BP][-08H]
    mov AX,[SI]                       and AX,WORD PTR [BP][-0AH]
    push AX                           pop DI
    pop CX                            mov [DI],AX
    pop AX
    and AX,CX
    push AX
    mov DI,SP
    mov DI,[DI][2]
    pop AX
    mov [DI],AX
    add SP,2
```

Die Rewrite-Rules werden wiederholt auf den Text angewandt, bis keine mehr paßt. Für
die Terminierung des Rewrite-Prozesses sorgt normalerweise die Tatsache, daß die
Optimierer-Regeln sämtlich verkürzend sind.

Für den seltenen Fall, daß nicht-verkürzende Regeln vorkommen sollen, hatten wir dem Anwender die Verantwortung überlassen, durch andere Maßnahmen für die Terminierung zu sorgen.

10. Symbolisches Debugging

Für das symbolische (= quellsprachbezogene) Debugging enthalten die Zwischensprache CAMIL und die als Zielsprache fungierende Assemblersprache Symbolinformation, die für jedes benannte Objekt, egal ob statisch oder dynamisch,

- die Überprüfung der Sichtbarkeit erlaubt,

- falls es sichtbar ist, die Berechnung der
  aktuellen Adresse ermöglicht, und

- eine typrichtige Darstellung unterstützt.

Außerdem ist noch die Zeilennummer des definierenden Auftretens des Symbols verfügbar.

In der Ladephase wird die Symbolinformation vom eigentlichen Code getrennt und in einer Datenbasis gesammelt (siehe Abb. 2).

In der Regel geschieht das Debugging über einen In-Circuit-Emulator, der über eine Datenkommunikationsleitung an den CAMIC-Rechner angeschlossen ist. CAMIC gestattet die Verwendung unterschiedlicher Emulatoren; ihre Bedienung ist durch das "Debug-Interface" weitestgehend vereinheitlicht. Der Benutzer arbeitet an seinem Terminal nur mit dem Debug-Interface; intern werden seine Anweisungen in die spezifischen Kommandos des jeweiligen Emulators umgewandelt und diesem geschickt.

Das Debug-Interface wertet die oben erwähnte Symbol-Datenbasis in zweierlei Hinsicht aus:

- Eingegebene CAMIC-Debug-Anweisungen (die Quell-Symbole und Zeilennummern enthalten können) werden in absolut adressierte Emulatorkommandos umgewandelt

- Rückmeldungen des Emulators werden analysiert und zum Teil mit Symbolinformation ergänzt; dazu ist ein Parsing der Emulatorausgaben nötig.

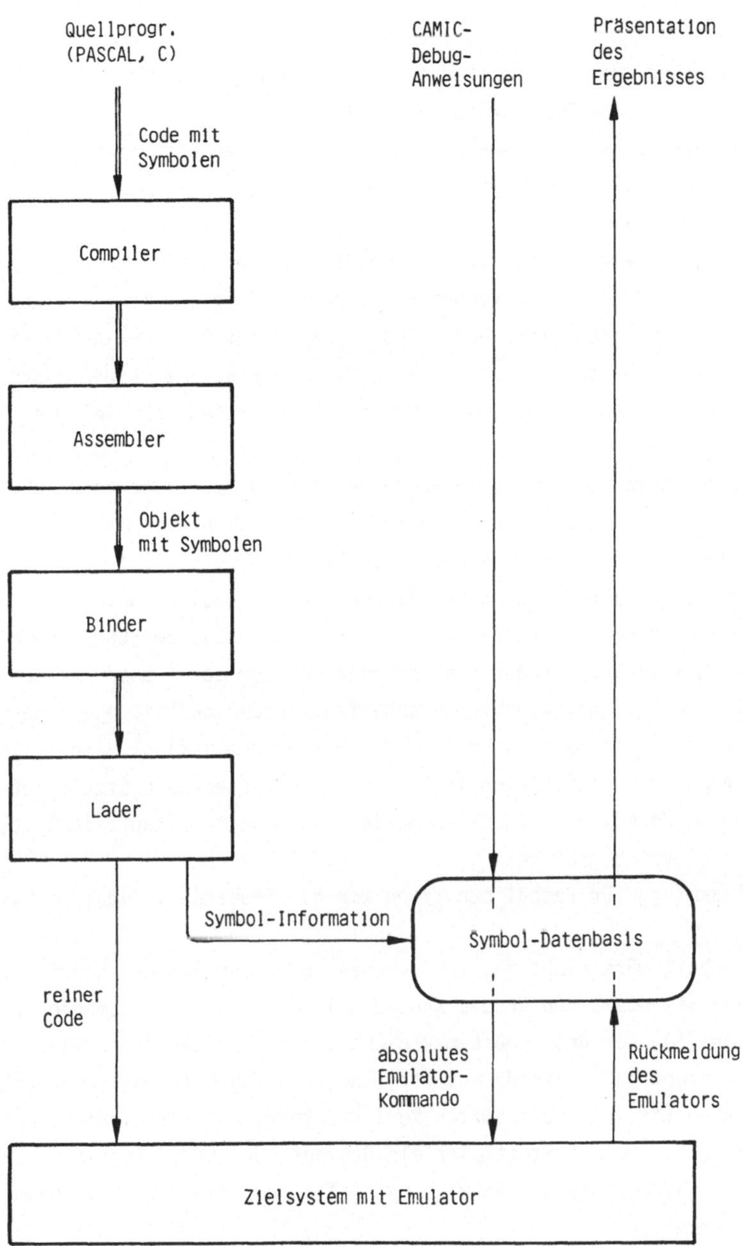

Abb. 2: CAMIC - Debug - Konzept

11. Realisierung

Die Implementierung des Compiler-Paketes erfolgte ausschließlich in C unter UNIX.
Dadurch, daß die gesamte Entwicklung mit Hilfe der bereits realisierten CAMIC-Teile
erfolgte, war dies auch ein ausgezeichneter Test der Anwendbarkeit der Basisfunk-
tionen unseres Entwicklungssystems.

Wo immer es möglich war (d. h. überall, wo "Syntax vorkam"), wurden Generatoren eingesetzt, vor allem der im UNIX vorhandene Compiler-Compiler YACC (7) und zum Teil
Scanner-Generator LEX (8). Wenn auch YACC in bezug auf Attributierung ziemlich
schwach ist, macht ihn doch seine einfache Handhabbarkeit zu einem ausgezeichneten
Werkzeug, gerade in den Händen von im Compilerbau unerfahrenen Kollegen.

Für den Test der Compiler-Oberteile wurde weitgehend der Zwischensprach-Interpreter
eingesetzt. Für den Test der Codegeneratoren und für den Gesamttest wurden Zielsysteme mit den jeweiligen Prozessoren beschafft und an die Entwicklungsmaschine
(VAX) gekoppelt. Für Z8000 und M68000 liefen die Zielsysteme auch unter UNIX, was
Kopplung und Bedienung sehr vereinfachte. Der Stackaufbau der CAMIC-Compiler ist
weitgehend einheitlich und dadurch abweichend von dem der C-Compiler auf den Ziel-
systemen. Um eine Laufzeitumgebung zu schaffen, wurden deshalb die Eingänge in den
Systemkern des Zielsystems (Systemdienste: UNIX-Dokumentation, Band 1, Kap. 2) durch
einen "Trap-Adapter", eine kleine in Assembler geschriebene Laufzeitroutine, modifiziert. Dann wurde mit dem CAMIC-C-Compiler das gesamte C-Laufzeit-System übersetzt
und auf das Zielsystem gebracht.
Als Beispielsammlung für Pascal benutzten wir die Tasmania Validation Suite (9).

Die gesamte Arbeit wäre nicht möglich gewesen ohne den Rat und die Mithilfe vieler
Kollegen, ganz besonders von Ursula Kresse, die mit uns CAMIL definierte, Bernd
Krieg-Brückner (*), der uns in einem Projektseminar entscheidende Tips für das Modularisierungskonzept gab, Alfred Laut (**), der den Z80-Code-Generator entwickelte,
Manfred Luckmann (**) als geschätzter Reviewpartner, Norbert Richter, der den Optimierer entwickelte, Helmut Stettmaier als Designer der CAMIC-Assembler und -Binder
und des Debugging-Konzepts und Ta Dinh Que (***), der die PASCAL-Strukturierung ent-
warf und implementierte.

(*)   jetzt Universität Bremen
(**)   PCS GmbH, München
(***)   jetzt Nixdorf AG, München

Literatur

(1) Ritchie, D.M.: A tour through the UNIX C compiler. In: UNIX Programmer's Manual,
     seventh edition, vol. 2B, ch. 33. Murray-Hill: Bell Telephone Laboratories 1979
(2) Joy, W.N., Graham, S.L., Haley, C.B.: Berkeley Pascal user's manual, vers. 2.0.
     University of California, Berkeley, Comp. Sc. Div., Dept. of Electr. Engin. and
     Comp. Science, 1980
(3) Joy, W.N., McKusick, M.K.: Berkeley Pascal px implementation notes. Wie bei (2),
     1979
(4) Fulton, C.A.: Micro Concurrent Pascal (mCP) user's guide. Enertec Inc.,
     Lansdale, PA, USA, 1980
(5) Tanenbaum, A.S., Stevenson, J.W., v.Staveren, H.: Description of an experimental
     machine architecture for use with block structured languages. Vrije Universiteit
     Amsterdam, Informatica Rapport IR-54, 1980
(6) Lamb, D.A.: Construction of a peephole optimizer. Software - Practice and Expe-
     rience 11, 639-647 (1981)
(7) Johnson, S.C.: Yacc - yet another compiler-compiler. Wie bei (1), ch. 19
(8) Feldman, S.I., Weinberger, P.J.: Lex - a lexical analyzer generator. Wie bei (1),
     ch. 20
(9) Wichmann, B.A., Ciechanowicz, Z.J.: Pascal compiler validation. Chichester-
     New York-Brisbane-Toronto-Singapore: Wiley & Sons 1983

<u>Anhang A</u>: Übersicht über die Operatoren der Zwischensprache CAMIL

DSEXPR, DSFLOAT, DSSTR	Belegung von Datenspeicher
DSFREE	Freihalten von Datenspeicher
XLABEL, CLABEL, DLABEL	Markendefinition in verschiedenen Bereichen
EXPORT, IMPORT	Exportierter / importierter Name
SYMBOL	Symboltabellen-Information
LINO	Zeilennummer
RCHECK, NIL	Bereichsprüfungen
BEGIN, END	Blockbeginn, -ende (statisch und dynamisch)
LOCVAR	Platz für lokale Variable reservieren
RESULT, GETRES	Übergabe des Funktionsergebnisses
NREF, SREF	Adresse einer Variablen laden
NVAL, SVAL	Wert einer Variablen laden
CON, CONFLOAT	Konstante laden
CONSET, NEWSET, GENSET	Konstante, leere, variable Menge laden
CONV	Universeller Konvertieroperator
DEREF	Dereferenzierung
FDEREF	Bitfeld-Dereferenzierung
INDEX	Adressenberechnung für Feldelement
ABS, COMPL, NEG, SQRT	monadische arithmetische Operatoren
NOT	logische Negation
CARD	Mengen-Kardinalität
ADD, SUB, DIV, MULT, MOD	dyadische arithmetische Operatoren
BITAND, BITOR, BITXOR	bitweise Verknüpfungen
LSHIFT, RSHIFT	Shifts
LAND, LOR	dyadische logische Operatoren
ADDSET, SUBSET, MULTSET	dyadische Mengenoperatoren
EQ, NEQ, LEQ, GT, GEQ, LT	arithmetische Vergleiche (boolesches Ergebn.)
EQSET, NEQSET, ..., LTSET, INSET, INCSET	Mengenvergleiche (")
EQSTR, NEQSTR, ..., LTSTR	Stringvergleiche (")
ASSIGN	Wertzuweisung (beliebiger Länge)
FASSIGN	Bitfeld-Wertzuweisung
ASPLUS, ASMINUS, ..., ASLSH, ASRSH	Wertzuweisung mit Operation (a := a op expr)
INCAFT	Dereferenzierung mit Post-Inkrement
CALL, CALLEND, SCALL	Funktions- und Prozeduraufruf
GOTO, NLGOTO	lokaler, nicht-lokaler Sprung
CASEH, CASEA	Auswahlsprung
IF	bedingter Sprung
IFEQ, IFNEQ, IFLEQ, IFGT, IFGEQ, IFLT	arithmetischer Vergleich und bedingter Sprung
IFEQSET, ..., IFINCSET	Mengenvergleich und bedingter Sprung
IFEQSTR, ..., IFLTSTR	Stringvergleich und bedingter Sprung
SDUP	oberstes Kellerelement verdoppeln
POP	oberstes Kellerelement entfernen
SYS	Anforderung von Interpreterfunktionen

<u>Merging High-level Language and Assembly Software:</u>
<u>Principles and Case Study</u>

Helmar Burkhart and Michael Moser
Elektronik, ETH
CH-8092 Zuerich

Yen Chao   *)
Beijing Polytechnic University
Beijing, China

ABSTRACT

Future programming environments are expected to offer the user a
variety of programming languages. Especially the co-operation of
high- and low-level language translators is desirable in order to
combine the benefits of abstraction with those of machine-
orientation. We outline methods for merging these two kinds of
languages. As a case study, we have chosen to embed an Assembler
into the existing MODULA-2/68K programming environment. We present
an overview of the Assembler implementation, and sketch the
programming rules by a sample demonstration program.

1. Towards integrated foreign language programming systems

The past two decades have been characterized by much progress in
the understanding of programming theory and language concepts
[WEG 76]. Today's programming environments, however, show a lack
of such widely accepted concepts. Therefore, in the next few years
the design of programming SYSTEMS not that of new languages is
expected to dominate the relevant field. One of the demanding
targets of an ideal programming system is to possess flexibility;
i.e. the system should be able to offer the user a variety of
programming tools at all language levels, and provide standard
techniques for the usage of foreign programming languages.
Powerful languages, like ADA, enable the user to construct program
parts written in foreign language. Translators are proposed [BWW
82] which accept these programs bodies and produce appropriate
containers in the program library, pretending everything to be
originally written in ADA.

As a step towards this goal we draw attention to the merging of
high-level and assembly language in order to combine the benefits
of well organized software structures with those of machine
orientation.

---

*) on leave 1981-83 at the Institute fuer Elektronik, ETH

2. Methods for merging high-level language and assembly programs

There are several approaches to include assembly parts into a high-level language program. A simple way is by means of a special procedure, for instance INCLUDE, that accepts assembly code specifications as argument.   In its simplest form only the hand-coded machine instructions are passed over.   When parsing the program the compiler is allowed to ignore these arguments.   During the code generation phase the bit sequence originated from the translation process is merged with the bit patterns from the INCLUDE routines.   The implementor's task is not difficult; however, for the programmer this method is cumbersome and prone to errors especially when a large amount of code has to be inserted.

A further improvement is the argument specification in assembly notation. If the compiler generates assembly output the same scheme as above holds.   All assembly parts are ignored till the phase of final merging with the code output stream.   The generated file will be processed by an independent assembler program.   PL/S [BM 74] and OMSI PASCAL-1 [OSI 80] are examples that provide this facility.   However, if the compiler generates machine code the situation is more complicated.   Having a compiler that translates language L to machine language M, and having an assembler that translates assembly language A to M, both software tools will be involved when a program mix has to be translated.   There are two main approaches to solve this problem:

Method A: Compiler and assembler communicate at the file interface

To meet the requirements of dividing a program into separate compilable and testable program pieces, modern programming languages furnish relevant language concepts (e.g."Package" in ADA, or "Module" in MODULA-2).   A linker program is then used to close all cross-references between the separately compiled modules. In order to generate the final code file that will be loaded and executed, the linker program has to accept the code file in the format defined by the compiler.   If we force the assembler to generate the same format as the compiler does, we can merge high-level and low-level language at the "module" level. Assembly lines may be encapsulated in a source file and replace corresponding high-level parts.   By this mean compiler, assembler and linker co-operate at the same file interface.   In order to provide universal extendibility of the language set a standard code file format is required.

Within this method we can define different levels of complexity and power:

+ Only a contiguous code stream defined in assembly language can be invoked by the compiler translated code at the entry point.

++ Self-contained software modules can be written in assembly
language. This implementation requires provisions for the data
structure part, e.g. reservation of memory space.

+++ Compiler and assembler share object files. Variables of the
high-level language program may be used in the assembly parts
and vice-versa.

This module-wise merging takes care of software engineering
principles:

* Universality is provided because additional translators may be
added to the language set.

* As no further machine specific parts are introduced into the
language and the compiler, portability is the same as for the
stand-alone compiler.

* Modularity of software is favoured in this method. Programmers
with different language backgrounds may co-operate with precise
interface specifications.

The only problem with this method is that selective embedding of
diminutive machine-oriented features must also be oriented on the
module structure; if we only want to optimize a single procedure
or a few statements (eg. a tight loop), the whole module must be
written in assembly language or the logical module structure has
to be rearranged.

To overcome this problem one solution is the introduction of a
preprocessor pass. Before the actual compilation takes place, the
assembler is invoked to transform all assembly parts into an
appropriate intermediate form or into the final machine code which
may later be merged with the generated code stream. However, since
all the high-level portions would have to be skipped in the
preprocessing phase the translation process is slowed down. To
overcome this deficiency a tighter co-operation is necessary.

Method B: Compiler and assembler share internal data structures

A faster method is not only to immediately start with the actual
compiling process, but to provide a switching facility to the
assembler when "foreign" statements are detected by the compiler.

For the sake of proper code generation, the translators are
allowed to check the state when switching in the control flow
takes place. For instance when the compilation is interrupted,
certain machine registers are used in the code generation part. If
the programmer now wants to use these registers for other purposes
in the assembly part, these registers have first to be freed by
pushing the contents onto the stack. However, because of its time
influence this saving should only occur if really necessary. Thus
the assembler needs to have the right to check the register
allocation state.

Another data structure made accessible to both translators is the
"symbol table". If we allow cross-references to objects, e.g. move
the contents of a variable into a specific register in order to
check wether the object is well defined, the assembler is forced

to take access to the symbol table.

As in method A we could define different levels of complexity. The more power we impose onto the merging facility, the more the assembler degenerates to a specific part of the compiler.   If we can insert machine dependent code whereever we want, portability of the software decreases dramatically.   Limiting such insertions to the level of existing language constructs can help to keep this loss relatively small , but requires slight modifications of the language (e.g "foreign procedures", or even "foreign statements"). Therefore, according to software engineering principles, method B should only be applied when machine orientation is essential.

In conclusion: a modern programming system should provide the integrated usage of several languages as described in method A. This can be achieved at the level of separate compilable software pieces and does not affect the programming language.   A specific system may be tuned by additional implementation of method B when optimization reasons out-weigh the loss of portability.   In our environment the benefits of method A had priority; the subsequent case study outlines this implementation.

3. Case study: Merging MODULA-2 and assembly programs

MODULA-2 was designed in 1978 by PASCAL author Niklaus Wirth as a tool for building complex software systems.   The most prominent concept in the language is the module construct that leads to structuring software into self-contained program parts with a precise interface to the environment (IMPORT-EXPORT lists) [WIR 82]. Programming security is enhanced by full type checking including even the separately compiled modules. Advanced language features are the support of coroutines, the procedure type construct, a general loop statement, dynamic array parameters and low-level machine access facilities.

3.1 Merging machine code and MODULA-2 in the early implementations

The MODULA-2 language provides a modest feature to incorporate machine code into a MODULA-2 program. The construct of a procedure type may be used in combination with a variant record definition:

```
TYPE ExternalProcedure =
     RECORD
       CASE BOOLEAN OF
         FALSE: Code: ARRAY [1..Length] OF WORD
                  (* to be filled with machine code *)
            |
         TRUE: p:PROC (* to be activated afterwards *)
       END
     END
```

A variable of the above type must first be filled with the machine code and can then be activated as a procedure by using the second alternative.

In the project SMILER [SEI 83] the "CODE"-facility has been added to the MODULA-2 language. Machine code has to be specified like procedure argument values. The run-time system module SYSTEMX is written with heavy use of this code feature.

The MODULA-2 language provides two views of a software module which play significant roles in our work. The DEFINITION module specifies the conceptual view ("WHAT is specified ?"), while the IMPLEMENTATION module reflects the physical view ("HOW is the internal representation specified ?"). This language construct conceives a solution by which all conceptual parts remain in the MODULA-2 environment, while the implementation parts can be written in assembly (or another) language. The VAX-11 implementation [EKMP 83] goes in this direction and includes the concept of a "Foreign" definition module to provide access to other languages of the VAX-11 system. As further parameter passing techniques are asked in those foreign languages (immediate value, reference passing, passing by string descriptor etc.), the syntactical prefix "FOREIGN" has been introduced to notify the compiler when it should tolerate nonconformant MODULA-2 parameter techniques.

In order to explore merging techniques at different levels of complexity and power, we designed a MOTOROLA 68000 assembler that operates both independently and compiler- controlled. We describe this assembler implementation in the subsequent parts of this paper.

3.2 The MODULA-2/68K programming environment

Project M3 (Modular Multi-Microprocessor) was started in spring 1981 to explore the main research topics in the multiprocessor field. A multiprocessor prototype and several single processor work stations have been built forming the core of our laboratory for multiprocessor experiments. The M3 system design is based on modern tools: The 16 bit microprocessor MOTOROLA MC68000 and the high-level language MODULA-2 have been chosen as the basic elements on hardware and on software side, respectively.

The MODULA-2/68K implementation is based both on the original PDP-11 system and the Cross-Development System SMILER-2. The overall structure defined by the PDP-11 implementation has been taken over: system components are a 5 pass compiler, a linker, a post-mortem dump analyzer, and a system specific run-time package. The code generation, however, had to be replaced by a MC68000 code generator adopted from the SMILER-2 cross development system.

3.3 Co-operation of assembler and MODULA-2 compiler

The base of the merging facilities is a resident MC68000 assembler that has been developed with MODULA-2 as implementation language ([YEN 83], [MOS 83]). Its user interface (e.g. directives) has been chosen to be similar to the MOTOROLA Cross-Assembler [MOT 79] that runs on the EXORCISOR development system. The assembler comprises 12 logically related modules among them only 3 modules need to be modified according to different instruction sets. The assembler is designed to accomplish its translation in two passes: During the first pass it scans the source program line by line and checks out syntactical errors. Labels encountered in the source text are inserted into a symbol table. If an instruction can be fully translated, the generated code is stored; if forward references exist, the detected state is put onto an intermediate file. After gathering all information the final code is produced in pass 2 or an error handling routine is activated, respectively.

For the implementation of Method A two modules (input/output; symbol table construction) of the independent version had to be modified and two modules (generation of structured code file and for the reading of symbol files) were added to form the merged version. While the processing of the definition part remains inside the MODULA-2 environment, i.e. the symbol file is generated by the compiler, the assembly program is encapsulated in an "implementation module"-like file (Fig. 1). The assembler is responsible to translate the contents of this file into corresponding machine code and to provide limited security against oversights. The symbol file in turn is read from a module in the assembler which creates a file possessing the same code file format as the compiler does, e.g. heading with Link Code Version, Separated Compiled Module Header etc.; but the main block in this file is the assembler generated object code.

In order to implement the merging facility certain features of the independent assembler have been modified :

* The directives 'ORG' and 'RORG' that serve for the program counter specification in an independent assembly program are omitted. Instead, the relevant task is reserved for the standard MODULA-2 linker to accomplish.

* The compiler processes the definition module and generates a symbol file that contains all specified objects in compact representation. Thus, procedure objects get a unique number that is later used by the linker. To identify the assembly parts that correspond to the MODULA-2 procedure definition, new directives "PROCEDURE" and "ENDPROC" have been introduced. When a "foreign" implementation module is written, the directive "PROCEDURE" opens a new block. It must be followed by the procedure number. Procedure number 0 represents the initialisation code of the module (if there is any). The following numbers [1..n] are reserved for the exported procedures in the order of textual occurence in the definition module and are used for labelling the corresponding assembly pieces. All higher numbers are free and may be used for module internal procedures. The assembler checks the correct assignment: all exported procedures have to be defined, but no number may be used twice.

* As in a MODULA-2 program, the definition of global variables and constants only appear at the outset of a module (Assembler directives DC = Define_Constant, DS = Define_Storage). After the first "PROCEDURE" directive further DC/DS usage is prohibited. Variables local to a procedure must be allocated on the stack as in the compiler.

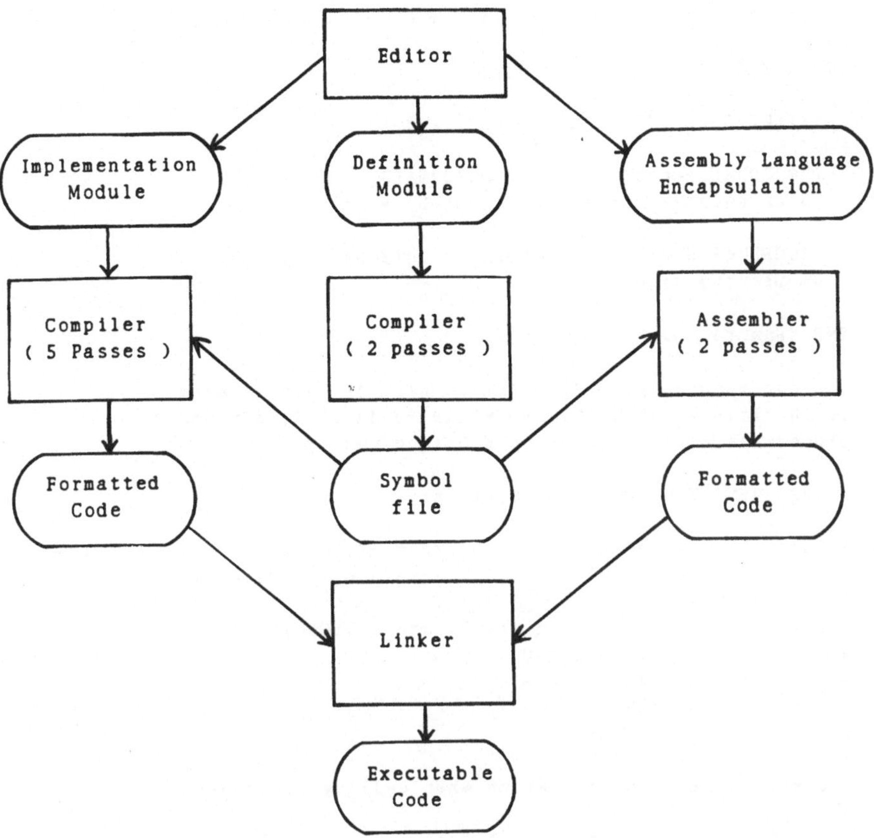

Fig 1 . Data flow in the MODULA-2 tool set

3.4 Example Session

To illustrate the programming rules introduced above we cite a simple demonstration program that has been translated according to the merging principle of the method A level [MOS 83].

Two functions

    Function(a,b) = Sign(a-b) * (a+b)^2

    Sign(x) = +1 for x > 0
               0 for x = 0
              -1 for x < 0

are calculated with assembly language support.

We first specify the definition module in MODULA-2 syntax:

```
DEFINITION MODULE XFunctions;

   EXPORT QUALIFIED  Function, Sign;

   PROCEDURE Function (a,b : CARDINAL) : INTEGER;
   (* calculates function (Sign(a-b) * (a+b)^2) *)

   PROCEDURE Sign (x : INTEGER) : INTEGER;
   (* returns sign of x *)

END XFunctions.
```

The corresponding implementation part is encapsulated
in the file XFUNCT.ASM. The whole "module" is divided in 6
procedures, each possessing a unique number.

```
* IMPLEMENTATION MODULE XFunctions;
*
* Function:  with two CARDINAL arguments a and b this procedure
*            calculates the INTEGER-function 'Sign(a-b)*(a+b)^2'
*
* Sign:      argument and result are INTEGER.
*                 1 if x > 0
*                 0 if x = 0
*                -1 if x < 0
*
*
* Compiler stack organisation when calling procedures:
*
*    ^ Addresses (counted in bytes)
*    |
*    |    +------------------------------+
*    |    | space for function-result    |
*    |    +------------------------------+
*    |    | arguments (in reverse order  |
*    |    | of textual appearence in     |
*    |    | source text)                 |
*    |    +------------------------------+
*    |    | return address (two words)   |
*    +    +------------------------------+ <--- current stack pointer
*
*
* Procedures 1and 2 are exported, 3-5 are for internal use only.
* Procedure 0 would be initialisation code (not used).
*
              PROCEDURE 3

Reg_Sign      TST      D0
              BEQ      EndReg_Sign      x = 0 ?
              BMI      Minus
              MOVEQ    #1,D0            x > 0
              BRA      EndReg_Sign
Minus         MOVEQ    #-1,D0           x < 0
EndReg_Sign   RTS                       D0 := Sign(D0)
              ENDPROC  Reg_Sign
```

```
*----------------------------------------------------------------
            PROCEDURE 4

Sum         MOVE.W   $8(A6),D1      D1 := a
            ADD.W    $A(A6),D1      D1 := a + b
            RTS
            ENDPROC Sum
*----------------------------------------------------------------
            PROCEDURE 5

Diff        MOVE.W   $8(A6),D0      D0 := a
            SUB.W    $A(A6),D0      D0 := a - b
            RTS
            ENDPROC Diff
*----------------------------------------------------------------
*           exported Functions:
*----------------------------------------------------------------
            PROCEDURE 1

Function    LINK     A6,#0
            JSR      Diff          D0 := a-b
            JSR      Reg_Sign      D0 := Sign(D0)
            JSR      Sum           D1 := a+b
            MOVE.W   D1,D2         D2 := D1
            MULU     D1,D2         D2 := D1 * D2  (=(a+b)^2)
            MULS     D2,D0         D0 := D2 * D0
            MOVE.W   D0,$C(A6)     Result := D0
            UNLK     A6
            RTS
            ENDPROC Function
*----------------------------------------------------------------
            PROCEDURE 2

Sign        MOVE.W   $4(SP),D0
            JSR      Reg_Sign
EndSign     MOVE.W   D0,$6(SP)
            RTS
            ENDPROC Sign
*----------------------------------------------------------------
            END XFunctions.
```

When the above assembly file is handed to the merged version
assembler, both symbol table, code listing, and code in universal
linker format are generated. At this stage of merging, still a
sound knowledge of the MODULA-2 internal organization is required
from the user. The programmer has to obey strictly the parameter
passing techniques defined by the compiler.

The current implementation offers a notable increase in
programming comfort, e.g. the previous hand-coded run-time system
module SYSTEMX can now be rewritten in assembly language and thus
becomes both well-documented and easier adaptable. As shown above
there are still awkward inconveniences and a lot of details to be
remembered by the programmer. Improved merging facilities are
under development. The next step will be providing the ability to
interpret symbol files; thus, imports from other modules become
feasible. This will also emancipate the programmer from the
cumbersome manual organisation of procedure numbers and offer
tests against undefined hidden types and procedures during
translation.

4. Conclusions

Many software engineering aspects urge upon the usage of high-
level languages, but in many cases the necessity of assembly usage
still exists. We gained a remarkably improved flexibility of our
programming environment without affecting the used high-level
language. This was done by concentration Bon the compiler/linker
interface. Complex software systems demand an even wider scale of
languages. Therefore, work towards standardized interface
specifications of the concerned programming tools (program
editors, translators, linkers, configurators, debuggers etc.) is
mandatory. Standards like that proposed by the IEEE P695 working
group [IEE 83] go this direction and might pave the way for future
integrated programming systems.

ACKNOWLEDGEMENT

The existence of the MODULA-2/68K system software, which is
partial outcome of the Project "Portabilitaet interaktiver
Systeme" sponsored by "Schweizerischer Schulrat", has been a precondition for the presented Assembler implementation and
embedding.

REFERENCES

[BM 74]   W.R. Brittenham and B.F. Melkun: "The Systems
          Programming Language Problem", Proc. of the IFIP
          Working Conference on Machine Oriented Higher
          Level Languages, pp. 29-42, 1974

[BWW 82] W. Babich, L. Weissman, M. Wolfe: " Design
          considerations in language processing tools for
          ADA", in Proc. of the 6th Int. Conf. on Software
          Engineering, Tokyo, pp. 40-47, (Oct. 1982)

[EKMP83] H. Eckhard, J. Koch, M. Mall, P. Putfarken: "VAX-11
          MODULA-2 User's Guide", DPLM Memo 41-83, Informatik
          University of Hamburg, 1983

[IEE 83] IEEE P695: "The Microprocessor Universal Format for
          Object Modules", in IEEE Micro Vol. 3, No. 4, pp. 48
          - 66 (Aug. 83).

[MOS 83] M. Moser: "Resident assembler for M3 and the merging
          with MODULA-2 programs"; diploma thesis
          Elektronik ETH, July 1983

[MOT 79] MOTOROLA Inc.: "M68000 Macro Assembler Reference Manual"
          July,1979

[OSI 80] Oregon Software Inc.: "OMSI Pascal-1 V1.2/RT-11 User's
          Guide", August 1980

[SEI 83] H. Seiler: "SMILERX: MODULA-2 Cross-compiler for the
          MC68000, Computer Center ETH, 1983.

[WEG 76] P. Wegner: "Programming languages: The first 25
          years", IEEE Trans. on Computers, pp. 1207-1225,
          (Dec. 1976)

[WIR 82] N. Wirth: "Programming in MODULA-2", Springer
          Verlag, 1982

[YEN 83] Yen Chao: "A Type Adaptable Microcomputer Modular
          Cross Assembler : A 68000 Cross Assembler
          Implementation"; Technical report Elektronik, ETH

How to Implement a System for Manipulation of Attributed Trees

Ulrich Möncke[*], Beatrix Weisgerber[+], Reinhard Wilhelm
Fachbereich 10 - Informatik
Universität des Saarlandes
6600 Saarbrücken

Abstract:

The transformation of attributed trees is a very elegant and powerful method to deal
with problems like code optimization in compilers, language-based editors, theorem
proving, source-to-source translation (such as high level programming language to
high level programming language, high level intermediate language to low level
intermediate language) and translation of natural languages. The specification
language OPTRAN has been designed to describe transformations statically. Transformations, which logically belong together, are collected in modules. A system for
transforming attributed trees is generated separately for each of those modules. Such
a system mainly consists of an attribute evaluator, a tree analyser, a transformer
and an attribute reevaluator.

Zusammenfassung:

Die Transformation attributierter Bäume ist eine elegante und sehr mächtige Methode
zur Bearbeitung von Problemen wie Codeoptimierung in Compilern, rechnergestützte
Programmentwicklung, automatische Beweiser, source-to-source-Übersetzung (wie Programmiersprache nach Programmiersprache, hohe Zwischensprache nach niedriger Zwischensprache) und maschinelle Übersetzung natürlicher Sprachen. Transformationen
können statisch beschrieben werden mithilfe der Spezifikationssprache OPTRAN. Logisch
zusammengehörige Transformationen werden zu Moduln zusammengefaßt. Ein System zur
Transformation attributierter Bäume wird anhand einer solchen Spezifikation jeweils
für ein Modul generiert. Hauptbestandteile eines solchen Systems sind ein Attribut-
auswerter (Erstattributierer), ein Baumanalysator, ein Transformator und ein Reattri-
butierer.

1. Introduction

The specification language OPTRAN has been developed as a tool for static
description of transformations of attributed trees ([GLMW]). The level of the
language corresponds to the level of other description mechanisms used for
translators of programming languages. As the context-free grammar of a programming
language abstracts from the possible mechanisms of syntax analysis and its technical
realization, an OPTRAN-program abstracts from the representation of the tree, from

---

[*] work supported by the DFG-project "Manipulation of Attributed Trees"
[+] work supported by the SFB-project "VLSI-Design and Parallelism"

the space management technique for attributes, from the pattern matching algorithm and the way successive transformation steps co-operate. Only the structure of the trees to be manipulated is determined by means of a tree grammar, attributes are associated with nodes of the tree and the functional relation of attribute values is specified. The transformation process is described by a set of transformation rules, each consisting of a syntactic part (describing the syntactic pattern to be found and the local modification) and an applicability restriction on attributes of the considered region of the tree.

In general, it is not possible to find out automatically the "right" transformation strategy, because different application sequences may have different results. Therefore, the user has to determine a strategy.

In OPTRAN, transformation rules which logically belong together can be collected into transformation units (t-units). By means of an attribute tree grammar each t-unit specifies the objects which are to be manipulated by its rules. Each tree transformed by the rules of a t-unit must remain within this language ("pure" transformation) or is translated from one language into another (transfer transformation). The dynamic sequence of application of t-units is determined by the textual sequence.

The OPTRAN-system translates each t-unit into a transformation system. What do we need? First of all, the attributes of the tree to be manipulated must be evaluated according to the t-unit's attribute grammar. For this purpose an attribute evaluator is generated: the attribution is partitioned and an adequate evaluation strategy is determined for each component.

In order to find nodes in a syntax tree, where transformations are applicable, the tree must be analysed. For this purpose, a tree analyser is generated from the input templates.

Predicates (as well as semantic and explicit rules), written in PASCAL-like notation, are immediately translated, whereby attribute names are transformed into memory accesses. A rule is applicable, if the tree analyser signals a match of an input template and the predicate (belonging to the same rule) delivers "true".

The transformer, which restructures the tree, is generated from input and output templates (cf. [Wilh81]).

Certain attributes, so-called imported attributes, receive values by the translated explicit rules.

When restructuring the tree, some attributes may become inconsistent. Those attributes have to be reevaluated, the change must be propagated. This task is done by the attribute reevaluator. Its tables can be generated at generator time.
The whole system is shown in figure 1.

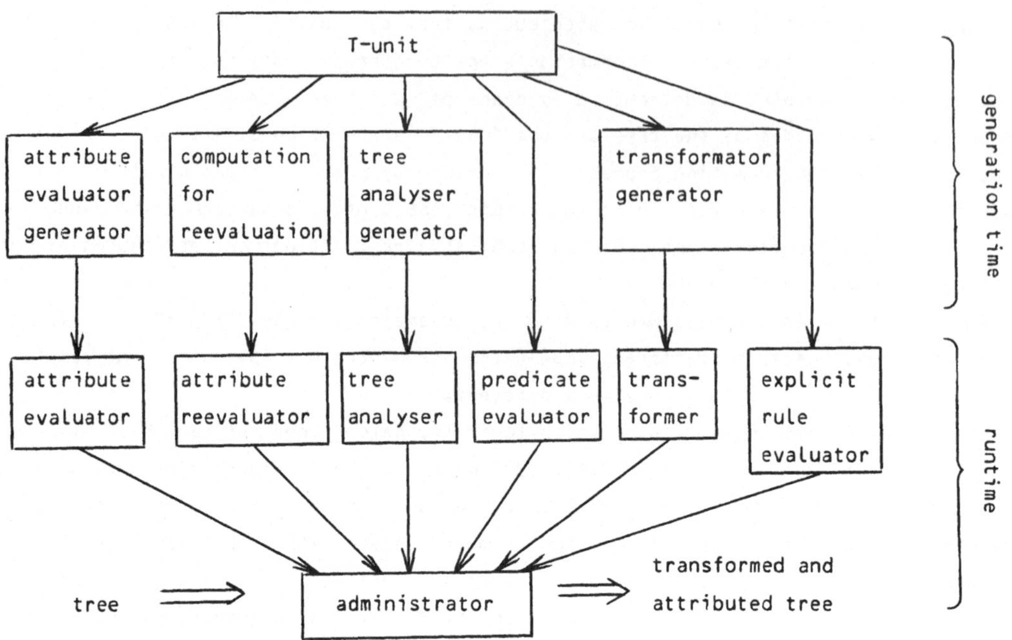

Figure 1

2. The attribute tree grammar

Abstract trees - as used in OPTRAN - can be described by a context free grammar. This way of description corresponds to the tree part of a string-to-tree grammar and hence allows the linking with a compiler frontend, in our case a compiler generated by POCO [Eul] (cf. [GGMW], [PKPR], [KLMN]). Each node of a tree is labeled with a terminal, a so-called operator.

A _tree grammar_ is a 4-tupel $BG = (N,OP,P,S)$ with:

- N is a finite set of nonterminals,
- OP is a finite set of operators with fixed arity,
- $S \in N$ is the start symbol,
- P is a set of productions of the form:

$NT_0 ::= NT_1$ or

$NT_0 ::= <op,NT_1,...,NT_k>$

where $k \in IN_0$ is the arity of the operator op, $NT_0,...,NT_k$ are nonterminals, $<op,NT_0,...,NT_k>$ is the linear representation of a tree with depth 1. Each operator can appear in only one production.

A syntax tree of BG is a finite ordered tree, whose nodes are labeled with operators. Starting with the start symbol, a syntax tree is produced by successively replacing each nonterminal NT, appearing in a sentential form, by the right side of a production p, whose left side is NT (p is _applied_).
Example 1:

S ::= EXPR;   EXPR ::= <id>;
EXPR ::= PLUSEXPR;   EXPR ::= <const>;
EXPR ::= <neg,EXPR>; PLUSEXPR ::= <plus,EXPR,EXPR>;

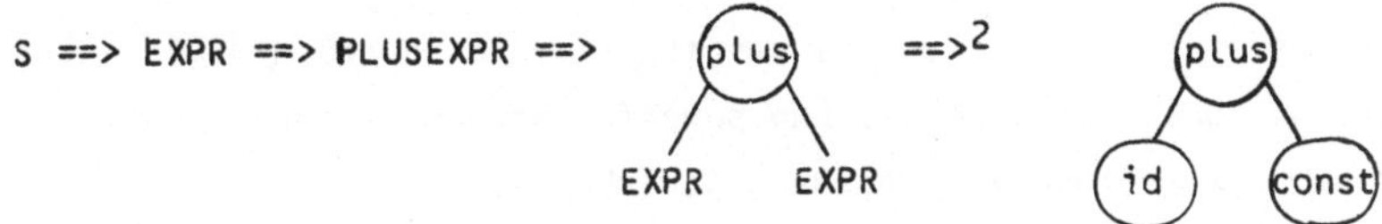

The set of all operators which can replace a nonterminal NT is called ROOTS(NT). Example 1: ROOTS(EXPR) = {neg,plus,id,const}.

Attributes transport semantic information. Each attribute has a type. With each operator op, two disjoint sets of attributes are associated, _instances_ of which are attached to every node of a syntax tree labeled with op. _Inherited_ attributes (I(op)) transport semantic information from the context to the subtree labeled op, _synthesized_ attributes (S(op)) from the subtree to the context. The set of all attributes of op is denoted A(op) = I(op) ∪ S(op). The set of _imported_ attributes of op (IM(op)) is a (possibly empty) subset of A(op).

Semantic rules specify locally to each production of the form NT_0 ::= $<op,NT_1,...,NT_k>$, how the synthesized attributes of op and the inherited attributes of the children are calculated from the inherited attributes of op and the synthesized attributes of the children. Attributes of a child i are related to attributes of the nonterminal NT_i. They have to be associated with _all_ operators in ROOTS(NT_i). Instances of attributes in IM(op) are assumed to receive their values by a preceding t-unit. Hence their occurrences need no semantic rules.

The _attribute dependency graph of a production p_ (DG(p)) represents the attribute dependencies given by the semantic rules. The set of nodes of DG(p) is the set of all attributes occurring in the tree part of p. There exists an edge from an attribute b at position i to an attribute a at position j, if the semantic function calculating a (at j) has b (at i) as an argument.
Example 2: inherited attributes are drawn at the left of a node, synthesized attributes at the right. Indices (/i) are used to distinguish different positions.
EXPR ::= <plus,EXPR/1,EXPR/2>   DG(p):
 a _of_ plus:=f(a _of_ EXPR/1,a _of_ EXPR/2;
 b _of_ EXPR/1:=g(b _of_ plus);
 b _of_ EXPR/2:=h(b _of_ plus);

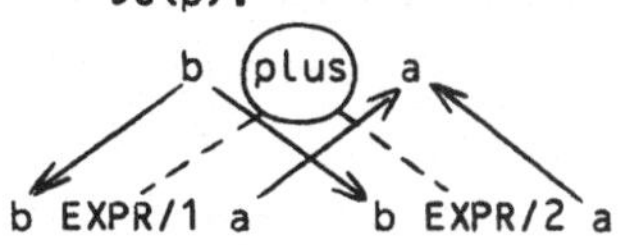

Composition of the dependency graphs of the tree deriving productions produces the attribute dependency graph of a syntax tree t (DG(t)). In the same way we get dependency graphs of subtrees (such as templates).

The attribution of an OPTRAN-tree grammar must be noncircular, that is, no dependency graph of a syntax tree may contain a cycle.

3. The transformation rules

OPTRAN allows the formulation of transformation rules, the application of which is not only dependent on structural conditions (as for example in the MENTOR-system [DHKL]) but also on context conditions. Hence, two powerful mechanisms are combined: attribute grammars and subtree replacement grammars ([Wilh74]).

An input template specifies the structural applicability condition of a transformation rule. Templates are trees, whose leaves may be labeled with distinguished symbols, so-called parameters. An instance of a template is obtained by replacing parameters by operator trees. A template matches all its instances.

Example 3:

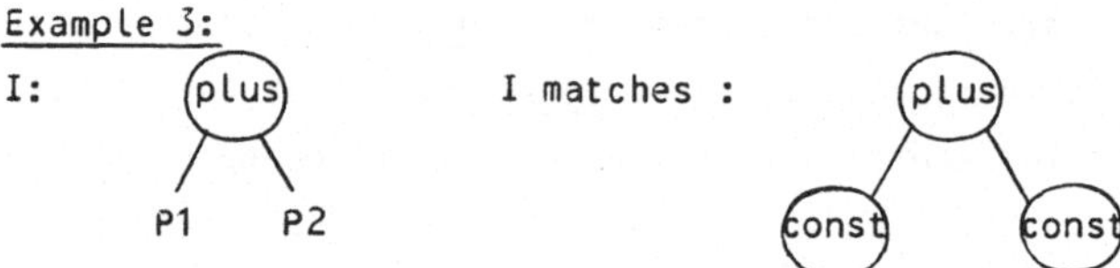

If attributes are associated with operators, predicates on attributes of the input template can be formulated additionally. Input template and predicate form the condition part of a rule. A rule is applicable, if the input template matches a tree at node n and the predicate, applied to the attributes of the instance, delivers "true". n is called transformation node.

The restructuring of the matched subtree is described in the action part of the rule. The output template, containing only parameters of the input template, specifies the structural change. Restructuring means:
- replace the instance of the input template by the output template
- replace every parameter by the subtree of the instance corresponding to the same
  parameter

Imported attributes - whose values must always be present in the tree - are computed in the region of the output template by explicit rules. They depend only on the attributes of the input template. Predicates and explicit rules are optional.

Example 4: cvalue ∈ IM(const)

OPTRAN: Transform <'plus','const'/1,<'neg','const'/2>>

      if cvalue of const/1 = cvalue of const/2

      into <'const'>

      apply cvalue of const := 0;

To simplify the following description, output templates consisting of a single parameter node are excluded (details in [MW]).

In this article only local transformation rules are described. Further concepts are proposed in [GLMW].

4. The t-unit

Each t-unit has a name. A t-unit mainly consists of an attribute tree grammar, a set of transformation rules and a specification of strategies coordinating application of rules. In general, several rules are applicable in a tree. But parallel application is problematic because of structural overlappings of several instances on the one hand and influence by attribution on the other hand ([Mön], [Weis]). Hence, one transformation node must be chosen.

A given strategy works as follows:

- some nodes, which should no longer be tested, are excluded. The criterion is dependent on preceding transformations. (For example: (proper) ancestors/descendants of a transformation node (=(strictly) monotonic) or no further specification (no exclusion))

- from the remaining set one node is chosen according to a certain condition. (For example: the leftmost (rightmost) outermost (innermost) (LR(RL)TD(BU)))

OPTRAN offers some fixed strategies composed of the examples above. (For example sBULR (strictly monotonic bottom up left to right): exclude the descendants of and the nodes left to the preceding transformation node, then choose the leftmost innermost of the remaining ones).

If there is more than one rule applicable at a node, the most specific rule must be chosen. Unfortunately, the problem of speciality of rules is undecidable considering the predicates. Therefore we take the rule containing the most specific input template. If the templates are incomparable the rule with one of the most specific input templates textually preceding all other rules considered is chosen.

Example 5:

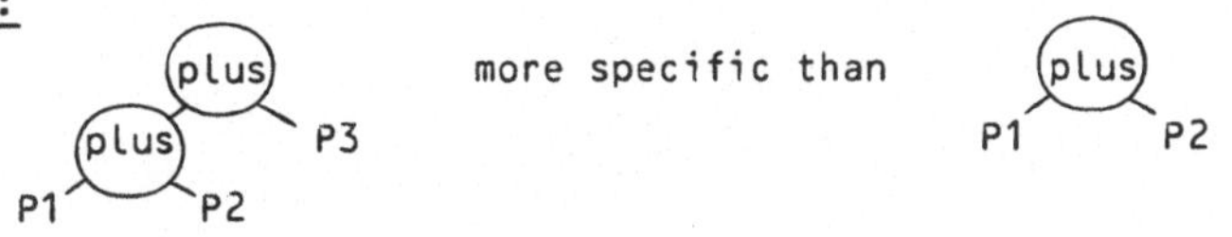

more specific than

After application of a transformation rule the tree obtained must allow further application tests of rules. This means that predicate attributes must have consistent values. The most simple way to achieve consistency, is to reevaluate the inconsistent attributes after each transformation. (Other concepts are proposed in [GiMW] and [GGMW]). The reevaluation of attributes according to the same attribute tree grammar is possible, if the transformed tree is still in the given tree language and if all imported attributes have defined values. The first condition can be guaranteed in certain cases inspecting input and output templates ([Weis]). The explicit rules provide for the second condition.

But in case of transfer transformation, trees appear during the transformation process containing subtrees of the source language as well as subtrees of the target language. To maintain consistent attribution, subtrees of different languages are separated by special (seperation) nodes and the flow of information is controlled by attributes of these nodes.

Suppose we have a textual and therefore also a dynamic sequence of t-units $T_1...T_{i-1}$ $T_i...T_n$. Each t-unit has its own local attribution. Before applying a t-unit T_i to a tree, the imported attributes obtain values of certain attributes belonging to the local attribution of the t-unit T_{i-1}, the dynamic immediate predecessor of T_i. The user specifies this process (call-by-value principle) in the heading of each t-unit: <imported attribute a of op in T_i> <== <exported attribute b of op in T_{i-1}>. That means, every instance of an attribute a at an node n labeled op in the tree obtains the last value of attribute instance b at the same node which is computed in t-unit T_{i-1}. Notice, that the value is transferred once. There is no further linkage to the attribution of T_{i-1}, which is not known in T_i. An extension to a call-by-reference mechanism is considered exporting whole attributions.

Beyond this, we plan the separation of declaration of t-units and description of runtime application (for example by regular expressions on t-unit names).

5. The evaluation of attributes

The attribute evaluator generator is based on the principle of partitioning the whole attribution into disjoint components ([Joch]). That is, we want to have a partition of the attribute <u>instances</u> of every individual syntax tree into disjoint components $A_1,..,A_j$. The components are arranged according to the flow of information between the components. Cycles of components are not allowed. In figure 2 such a partition is shown. The components are arranged on different levels. An edge --> is forbidden.

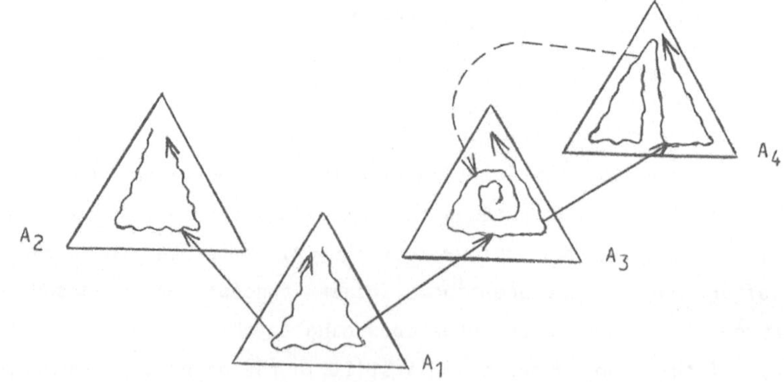

Figure 2

The attribute dependency graph of a tree is divided into dependency graphs for each component and some intercomponent edges. The dependencies within the individual components may vary in different and complicated ways. Each component has to be evaluated in an adequate manner, that is with an evaluation strategy which is just sufficiently powerful. An attribute evaluation strategy determines the sequence of evaluation.

The following evaluation strategies are used in OPTRAN:

- <u>simple-one-L(R,sweep)-pass-evaluators</u>: <u>all</u> instances corresponding to an attribute of a component are evaluated during one depth-first pass through the tree. The children of a node are visited from left to right (L) (right to left (R), in a permuted order fixed for each production (sweep)). Only membership to a component determines the moment of evaluation.

- <u>dynamic evaluators</u>: they decide at runtime which attributes are to be evaluated assisted by the dependency graph of the tree, further graph information and the evaluation states.

At generator time we have to "plan" such a partition for <u>all</u> individual trees regarding the attribute tree grammar. According to this precomputation, we know, that for every tree existing at runtime

(1) there exists a partition into at most, say, k components $A_1,...,A_k$,

(2) whether there is a connection between attribute instances of A_i and A_j,

(3) to which component an attribute instance a at node n is associated,

(4) which evaluation strategy can be applied to a component A_i.

In contrast to the conventional partition algorithms used for the attribution of concrete syntax trees, criterion (3) considers some context information. It is not sufficient to know the <u>attribute</u> a to find the partition, but instead the generator needs <u>operator-attribute</u> relations. That is, instances of <u>one</u> attribute associated with different operators may be contained in <u>different</u> components. This allows a refined partition into components. The generator produces a so-called compressed dependency graph, whose nodes are sets of operator-attribute relations extended by strategy information.

<u>Example 6:</u>

$\{(op_1,a_1),(op_2,a_2)\}\ S_1 \longrightarrow \{(op_3,a_3)\}\ S_2$

$\longrightarrow \{(op_2,a_1),(op_3,a_1)\}\ S_3$

$\downarrow$

$\{(op_1,a_3\}\ S_4$

The partition algorithms as well as the algorithms for determination of the strategies are modifications of the respective algorithms applied to concrete syntax trees in [RÿUk], [EnFi], [KeWa]. The determination of evaluation strategies for different components is tried according to the attribute evaluation hierarchy: simple-one-L or R-strategy, simple-one-sweep-strategy, strategies for absolutely noncircular and noncircular attribution (for more details see [MW], [Schm]).

6. The reevaluation of attributes

After each application of a transformation rule the attributes of the restructured
tree must be recalculated to guarantee a consistent attribution. Because reevaluation
is repeated over and over again during the transformation process, the reevaluation
technique must be carefully designed. A "good" reevaluation algorithm should have the
following properties:
- each attribute instance should be reevaluated at most once,
- an instance should be reevaluated only if the value of at least one of its
  arguments has changed,
- unnecessary tree walking should be avoided,
- the overhead of bookkeeping information should be limited.

Hence, the algorithms used for the (first time) evaluation of attributes are not
suitable. Because the reevaluation process is a central aspect of the OPTRAN-system,
we will go into further details (cf. [Mön], [MW], [Schü]).

In order to describe the reevaluation process used in OPTRAN it is assumed that
- attribute instances can be accessed via the nodes of the tree,
- every instance outside the output template region has a defined value,
- inside the output template region imported attributes and attributes at parameter
  positions have defined values. Structural transformation preserves the values of
  the non imported attributes at the transformation node.

The syntax tree is divided into the following regions:
- the output template region (central region)
- outside this region into regions of applied productions.

Each region is "governed" by a so-called "demon" controlling the reevaluation of his
attributes. Each demon knows about the position (relative to his root) leading to the
central region. This special position is denoted n^*. Beyond the dependency graph of
his region, each demon knows about the characteristic graphs of his borders according
to the following figure.

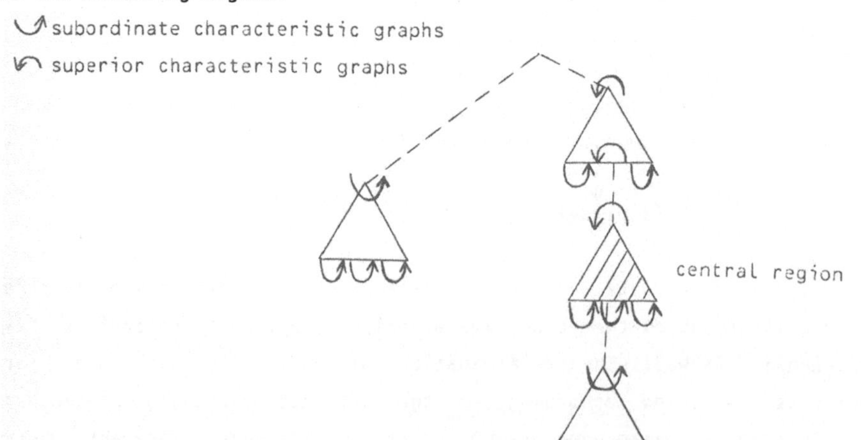

Characteristic graphs are the projections of the dependency graph of a syntax tree on a single node (see [Ml0Wi]).

Every region has <u>input</u> and <u>output attributes</u>:

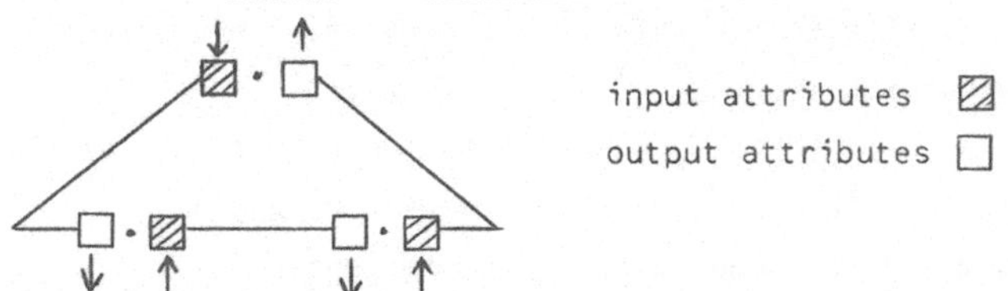

During the reevaluation process attributes are labeled: N for "not equal" (value changes), E for "equal" (value remains the same). Initially all attributes are unlabeled. Labels are the means of communication at the boundaries between regions. Each demon works according to the following instructions:

- non-central demon:

(1) semantic actions:

If every argument of an attribute a is labeled and at least one of the arguments has label N, then the new value of a is calculated. If the old and the new value are identical, a is labeled E, otherwise N.

(2) inner E-propagation:

If every argument of an output attribute a is labeled E, then the E-label is propagated to a.

(3) outer E-propagation

At non n*-positions an E-label is propagated along edges of characteristic graphs to an input attribute a, if all ancestors of a have an E-label. Thus, propagation along paths is saved.

(4) spontaneous E-label:

A spontaneous E-label can be generated for every imported attribute and for every <u>safe</u> attribute. (An input attribute is denoted safe, if it has no ancestors in the respective characteristic graph.)

(5) spontaneous E-label:

Attributes calculated by nullary semantic functions are labeled E.

The actions (3),(4) and (5) provide E-labels used in actions (1) and (2).

- central demon:

(1) as above

(3') if all ancestors of an input attribute a in a characteristic graph at non n*-positions are labeled E, then a must be labeled N, because the values of their descendants must be computed.

(4') imported and safe attributes are also labeled N,

(5') nullary functions must be applied. If their attributes are output attributes, they are labeled according to the comparison of old and new values, otherwise they are labeled N.

Every production demon D delays his actions (1) - (5), until his own activity seems to be "productive" to his n^*-neighbour. His work is "productive", if there is a N-labeled input attribute a at the n^*-position and every predecessor of an unlabeled descendant of a in $C(n^*)$ is labeled (in this case D produces a new result for his n^*-neighbour) or if every output attribute at n^* is labeled and there is still a N-labeled input attribute with unlabeled descendants (paths without feedback are collected). According to this principle, E-generation and propagation is delayed, until a new attribute to calculate is signaled by the n^*-neighbour.

Example 7:

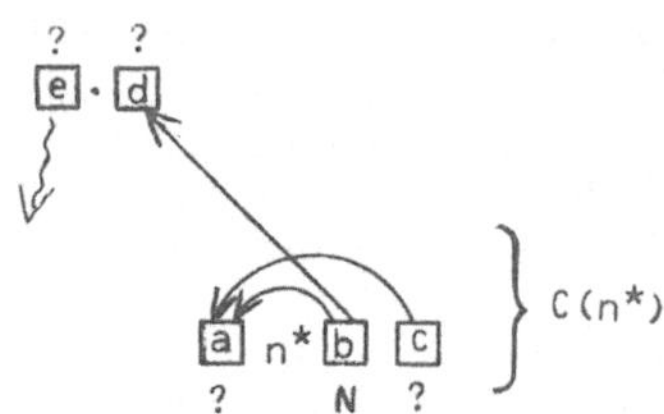

The calculation of d and the spontaneous E-labeling of e is delayed, until c is labeled. Now a is evaluable.

This basic algorithm can be modified to reduce time and space costs.

In order to speed up the work of the central demon, for all output templates "plans" can be generated at generator time using a topologic sorting of the dependency graphs (possibly extended by characteristic graphs). Now the new central demon only executes plans, when he is supplied with labels of certain input attributes.

Example 8: dependency graph of an output template

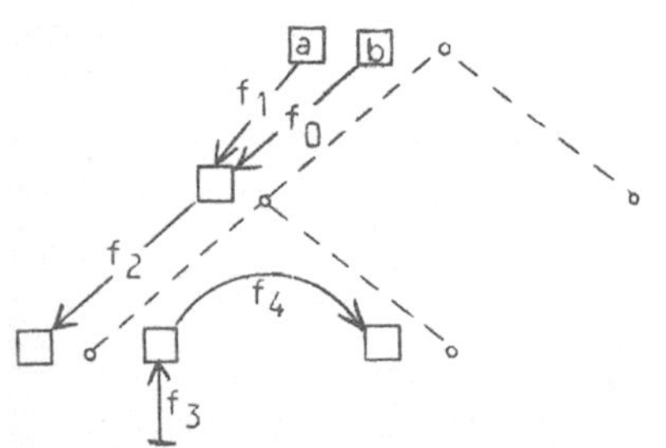

Plan $[f_3,f_4]$ can immmediately be executed. Label of b gives the impulse to carry out plan $[f_0]$ and then - if a is labeled - plan $[f_1,f_2]$ can be executed.

Until now the complete "affected region " (denoting the union of those regions containing at least one attribute to be recalculated) is labeled. But E-labeling of an attribute a is unnecessary, if it is guaranteed that no descendant of a must be recalculated. By using the informations obtained by the partition of the attribution, we obtain sufficient conditions to suppress E-labeling in certain cases (more details in [MW]).

In order to save space it seems useful to divide the syntax tree a priori into regions containing more than one production. Values of attributes are only retained at the borders of the regions. It is always possible that the complete output template region is contained in a single region. This region is now regarded as central region. Reevaluation is executed as above, but within a region every attribute, that depends on a N-labeled input attribute or whose value is needed as argument for an attribute which itself must be recalculated, must be reevaluated and is labeled N.

Example 9:

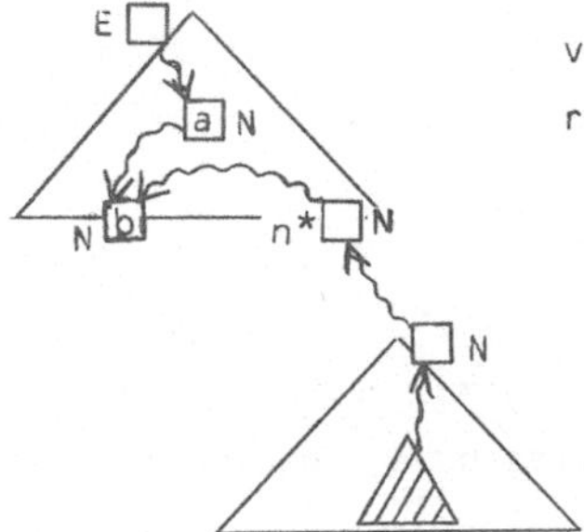

value of a remains the same, but has to be recalculated because of reevaluation of b.

Until now only characteristic graphs are used to illustrate attribute dependencies of the context. They give exact information but they are very expensive. At generator time for each operator a set of subordinate and superior characteristic graphs can be computed. Thus, at runtime every node can be supplied with its graphs by making first a bottom-up pass and then a top-down pass through the tree. Hence, time costs are shifted into generator time, but space problems caused by a possibly immense number of different graphs remain. Therefore it could be preferable to use approximative graphs as IO-graphs [KeWa] or dominating graphs instead of exact information([MöWi]). Any existing dependency is represented in an approximative graph, but the graph may contain edges, which represent no path in the original dependency graph. Therefore, the calculation of attribute values may be delayed and the E-propagation may be delayed or even prevented.

Example 10:

--> edges, which represent no path in the dependency graph

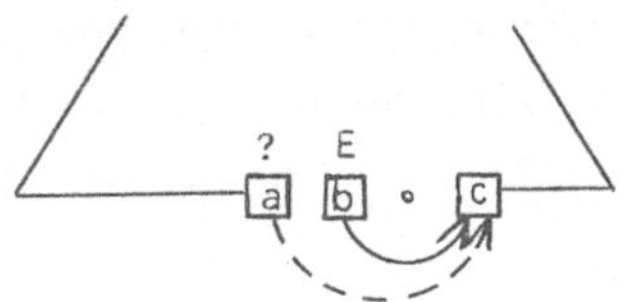

the propagation of the E-label is delayed until a is labeled E. If a is labeled N, the propagation is prevented.

D_2 becomes active only if a is labeled.

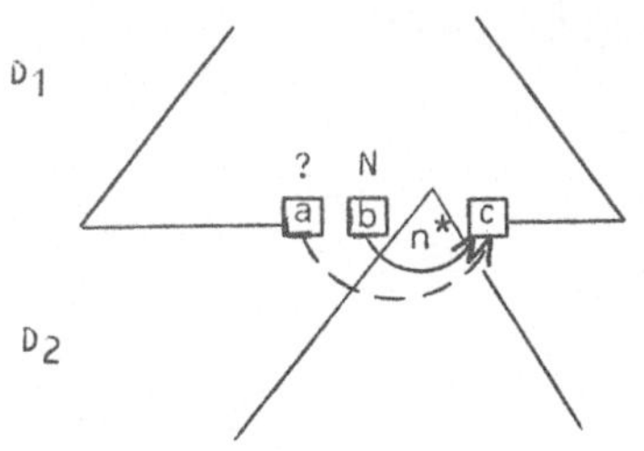

IO-graphs can only be used, if the attribution is absolutely noncircular. Another approximation can be achieved by calculating separately characteristic graphs only for attribution components and combining them (see [MÜn]).

In order to use the method of reevaluation of attributes for the initial evaluation of attribution components, we slightly change the mechanism:
- every region contains one production,
- only label N is used, the only instruction is: recalculate semantic actions and label the target attribute N,
- the principle of "productivity" remains the same, but a demon is additionally allowed to work, if a value of an attribute can be produced, which has no predecessor in $C(n^*)$. This allows the propagation of values from imported attributes and from attributes calculated by nullary functions.

The position of the central demon can be chosen arbitrarily. Choosing the root of the syntax tree leads to a method similar to the automaton driven evaluators of [KeWa] or [CoHa].

The essential differences to the method of [Reps] are the introduction of concurrency, usage of labels, further restriction of visits to attributes those values remain unchanged, prevention of unnecessary walking through the tree, considering the partition of attribution at reevaluation time and the possible exchange of characteristic graphs by approximations.

7. The tree analysis

Using the input templates of transformation rules, the OPTRAN-system generates a tree analyser which recognizes matches of templates in a syntax tree. The analyser visits every node of the tree bottom-up associating with each node N a state containing those (sub)templates matching the subtrees at n. Parameter nodes are not considered.

Example 11:

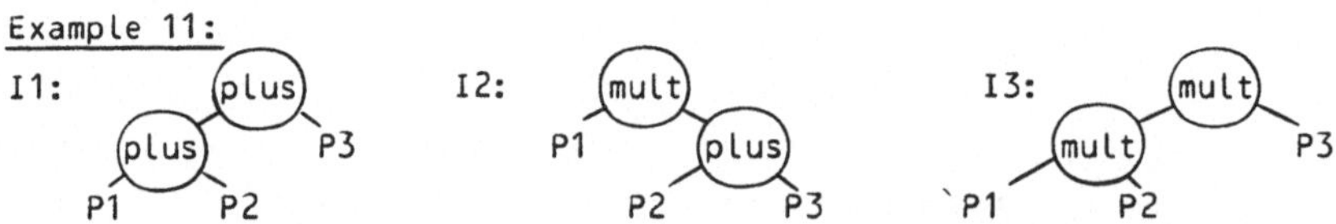

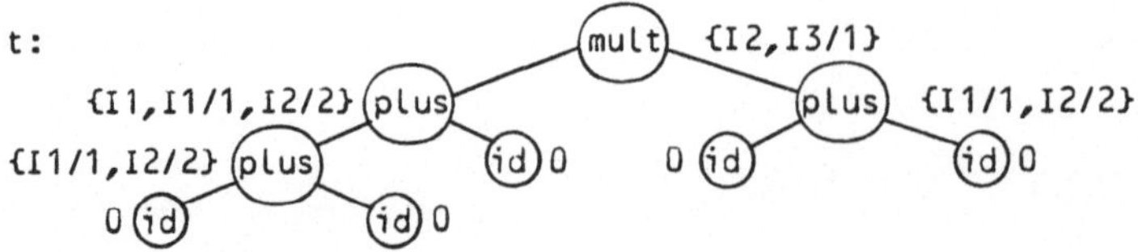

Ij/1: left subtemplate of Ij
Ij/2: right subtemplate of Ij

The state of a node is achieved as follows:
- collect all (sub)templates, which are possible matches only regarding the operator
  of the node,
- exclude successively (sub)templates regarding the states of children from left of
  right (different sequences can be imagined).

Example 12:

Regard the root of the example above. Only looking at the operator, I2, I3 and I3/1
are possible matches. Including the state of the left subtree, I3 is excluded,
because I3/1 is not contained in the state of this subtree. Regarding the state of
the right subtree, the match of I2 is confirmed because parameters match all operator
trees.

The tree analyser generator simulates this method. We get the following automaton
for the templates of example 11:

$\xrightarrow[\{s,..\}]{i}$:"regard the state at the ith child. If this state contains s, enter the target
state"

sub-automaton for the operator mult:

initializiation with

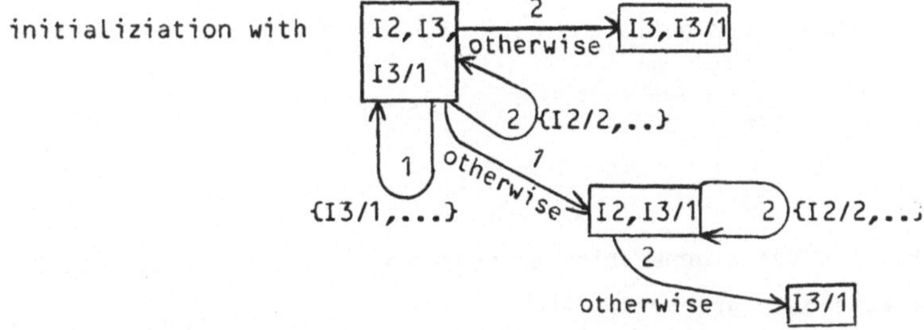

After each transformation only the states of the output template region (exclusive
parameter positions) and at most some predecessors of the transformation node
(limited by the height of the highest input template) must be recalculated.

8. State of implementation

Until now, we have realized the OPTRAN-compiler:
(1) The syntax analysis phase parses the description of a specific transformation
    system written in OPTRAN.
(2) Similar to conventional compilers, in the semantic analysis phase certain context
    conditions are checked (for example: circularity of the attribution, invariance
    of the language considering the transformation rules).
(3) The generation of the transformation-time operators (like tables for the
    attribute (re)evaluators and the tree analyser) corresponds to the code
    generation.

Currently, we work at the runtime system consisting of the skeletons of the attribute (re)evaluators, the tree analyser, the transformer and the administrator.

Conclusion

The mechanisms described above form a kernel system for a tree manipulation system realizing some of the concepts of [GlMW]. We now want to gain experience with practical applications of the system and to learn which extensions are essential. We consider for example the introduction of cyclic attribute grammars, more flexible transformation strategies and possiblities of user interaction. The final aim is a whole programming system allowing incremental development of OPTRAN-programs and interchange of transformation units between several users.

Acknowledgments

We would like to thank Michael Schmigalla and Alois Schütte for their contribution to the OPTRAN-project.

References

[CoHa] R.Cohen, E. Harry, Automatic generation of near-optimal linear-time translators for non-circular attribute grammars, POPL 6, 1979

[DHKL] V. Donzeau-Gouge, G. Huet, G. Kahn, B. Lang, Programming environments based on structured editors: the MENTOR-experience, INRIA, Research Report, 1980

[EnFi] J. Engelfriet, G. Filè, Formal properties of one-visit and multi-pass attribute grammars, Lecture Notes in Comp. Sci., 85, 1979

[Eul] M. Eulenstein, POCO, ein portables System zur Generierung portabler Compiler, Doctoral dissertation, Universität Saarbrücken, 1983

[GGMW] H. Ganzinger, R. Giegerich, U. Möncke, R. Wilhelm, A truly generative semantics-directed compiler generator, ACM Symp. on Compiler Construction, 1982

[GiMW] R. Giegerich, U. Möncke, R. Wilhelm, Invariance of approximative semantics with respect to program transformations, Informatik-Fachberichte 50, Springer 1981

[GlMW] I. Glasner, U. Möncke, R. Wilhelm, OPTRAN, a language for the specifcation of program transformations, Informatik-Fachberichte 34, Springer, March 1980

[Joch] G. Jochum, Automatische Konstruktion und einheitliche Darstellung von Attributauswertungsalgorithmen, Doctoral dissertation, TUM-Bericht, Technische Universität München, 1981

[JOR] M. Jazayeri, W.F. Ogden, W.C. Rounds, The intrinsically exponential complexity of the circularity problem for attribute grammars, POPL 2, 1975

[KeWa] K. Kennedy, S.K. Warren, Automatic generation of efficient evaluators for attribute grammars, POPL 3, 1976

[KLMM] G. Kahn, B. Lang, B. Mélèse, E. Morcos, Metal: A formalism to specified formalisms, INRIA, Research Report, 1983

[Mön] U. Möncke, Doctoral dissertation, Universität Saarbrücken, forthcoming

[MöWi] U. Möncke, R. Wilhelm, Iterative algorithms on grammar graphs, Proc.of the 8th Conf. on Graphtheoretic Concepts in Computer Science, Hanser, 1982

[MW] U. Möncke, B. Weisgerber, Implementation of a system for transformation of attributed trees, Universität Saarbrücken, internal report, forthcoming

[PKPR] T. Payton, S. Keller, J. Perkins, S. Rowan, S. Mardinly, SSAGS: A syntax and semantics analysis and generation system, IEEE, 1982

[RäUk] K.J. Räihä, E. Ukkonen, Minimizing the numbers of evaluation passes for attribute grammars, Report C-1979-121, University of Helsinki, 1979

[Reps] Th. Reps, Generating language-based environments, PhD-thesis, Cornell University, 1982

[Schm] M. Schmigalla, Attributierte Transformationsgrammatiken: Die Erstattributierung, Diplomarbeit, Universität Saarbrücken, 1983,

[Schü] A. Schütte, Attributierte Transformationsgrammatiken: Die Reattributierung, Diplomarbeit, Universität Saarbrücken, 1983

[Weis] B. Weisgerber, Attributierte Transformationsgrammatiken: Die Baumanalyse und Untersuchungen zu Transformationsstrategien, Diplomarbeit, Universität Saarbrücken, 1983

[Wilh74] R. Wilhelm, Code-Optimierung mittels attributierter Transformationsgrammatiken, Lecture Notes in Comp. Science 26, Springer, 1974

[Wilh81] R. Wilhelm, A modified tree-to-tree correction problem, Information processing letters, Vol. 12, North-Holland, 1981

<u>Context Relations - a concept for incremental context analysis</u>
<u>in program fragments</u>

W. Henhapl, G. Snelting[*]

Institut für praktische Informatik
Technische Hochschule Darmstadt

Abstract

For the generation of programming environments formal specification methods of programming languages are required, which support the specific features of the generated environment. In the case of the Programming System Generator developed in Darmstadt the central feature is the possibility to edit, interpret and catalogue arbitrary program fragments. Therefore, a specification method is necessary for the context analysis, which allows earliest possible context error detection even in incomplete programs.
In this paper a method of specifying the operator-operands compatability is presented, which can be used as a very natural definitional tool and futhermore interpreted as a typing algorithm for the expressions in a fragment even in absence of declarations.
The translator of the specification into the incremental context analysis is implemented and successfully applied to Pascal.

1. Requirements

A programming environment for a programming language should support the stepwise construction of correct programs. Correctness at least includes syntactic correctness and in case of typed programming languages wellformedness according to the context conditions of the language.

In this paper only the aspect of context conditions will be discussed. Correctness of the final program is secured, if all incomplete program versions occuring during the stepwise construction are correct. The most general form of an inclomplete program is a sentential form of some nonterminal of the language. In the following these forms (and their representations as abstract trees) will be called fragments.

On the basis of fragments as construction and library units each programming style can be followed or enforced by a suitable selection of those nonterminals

---

* Work of this author was supported by the "Deutsche Forschungsgemeinschaft", grant He 1170/2-2

in the fragment, which are to be refined or replaced by an already constructed fragment catalogued in the library.

As a consequence we can state our first requirement:

> The checking algorithm of the context conditions must be applicable
> to each fragment of the language.

A fragment is correct, if it is a correct complete program or can be embedded in a correct program.

> The checking algorithm must detect error situations immediately.

For practical reasons analysing the refinements is not enough. It is important that the user of the environment can ask for the types of variables and expressions. In general a variable need not have a uniquely determined type in a fragment. For the support of the user however the algorithm must fulfil the third requirement:

> The algorithm computes all the type information, which is valid
> for all extensions to correct programs.

Finally to guarantee syntax oriented evaluation and efficiency the typing algorithm must commute with the refinement operation:

> The type information of a composed fragment can be evaluated from the
> type informations of the subfragments.

In the next chapter we present a concept and theory for an incremental context analysis satisfying these requirements.

2. The Concept Of Context Relations

Within the Programming Sytem Generator developed at Darmstadt ([Bahl82b]) the definition of the abstract syntax is the core of any language definition. Thus, we assume that the generated structure-oriented editor has produced an arbitrary fragment (i.e the part of an abstract syntax tree), which then becomes the object of context analysis.

For purposes of context analysis, we associate a (possibly structured) attribute value with each node of the fragment. However, it will be impossible to compute an uniquely determined attribute value for each node, as in an incomplete tree important information (e.g. variable declarations) may be missing.

A well-known method to handle such problems is, for example, the introduction of special "default" attribute values ([Reps83]). In the contrary, we explicitly pass over from attribute values to sets of "still possible" attribute values. The basic idea is as follows:

An arbitrary correct program fragment can be embedded into a (usually infinite) set of complete programs. These programs can be attributed, thus yielding a set of attribute assignments. The restriction of all these assignments onto the fragment in question results in a set of attribute assignments for the fragment, which represents exactly the context information corresponding to the fragment. As attribute values are associated with tree nodes, such a collection of attribute assignments can be seen as a relation in the sense of relational data base theory (see [Ahob79]): the columns of such a relation are labelled with the tree nodes[1], tuple elements are attribute values, and each tuple represents a possible attribute assignment for the fragment. Thus, the relation represents the set of all assignments of attribute values to tree nodes, which are possible for a specific fragment. Such a relation is called a <u>context relation</u> and is uniquely determined by the underlying fragment: there are no superfluous tuples, as each tuple represents a possible assignment of attribute values to tree nodes, and there are no missing tuples, as all "still possible" attribute assignments must be present in the context relation. If the fragment is complete, the relation will contain exactly one tuple, as there is exactly one possible attribute assignment in complete programs. In case of a context error, the relation will become empty, as no correct assignment of attribute values to tree nodes exists. Note that a context relation may be of infinite size, if the set of underlying attribute values is infinite.

<u>Example</u> Assume we have a language with real, integer, boolean and array variables, where integers are convertable to reals, array elements must be basic, and array indices must be integer. The language contains variable declarations, expressions and assignments. For assignments and expressions we assume the usual context conditions. Attribute values are (for simplicity) type descriptors. We consider the following four program fragments:

    (1) a[i] :=   (an incomplete assignment)

    (2) i+1   (an expression)

    (3) i and true   (an expression)

    (4) var i:integer (a variable declaration)

with corresponding abstract syntax trees:

---

[1] These column labels are called "attributes" in relational data base theory. We do not use this term in order to avoid misunderstandings

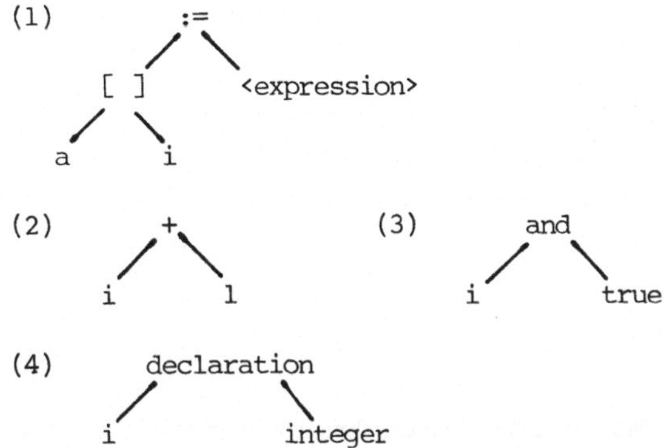

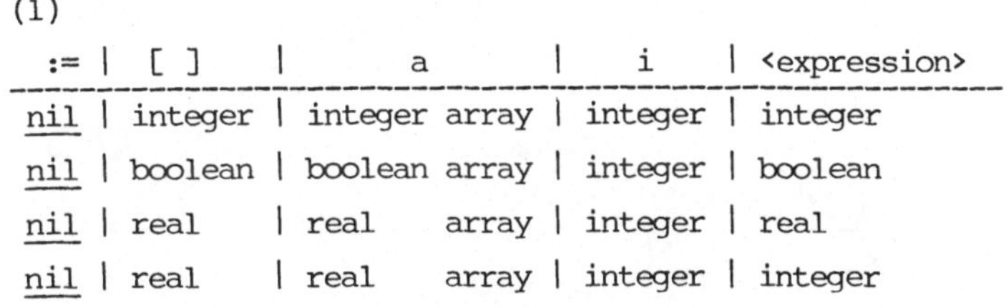

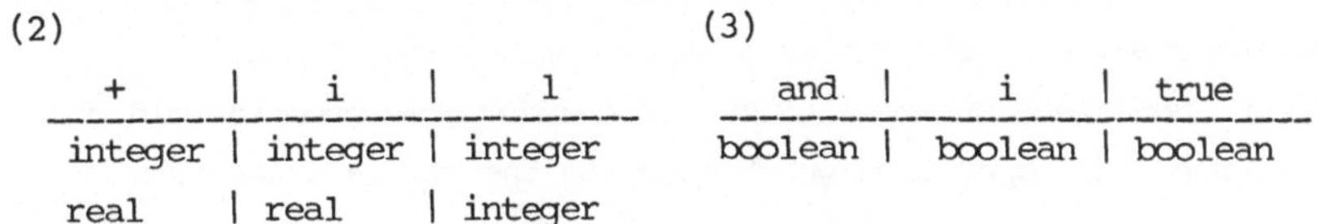

The corresponding context relations are:

(1)

:=	[ ]	a	i	<expression>
nil	integer	integer array	integer	integer
nil	boolean	boolean array	integer	boolean
nil	real	real array	integer	real
nil	real	real array	integer	integer

(2)

+	i	1
integer	integer	integer
real	real	integer

(3)

and	i	true
boolean	boolean	boolean

(4)

declaration	i	integer
nil	integer	integer

Note: assignment and declaration nodes have no type. This is indicated by the special attribute nil.

We observe, that in example (4) the relation contains only one tuple, i.e. the context information concerning the declared variable is uniquely determined. Thus, the presence of a complete declaration increases the precision of the context information (i.e reduces the number of tuples), but plays no special role. It is even possible, that uniquely defined context information can be computed without any declarations present in the fragment, as can be seen in example (3).

Formally, the context relation CR(F) associated with a program fragment F is a set of mappings

$$\{t:N \rightarrow A\}$$

where N is the set of nodes of F, and A is the underlying set of attribute values.

One should note, however, that identifier nodes occur only once as column labels in a context relation, even if the underlying syntax tree contains several occurences of the identifier. Therefore, in the first part of context analysis, several occurences of an identifier are "bound together". This process is called identifier identification and must of course observe scope and visibility rules. For details see [Aust81].

The composition of context relations during program development

During an editor session, a fragment is produced step by step by composing a bigger tree from smaller trees: subtree placeholders(templates) will be replaced by subtrees.

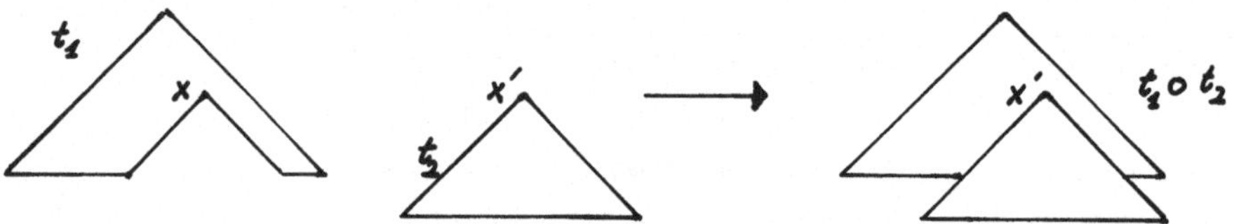

x denotes a template node, indicating a missing subtree, x' is the root of the subtree to be inserted, and "o" denotes subtree composition at node x.

But how do we get the context relation for the new tree from the old context relations? We need an operation which computes the new relation from the old ones, in order to obtain an incremental context analysis algorithm.

It is not a surprising fact, that relational data base theory can be used here: the operation we are looking for is just the natural join of relations (as known from data base theory, see [Ahob79]). We demonstrate this with examples:

(a) We compose trees (1) and (2) from the above example and obtain the assignment

    a[i]:=i+1

with corresponding abstract syntax tree

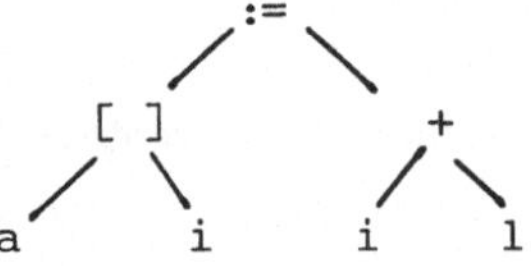

The "<expression>" node from (1) is identified with the "+" node from (2), and afterwards the join of relations (1) and (2) is computed. The resulting context relation is:

:=	[ ]	a	i	+	1
nil	integer	integer array	integer	integer	integer
nil	real	real array	integer	integer	integer

We see, that the original relations are in some sense "intersected"; the result is a relation which represents more detailed context information, as the number of tuples has decreased.

(b) In order to demonstrate the possibility to detect context errors as soon as possible, we compose trees (1) and (3), thus getting the assignment

$$a[i]:=i \text{ and true}$$

with corresponding abstract syntax tree

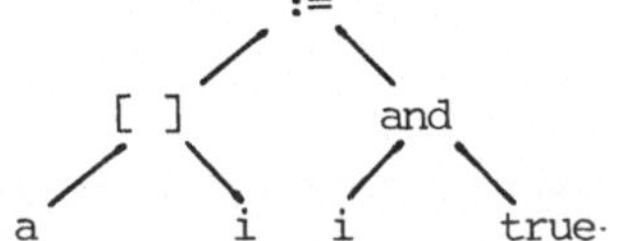

Joining relations (1) and (3), we obtain the empty relation

:=	[ ]	a	i	and	true

as the columns for "i" have no common attribute value. Thus, we have discovered a context error (i cannot be boolean and integer at the same time), although there are no variable declarations. This demonstrates, that context errors are detected as early as possible even in arbitrary incomplete fragments. "As early as possible" means: as soon as the fragment cannot be embedded into a correct program. The reason for this fact is, that context relations represent <u>exactly</u> the context information of a fragment; in this sense, context relations behave <u>optimal</u>.

Formally, the natural join of relations R_1, R_2 with column label sets N_1 resp. N_2 is defined as follows ([Ahob79]):

$$R_1 \bowtie R_2 := \{t:N_1 \ N_2 \to A \mid t/N_1 \in R_1 \text{ and } t/N_2 \in R_2 \}$$

where t/N is the projection of tuple t onto column label set N:

$$t/N \ (n) := \begin{cases} t(n) & n \in N \\ \text{undefined} & \text{otherwise} \end{cases}$$

Thus, if subtree composition at a certain node is denoted by o, we have the property

$$CR(T_1 \ o \ T_2) = CR(T_1) \bowtie CR(T_2).$$

This allows us to compute context relations incrementally during an editing session.

The specification method

We have seen, how to construct context relations incrementally. However, there must be some relations to start with! These basic relations are obtained as follows:

Each syntax tree can be composed from rudimentary trees of the form

which is a single terminal leaf, corresponding to a terminal symbol of the abstract syntax, and elementary trees of the form

which corresponds to a node rule of the abstract syntax. Therefore, the language definer, acting as "deus ex machina", has to specify basic relations for all terminals and all node rules of a given abstract syntax. In our sample language, the basic relation for assignments

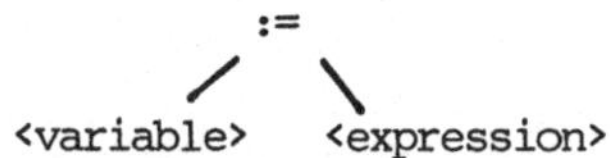

would look as follows:

:=	<variable>	<expression>
nil	integer	integer
nil	real	real
nil	boolean	boolean
nil	real	integer

The specification of these basic relations, using appropriate attributes, is sufficient to compute context information for any fragment (under the assumption that the abstract syntax has already been defined)[1]. However the specification could be a tedious job, as context relations are usually infinite!

---

1 The historical origins of this method can be found in the "operator-
-operand compatibility tables", which were used to specify context conditions of e.g. Algol and Fortran

The representation of context relations

In order to prevent the language definer from specifying infinite relations and to preserve the computer from joining infinite relations, one has to construct a finite representation for context relations. The basic idea is to use a grammar: We assume that the underlying set of attribute values can be described by an abstract syntax. Such a grammar is called a data attribute grammar[2]. Context relations are then represented by so-called attribute form relations, which are defined as follows: The column label set of an attribute form relation is the same as that of the represented context relation. However, instead of using attribute values as tuple components, a tuple consists of several incomplete data attribute trees (data attribute tree forms) according to the underlying data attribute grammar. Each data attribute tree form defines a (posssibly infinite) set of attribute values, namely those attribute values which can be derived from it. A tuple of an attribute form relation represents a (possibly infinite) context relation which contains those tuples, the components of which (i.e. attribute values) can be derived from the corresponding attribute form tuple components (which are attribute tree forms). An attribute form relation represents the union of the context relations represented by its tuples.

A data attribute grammar for our sample language might look as follows:

```
attribute = nil | type
type      = basic | arraytype
basic     = arithmetic | ordinal
arithmetic= integer | real
ordinal   = integer | boolean
arraytype :: Int Int basic
```

"integer", "real" and "boolean" are terminals; "Int" is a structured terminal which can be seen as an additional, implicitly defined syntactic class:

```
Int = 0 | 1 | 2 | 3 | ...        .
```

Note that this grammar is ambiguous, as "integer" belongs to "arithmetic" as well as "ordinal", which might be useful in some situations. In addition to the examples given above, an array attribute now includes not only the component type, but also the index bounds.

The incomplete data attribute tree

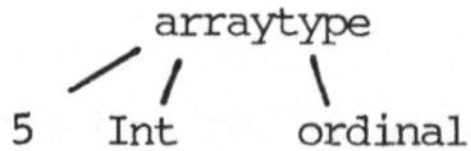

represents the infinite set of attribute values consisting of all array attributes with lower bound 5, unknown upper bound and component type "integer" or "boolean". The attribute form relation

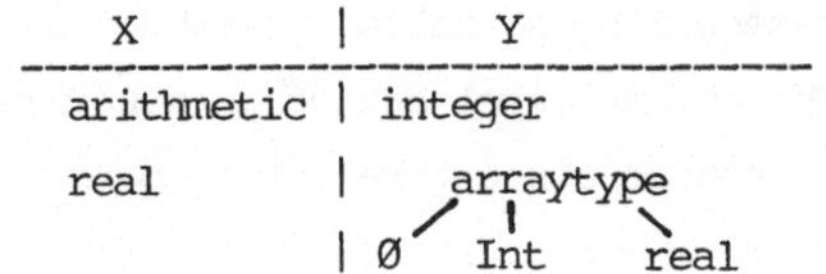

represents the infinite context relation

X	Y
integer	integer
real	integer
real	arraytype ∅ ∅ real
real	arraytype ∅ 1 real
real	arraytype ∅ 2 real
.	.
.	.
.	.

Formally, an attribute form relation is a set of mappings

$$\{t:N \rightarrow TF(G)\}$$

where G is the data attribute grammar and $TF(G)$ is the set of all attribute tree forms according to G. Given an attribute form relation r, the represented context relation $R[\![r]\!]$ is defined as

$$R[\![r]\!] := \{t:N \rightarrow A \mid \exists\, t' \in r\ \forall\, s \in N:\ t'(s) \overset{*}{\rightarrow} t(s)\}$$

where $\overset{*}{\rightarrow}$ means "is a derivative of", and $A=L(G)$, the language defined by G.

But what about the join operator? Of course, an operator should exist for attribute form relations which models exactly the join operation of context relations. This operation is quite complicated and can formally be defined as follows: Let r_1, r_2 be attribute form relations with column label sets N_1 resp. N_2, then

$$r_1 \sqcap r_2 := \{t: N_1 \cup N_2 \to TF(G) \mid \exists t_1 \in r_1 \; \exists t_2 \in r_2 \; \forall s \in N_1 \cup N_2:$$
$$t(s) = uni(t_1(s), t_2(s)) \text{ and } t(s) \neq \underline{\bot} \}$$

Here "uni" is the unification of data attribute tree forms, which is the "smallest" tree which can be derived from both original trees. For example,

$$uni\left(\begin{array}{c} \text{arraytype} \\ \diagup \; \mid \; \diagdown \\ 5 \quad \text{Int} \quad \text{ordinal} \end{array} \; , \; \begin{array}{c} \text{arraytype} \\ \diagup \; \mid \; \diagdown \\ \text{Int} \quad 10 \quad \text{arithmetic} \end{array} \right) = \begin{array}{c} \text{arraytype} \\ \diagup \; \mid \; \diagdown \\ 5 \quad 10 \quad \text{integer} \end{array}$$

Of course, such an unification need not exist, in this case we write $uni(x,y) = \underline{\bot}$. If $t_1(s)$ resp. $t_2(s)$ does not exist, as $s \notin N_1$ resp. $s \notin N_2$, we assume that $t_1(s) = t_2(s) =$ "start symbol of the data attribute grammar", and of course $uni(x, \underline{\bot}) = uni(\underline{\bot}, x) = \underline{\bot}$.

One can then prove [Aust83] that

$$R[\![\; r_1 \sqcap r_2 \;]\!] = R[\![r_1]\!] \bowtie R[\![r_2]\!] \qquad .$$

Thus the join is exactly represented by the "$\sqcap$" operation.

Coupling data attribute trees

Before we return to example (a), we have to introduce another notion. Often it is neccessary to specify certain equality conditions for data attribute trees. For example, the basic relation for index reference might look as follows:

$$\begin{array}{cc} \begin{array}{c} [\;] \\ \diagup \; \diagdown \\ \text{<variable>} \quad \text{<expression>} \end{array} & \begin{array}{c|c|c} [\;] & \text{<variable>} & \text{<expression>} \\ \hline \text{basic} & \begin{array}{c} \text{arraytype} \\ \diagup \; \mid \; \diagdown \\ \text{Int} \; \text{Int} \; \text{basic} \end{array} & \text{integer} \end{array} \end{array}$$

Here, the two occurences of "basic" are not independent: they must always derive identical attribute values, as the type of the index reference must be the same as the array component type. However, the definition of the representation function R in the previous section allows, that the two "basic"'s derive independent, and therefore possibly different, attribute values. Thus, we need some kind of coupling mechanism which allows a restriction of the function R. This mechanism should guarantee, that the above attribute form relation represents the corresponding basic context relation correctly.

In order to specify the coupling mechanism, we introduce attribute <u>variables</u>. These variables are placehoulders for attribute trees. The representation function R is modified, such that attribute variables are replaced <u>uniformly</u> by data attribute (sub)trees. Thus, we introduce some kind of uniform replacement rule.

Formally, an attribute form relation with variables is a set of mappings

$$\{t: N \to TFV(G) \}$$

where TFV(G) is the set of all incomplete data attribute trees which may contain variables instead of certain subtrees. The new representation function is then defined as

$$RV[\![r]\!] := \{t:N \rightarrow A \mid \exists\, t' \in r\, \exists\, e \in E\ \forall\, s \in N:\ e^{*}(t'(s)) \xrightarrow{*} t(s)\ \}$$

Here, r is an attribute form relation with variables, e is a substitution mapping (an environment) which maps variables to data attribute (sub)trees, e^{*} is the extension of e to data attribute tree forms, and E is the set of all substitution mappings.

Again we have to construct an operation for attribute form relations with variables, which models the natural join of context relations. Such a construction is possible indeed, but quite complicated (see [Aust83]). Due to space limitations, we will not show it in detail. The resulting operator is denoted by "⋈". It can be proved that

$$RV[\![r_1 \bowtie r_2]\!] = RV[\![r_1]\!] \times RV[\![r_2]\!] \quad .$$

Intuitively, "⋈" works as follows: for each pair of tuples in r_1 resp. r_2, the attribute trees of corresponding columns are unified in the sense of [Robi65], [Mart82]. If the unification does not fail, the resulting tuple will be included into the new relation.

<u>Example (a) revisited</u>

We reconsider example (a), using the notions of attribute form relations with variables. Attribute variables are written in capital letters and named like nonterminals of the data attribute grammar, thus indicating the kind of the attribute to be substituted[3].

The initial syntax trees and relations are:

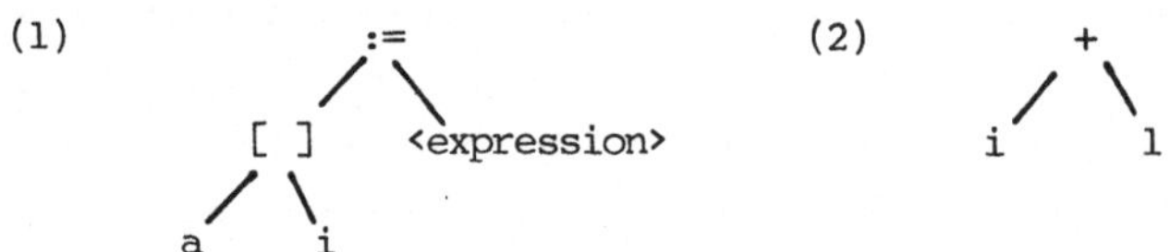

---

3 This naming convention codes parts of the environment into the variable names

```
(1):   := | [ ]  |     a         |   i   | <expression>
     ---------------------------------------------------------
       nil | BASIC | arraytype     | integer | BASIC
           |       | Int Int BASIC |         |

       nil | real  | arraytype     | integer | integer
           |       | Int Int real  |         |


(2):    +    |    i    |   1
      --------------------------------
      ARITHMETIC | ARITHMETIC | integer
```

Now we have to compute (1)⋈(2). This works similar to the join, but instead of looking for identical attribute values in corresponding columns, we have to compute the unification of attribute trees. For the column "i" we find that the unification of ARITHMETIC and integer is integer, for the column "<expression>" resp. "+" the unification of BASIC and ARITHMETIC is ARITHMETIC, which has already been substituted by integer (the substitution mapping is always updated at once!). Therefore, the result is, as one has expected

```
 := |  [ ]    |     a           |   i    |   +     |   1
 ---------------------------------------------------------------
 nil | integer | arraytype       | integer | integer | integer
     |         | Int Int integer |         |         |

 nil | real    | arraytype       | integer | integer | integer
     |         | Int Int  real   |         |         |
```

<u>Some notes on the implementation</u>

The incremental context analysis, as a part of the Programming System Generator, is implemented in Pascal on Siemens BS2000 machines. Rehosting of the system for UNIX machines is currently under work.

The generator for the context analyser consists of ca. 3000 source lines. For a language like Pascal, the definition of context conditions consists of 500 lines of meta language, which, as input to the generator, results in 8000 lines Pascal code which initialises language-specific tables at editor runtime. The context analysis itself consists of 6500 source lines. Several extensions have been necessary, which are not described in this paper, especially for the incremental modification of abstract syntax trees, for attributes which are lists and for arithmetic and list operators.

The context analyser can be seen as an inference engine. An extended version of Corbins "rehabilited robinson" unification algorithm [Corb83] is used. It computes about 1000 logic inferences per second. Depending on the size of the language definition and of the program which is analysed, this results in context analysis runtimes between 0.1 and 5 CPU seconds per editor step. To analyse a Pascal program of 250 lines, the method needs 100 kbyte virtual memory.

Context relation lattices

In addition to the more practical aspects of context relations in connection with programming environments, we present some mathematical properties (see [Snel83] for proofs).

The ⋈ -operator has some properties of an intersection operator: given two context relations, it computes a relation which represents the maximal context information compatible with both input relations. Formally, ⋈ is commutative, idempotent and associative and thus induces an upper semilattice of context relations together with a partial order on the set of context relations. One can define the counterpart of ⋈ by

$$R_1 \mathbin{⧖} R_2 := R_1/(N_1 \cap N_2) \cup R_2{}^{/(N_1 \cap N_2)}$$

which is something like a union operator: given two context relations R_1, R_2, it computes the minimal information compatible with either R_1 or R_2.

Example: consider the relations (2) and (3) from the previous examples.

i	1	+
integer	integer	integer
real	integer	real

⧖

i	and	true
boolean	boolean	boolean

=

i
integer
real
boolean

In a programming environment, the "⧖" operator can be used to compute context information concerning more than one fragment: for variables occuring in several different fragments the "union" operator computes the minimal context information which does not conflict with any of the relations induced by the fragments in question.

One can show, that the algebra $\underline{CR}$ = (CR; ⋈, ⧖) where CR is the set of all context relations, forms a complete lattice. The partial order induced by ⋈ and ⧖ is given by

$$R_1 \preccurlyeq R_2 \text{ iff } N_1 \quad N_2 \text{ and } R_2{}^{/N_1} \quad R_1$$

For attribute form relations, there is an operator ⊔ which is the counterpart of ⌐ :

$$r_1 \mathbin{⊔} r_2 := r_1/(N_1 \cap N_2) \cup r_2/(N_1 \cap N_2)$$

One can show that

$$R[r_1 \mathbin{⊔} r_2] = R[r_1] \mathbin{⧖} R[r_2] \quad .$$

This means that the lattice $\underline{CR}$ is a homomorphic image of the algebra

$\underline{AFR}$:= $(AFR; \sqcap, \sqcup)$ where AFR is the set of all attribute form relations. The homomorphism is just the function R.

Finally, for attribute form relations with variables, one can define an operator $\bowtie$ analogeously to x and $\sqcup$ such that

$$RV[\![r_1 \bowtie r_2]\!] = RV[\![r_1]\!] \; \text{⅄} \; RV[\![r_2]\!]$$

Thus, $\underline{CR}$ is a homomorphic image of the algebra $\underline{AFRV}$:=$(AFRV; \sqcap, \bowtie)$ where AFRV is the set of all attribute form relations with variables. Note, however, that CR$\subseteq$AFR and CR$\subseteq$AFRV .

3. Comparison with other methods

Comparing our system with others, we have to distinguish between language specification methods (e.g. Attributed Grammars [Knu68], Two Level Grammars [Wegn80]) and typing schemas for specific languages.

With the general specification tools the requirements of chapter 1 can be fulfilled according to their power. Their current methodology to specify the context conditions of a programming language however violates requirement 1 and 2 (applicable to each fragment and immediate error detection). A specification based on Attributed Grammars or Two Level Grammars has always the scheme: first build up the environment inspecting the declarations, then check the expression in this environment. Therefore fragments without declarations cannot be checked. No formal rules are known to the authors, which transform a specification written in the usual style in to a style suitable for incremental context analysis. Even the incremental evaluation of context conditions [Reps83] can not handle the occurence of undeclared variables, if usual-style attribute grammars are used as specification tool. Note, some similarities between Two Level Grammars and our system can be found: the metarules correspond to the data attribute grammar, a hyperrule to a rule of the abstract syntax together with a tuple of compatible data attributes and the concept of derivation to the composition of fragments and the join of relations. Although there exists some correpondence, no computable parsing algorithm for arbitrary fragments is known to the authors.

Existing type inference schemes for specific languages satisfy partially our requirements, but are not generalized to specification tools for programming languages. The type inference scheme in ML [Miln78] evaluates the most general polymorphic type of an expression in form of a type expression with variables. The scheme looks similar to our system, but differs in an important aspect: our system does not allow overloading and polymorphism, except for overloaded constants. However, work is done to include overloading, coercions and polymorphism into our concept.

A different approach of type inference of expressions can be found in the data
flow analysis of languages without static typing [Tene74,Jone76, Kapl80]. The
main difference to our system is that we assume a variable has just one final
type, whereas in untyped languages a variable can get several types depending on
the flow of control. Therefore in our system the knowledge about the data
attributes of a variable can only increase, whereas in the other case it can
also decrease. A comparison is due to the different assumptions not possible.

4. Final Remarks

The basic idea of the method is described in [Henh80]. The proof, that the
method is wellfounded and has the immediate error detection property is part of
the thesis [Aust83] as well as that the method is applicable to Pascal.
The generator, which translates the context specification into the context
analysis module of a programming environment was implemented by a series of
master thesis [Schm83,Hunk83]. The generator is succesfully applied to Pascal;
however, some extensions of the method have been neccesary which are not
described in this paper.
All the work was done within the frame of the PSG-Project supported by DFG
grants He-1170/1 and He-1170/2-2.The success of the incremenmtal context
analysis would not have been possible without the permanent inspiring discus-
sions with the other members of the project especially R. Bahlke and T.
Letschert.

References

[Ahob78]   A.V. Aho, C. Beeri, J.D. Ullman: The theory of joins in
             relational databases. ACM transactions on database systems
             4 (1979) S. 297-314.

[Aust81]   B. Austermühl, W. Henhapl: A generalised approach to the speci-
             fication of context conditions, Bericht PU1R10/81,
             Technische Hochschule Darmstadt, Dezember 1981.

[Aust82]   B. Austermühl: Context conditions of standard Pascal,
             Bericht PU1R14/81, Techn. Hochschule Darmstadt, April 1982.

[Aust83]   B. Austermühl: Ein relationaler Ansatz zur Spezifikation
             der statischen Semantik von Programmiersprachen, Dissertation,
             Techn. Hochschule Darmstadt, Juli 1983.

[Bahl82a]   R. Bahlke, W. Henhapl, T. Letschert:
             Forschungsvorhaben Programmiersystemgenerator - Arbeits-
             bericht. Bericht PU1R8/82, Techn. Hochschule Darmstadt,
             März 1982.

[Bahl82b]   R. Bahlke, T. Letschert: The BLKS system: towards the generation of
             programming environments, in: GI-Fachausschuss Compiler-
             -Compiler, 3. Fachgespräch, 1982.

[Corb83]   J. Corbin, M. Codoit: A rehabilitation of Robinsons unification algorithm, Proceedings of the IFIP 9th world computer congres, North-Holland, September 1983.

[Henh80] W. Henhapl: Context conditions in program fragments, Bericht PU1R1/80, Techn. Hochschule Darmstadt, Januar 1980.

[Hunk83] M. Hunkel: Kontextanalyse im PSG-Editor, Diplomarbeit, Techn. Hochschule Darmstadt (forthcoming).

[Jone76] N.D. Jones, S.S. Muchnick: Binding time optimization in programming languages: Some thoughts toward the design of an ideal language, 3. Annual ACM Symposium on Principles of Programming languages 1976, 77-94.

[Kapl80] M. Kaplan, J. Ullman: A scheme for the automatic inference of variable types, Journal of the ACM 27 (1980), 128-145.

[Knut68] D. E. Knuth: Semantics of context-free languages, Math. systems theory 2 (1968), 127-145.

[Mart82] A. Martelli, U. Montanari: An efficient unification algorithm, ACM Transactions on programming languages and sytems 4 (1982), 258-282.

[Miln78] R. Milner: A theory of type polymorphism in programming languages, Journal of omputer and System sciences 17 (1978), 348-375.

[Reps83] T. Reps, T. Teitelbaum, A. Demers: Incremental context- -dependent analysis for language-based editors, ACM Trans- actions on programming languages and systems 5 (1983), 3, 449-477.

[Robi65] J.A. Robinson: A machine-oriented logic based on the resolution principle, Journal of the ACM 12 (1965), 1, 23-41.

[Schm83] H. Schmitt: Bezeichneridentifikation im PSG-Editor, Diplomarbeit, Techn. Hochschule Darmstadt (forthcoming).

[Snel83] G. Snelting: Kontextrelationenverbände, Bericht PU1R9/83, Technische Hochschule Darmstadt, September 1983.

[Tene74] A.M. Tenenbaum: Type determination for very high level languages, Report NSO-3, Courant Institute of Mathematical science, Computer Science Department, New York University 1974.

[Wegn80] L.M. Wegner: On parsing two-level grammars, Acta Informatica 14 (1980), 175-193.

An Environment for High-level Program Development*

Peter Grogono

V.S. Alagar

Department of Computer Science

Concordia University

Abstract

TAPE, a Typed Applicative Programming Environment, is a system that facilitates the prototyping and development of software. By supporting a family of related languages at different levels, TAPE allows programmers to address the various problems of software development at an appropriate level of abstraction. The highest level supported by TAPE is an applicative language with automatic type inference and representation selection, used primarily for prototyping. During program development, a programmer can interact with the system, refining its typing decisions and selecting appropriate representations and optimizations.

1 Introduction

A "programming environment," as the term is understood today, incorporates a number of software tools designed to assist programmers in the production of software. The effectiveness of the environment depends on both the nature of the tools and the features of the programming language, or languages, supported. TAPE is a Typed Applicative Programming Environment. In this paper we discuss Dee, the language on which TAPE is based, rather than the related tools of the environment within which the languages are used. The language is named for John Dee (1527-1608), a British mathematician and alchemist.

2 Programming Environments

A programming environment provides a programmer, or a team of programmers, with facilities for the development of software. A programming environment is effective if it facilitates the rapid development of correct software.

In contrast to early programming environments, which provided minimal tools for developing programs in several languages, many recent programming environments are

* The research described in this paper was funded by the Natural Sciences and Engineering Research Council, le Fonds Formation de chercheurs et action concertee, and Concordia University.

dedicated to a single language and provide a high level of support for it. In this paper, we describe language features that are conducive to providing an effective environment. First we discuss the requirements of an effective environment and language features that can assist in achieving this environment.

2.1 Requirements

We can derive requirements for an effective programming environment by considering the characteristics of earlier programming languages that made them amenable to software development. The characteristics that we consider significant are enumerated below.

1. **Rapid prototyping.** It must be possible to obtain a working version of a program with minimal attention to detail. Rapid prototyping enables fundamental design and specification errors to be detected before a major investment in software development has been made [17].

2. **Modularity.** Separating the internal mechanism of a portion of the program from its external interface provides a powerful abstraction mechanism.

3. **Interaction.** The traditional edit/compile/test cycle is too slow for modern software development. Separate compilation of modules helps but may be insufficient. The environment must provide mechanisms for entering and testing code rapidly. This requires an incremental compiler and/or an interpreter.

4. **Type checking.** Few people now dispute the importance of type checking as a means of detecting errors in programs. A compiler can generate efficient code only if it can determine the type of each object in the program.

5. **Representation.** The programming environment should permit flexibility in the choice of representation and it should allow programmers to refine representations during program development.

6. **Semantics.** Explicit semantic principles are useful to both the designer of a language and its users [1]. We can reason about programs only if the language has a robust semantic foundation. Languages with expressive power can be constructed from a small set of appropriate semantic principles and well-chosen syntactic sugar.

7. **Efficiency.** Implementations of applicative languages tend to be inefficient. We do not share the opinion that cheaper and faster hardware will make efficiency considerations irrelevant.

8. **Conciseness.** Language designers must compromise between verbosity and hieroglyphics. As a general trend, however, we should expect programs to become shorter rather than longer.

These requirements are not independent. Some of them tend to go together: for example, postponing choice of representation is an important aid to rapid prototyping.

Others tend to be incompatible, at least if we base our experience on existing languages. For example, modularity and strong typing are associated with compiled, non-interactive languages, whereas interaction and rapid prototyping are associated with interpreted, untyped languages.

Nor are the requirements particularly novel. LISP fulfills many of them [16]. Most implementations of LISP, however, are not applicative, use dynamic scoping, and have call-by-value semantics. LISP programs are not amenable to source-to-source transformations and are difficult to maintain. APL is suitable for prototyping [8]. A number of recent languages, including Ada, Mesa, and Modula-2, provide facilities for creating program modules that can be separately compiled.

We do not expect TAPE to meet all of the requirements we have listed, but we hope that it will provide at least a novel balance of compromises.

2.2 Meeting the Requirements

TAPE is an experimental system, and we envisage an adaptable environment in which different techniques of program development can be explored. In designing TAPE, we considered all of the requirements listed above for a programming environment. We conclude this section by describing how features of the programming language Dee enable TAPE to meet these requirements. The following section provides an overview of the system.

1. **Applicative.** Dee is a purely applicative language; there is no assignment statement, and the value of an expression is determined by the environment in which it is evaluated. A small number of operations have side-effects, so that essential capabilities, such as input and output, can be implemented. Several researchers have described the benefits of applicative programming [2,4,5,18].

2. **Type checking and type inference.** Dee accepts, but does not require, type declarations. The principal type of every object in a program is inferred by the compiler.

3. **Abstraction.** The principle of abstraction in Dee is simple and powerful: any name can be abstracted from an expression, turning the expression into a function of which the name is a parameter. This abstraction mechanism provides polymorphic functions, higher-order functions, and abstract data types.

4. **Call-by-name semantics.** An applicative computation that terminates under call-by-value (applicative order) semantics also terminates under call-by-name (normal order) semantics; the converse is not true. Some program transformations are valid under call-by-name semantics or call-by-value semantics but not both.

5. **Modules.** Dee programs consist of modules that can import the environments of other modules and can export selected names to other modules. This contrasts with the "flat" name-space of APL and LISP.

6. **Multi-level.** There has been some recent interest in languages that permit problems to be expressed at different levels of abstraction; these "wide-spectrum" languages include CIP-L [3] and SETL [7]. Dee encourages separation of concern by providing several notations at different levels.

7. **Extensibility.** Dee has extensible syntax. Extensible languages were popular for a time but went out of favor because syntactic extensions are not useful without semantic power. We believe that the semantics of Dee, based on function application, are sufficiently powerful to provide a basis for a variety of useful syntactic extensions.

8. **Compilation.** Even with today's fast and cheap hardware, high-level interpreted languages make heavy demands on both time and space. Any system intended for software development must be capable of translating programs into object code of reasonable quality.

3 An Overview of Dee

Dee is based on a very simple model of computation: the evaluation of an expression in an environment. The syntax of the language provides ways of defining expressions and environments for their evaluation, and the semantics describe the evaluation of expressions.

Dee consists of a hierarchy of notations. Noar the top of the hierarchy, there is a language called L2. L2 is important because it is a **canonical form** in which all Dee programs are expressed during their development. L2 has external and internal representations. The two representations are closely related, in a similar way to the representations of S-expressions in LISP, and moving from one to the other is a trivial operation.

The highest level in the language hierarchy consists of a language called L1. L1 has several dialects which vary syntactically according to the application, but each dialect can be translated into L2. We are currently using only a "general purpose" dialect of L1. We anticipate the development of other dialects with syntax appropriate for appplications such as symbolic algebra and database query languages.

The notations below L2 in the hierarchy are intermediate representations used by the Dee processors. Unlike L1 and L2, they are not usually seen by users.

3.1 Objects, Environments, and Expressions

An **object** in Dee possesses a **name**, a **type**, and a **value**. In general, the object's type is determined during compilation and its value is determined during execution. New objects are introduced in a Dee program by **definitions** of the form

    x = e

in which x is the name of the new object and e is an expression. An **expression** is an abstraction, an application, or a constant. An **abstraction** has the form

    [p1,p2,...,pn] -> e

in which p1,p2,...,pn are names abstracted from the expression e. The result of evaluating this expression is a function of n arguments. The free variables in e are bound statically within the environment of the definition. An **application** has the form

    f(x1,x2,...,xn)

in which an expression f is applied to arguments x1,x2,...,xn. The function receives its arguments in unevaluated form and evaluates them only when necessary. A **constant** is an object whose type and value are predefined. The class of constants includes predefined functions in addition to objects such as 0 and **false.**

An **environment** is a collection of objects. (Unfortunately, this use of the word "environment" conflicts with its use in the term "programming environment." We hope that in this paper the intended use will be clear from the context.) An environment may be given a name and packaged in a **module.** Dee uses modules to control the scope of names and hence to facilitate data abstraction and information hiding.

The foregoing elements constitute the language L2. The language L1 is semantically equivalent to L2 but has a layer of syntactic sugar that makes it more palatable to the programmer but does not increase its semantic power. We illustrate the effect of the additional syntax in Section 4.

3.2 Types

The language described so far is a sweetened lambda-calculus. Its expressiveness is extended further by the provision of type declarations, type inference, and type checking.

Existing programming languages are, for the most part, either typeless (LISP, SNOBOL, APL) or strongly typed (Algol-68, Pascal, Modula-2). Both extremes have well-known disadvantages. Several recent programming languages attempt to overcome these deficiencies by providing more advanced features for type manipulation: for example, Russell [6], ML [9], MARY/2 [14], and Maple [19]. The Dee approach to types is based on the following objectives.

1. The programmer should not have to declare the type of every object.
2. The programmer should be able to define and use new types.
3. Both polymorphic and generic functions should be permitted.
4. The compiler should detect and report type errors.
5. The compiler should use inferred type information to generate efficient code.

Dee provides predefined types such as bool (Boolean) and int (integers). **Type-formers** are predefined functions that take types as arguments and return new types. For example,

    T3 = cp(T1,T2)

defines a new type, T3, as the Cartesian product of types T1 and T2. Similarly, du returns the disjoint union of its arguments; map(T1,T2) returns the type of functions from type T1 to type T2; and list(T) returns the type of objects that are lists with components of type T. In L1, the infix operators "*", "+", and "->" may be used to denote cp, du , and map , and the prefix operator "#" may be used to denote list .

Dee provides both polymorphic and generic functions. The expression denoting the type of a polymorphic function contains one or more universally quantified type variables. For example, the type of null , the predicate that recognizes an empty list, is

    for all types T: #T -> bool

An expression of this form is called a **type scheme** [12].

The term "generic function" denotes a convention whereby the members of a set of functions share the same name. The name of a generic function is said to be "overloaded." When a generic function is applied, the appropriate member of the set is selected by type comparison. The "type" of a generic function is actually a set of types. If we use plus as a generic function to add integers or rationals, for example, we can express its type as

    {int * int -> int, rat * rat -> rat}

Overloaded names complicate the task of type inference. Type inference in Dee is based on an algorithm described by Milner [12], extended to handle overloaded names

[10]. Type inference involves the application of rules requiring that the types of certain objects be equal. For example, if a function of type T1->T2 is applied to an object of type T3, the equation T1 = T3 must be satisfied. If T1 and T3 are type schemes, this equation can be satisfied if T1 and T3 can be **unified.** Type schemes can be unified if there is an assignment to their free variables that makes them equal; if any such assignment exists, the most general assignment can be found by unification [15].

We hope that further research will help us to avoid two disadvantages of the present type system. The first disadvantage is that the type inference algorithm fails in the presence of subtypes because it requires that the type of every constant be manifest. Second, implicit coercions are hard to manage in the absence of type declarations.

3.3 Evaluating Expressions

An expression is evaluated within an environment. The environment must contain bindings for all of the names in the expression when the expression is evaluated. Otherwise, the evaluator reports an error.

The evaluation of an expression in an environment is a central concept in Dee. Important features of the language exist for the purpose of creating or modifying environments.

1. An application ([x]->e)(a) in the environment env is evaluated by adding the binding x = a to env and then evaluating e . Under call-by-name semantics, a is not evaluated until it is required during the evaluation of the function body.
2. LET and WHERE expressions create local environments for the evaluation of their sub-expressions by using the mechanism of application.
3. A module creates an environment.
4. The directive IMPORT , followed by a list of module names, and the directive EXPORT , followed by a list of object names, modify the environment created by the module containing them.

3.4 Compilation

The general philosophy of Dee is that the compiler should extract and use as much information as possible about the source program but that it should not request more information from the user unless it cannot proceed. For example, the application of an undefined function would provoke an error. At the same time, the system should make all reasonable checks so that the considerable advantages of strong typing are not sacrificed.

The use of a very high-level applicative language is to some extent incompatible with the requirement of efficient object code. Extensive optimization is required if acceptable code is to be generated. The multi-level structure of Dee, however, permits optimizations of different kinds to be performed at the appropriate level. For example, transformations such as recursion removal are performed in L2. Simple transformations are performed automatically, but complex transformations may require direction from the user. By compiling first to an intermediate level language rather than to machine language, the loss of information useful to an optimizer can be avoided.

The L1 compiler removes syntactic sugar and constructs a symbol table. The result of compiling an L1 program, P1, is an L2 program, P2. Optimizing source-to-source transformations are applied to P2, both automatically and with user guidance. Eventually, P2 reaches a canonical form in which no further transformations are effective. Although L2 has call-by-name semantics, the compiler detects most situations in which parameters can be passed by value [13], and only in the worst case does it revert to call-by-need, passing a closure to the called function. The L2 compiler compiles P2 into an L3 program, P3. L3 is a procedural language which can be further compiled or directly interpreted. In the current version of Dee, L3 is suited to execution by a single processor. We hope that future versions will realize the potential for concurrent evaluation offered by applicative semantics and multiprocessor systems.

The compiler can operate in either of two modes. In "incremental" mode, modules are compiled separately. A module cannot be compiled until the modules that it imports have been compiled; this requirement imposes a partial ordering on the compilation. As in other modular languages, recompilation of one module may require recompilation of dependent modules.

In the other mode, which is called "global," the compiler performs a global analysis of all modules. Global compilation requires more time, but enables more efficient code to be generated for generic functions [10]. This gives the user a further opportunity to choose between development and production modes.

4 Examples

First, we develop a simple example to illustrate the notational conventions and use of abstraction in L1. The function even recognizes even integers.

    even = [n] -> eq(mod(n,2),0)

Using the syntactic sugar of L1, we can write this in the form:

```
even = [n] -> n\2 = 0
```

The function filteven selects even integers from a list of integers. The names null ,
car , cdr , and cons are borrowed from LISP.   Null recognizes the empty list, car
and cdr select the head and tail of a list, and cons constructs a list from its head
and tail.

```
filteven = [x] -> IF null(x)
                    THEN nil
                  ELSE IF even(car(x))
                      THEN cons(car(x),filteven(cdr(x)))
                  ELSE filteven(cdr(x))
```

Nil is a fixed point of so many list functions that it is useful to embody this property in
a second-order function scan with type $(T * \#T \to \#T) \to (\#T \to \#T)$.

```
scan = [f] -> [x] -> IF null(x)
                       THEN nil
                       ELSE f(car(x),cdr(x))
```

The concept of filtering with respect to an arbitrary predicate can also be abstracted
from the definition of filteven . The function filter requires a predicate as its
argument. In this definition we also introduce "." as the infix cons operator.

```
filter = [p] -> scan([a,x] -> LET f = filter(p)(x)
                              IN IF p(a)
                                  THEN a.f
                                  ELSE f
```

The function filteven can now be defined succinctly by

```
filteven = filter(even)
```

The system can infer the type of filteven , which is $\#int \to \#int$, from the type of
filter , $(T \to bool) \to (\#T \to \#T)$, and the type of even , $int \to bool$.

The next example illustrates modules. The integer functions plus , times , div, and
gcd are predefined in L2.   The following module extends the domain of plus and
minus to the rational numbers. The infix operators "+", "*", and "/", used in L1, are
associated with the names "plus", "times", and "div", not with the operations. Thus "+"
may be used for rationals as soon as "plus" has been defined for rationals. There is no
predefined infix operator corresponding to the name "cancel" and so the operator "//" is

defined with appropriate left and right precedence within the module. The exported functions cons-rat , plus , and times may be used with rational numbers within any module that includes the directive

IMPORT rational

The function selectors takes a Cartesian product type as argument and returns functions that select the components of the type. The function constructor is similar but returns a function that constructs an object of the type. The notation was introduced by Burge [4].

```
MODULE rational
  EXPORT cons-rat, plus, times
  rat = int * int
  num, den = selectors(rat)
  cons-rat = constructor(rat)
  cancel = [m,n] ->
              LET g = gcd(m,n)
              IN cons-rat(m/g, n/g)
  // = infix(cancel,40,50)
  LET nu = num(u), du = den(u), nv = num(v), dv = den(v)
  IN plus = [u,v] -> nu * dv + nv * du // du * dv
     times = [u,v] -> nu * nv // du * dv
END
```

Within any module that imports rational the type of plus is

$$\{int * int -> int, rat * rat -> rat\} \tag{1}$$

The function plus defined below adds the corresponding components of two lists. It could be used, for example, to add polynomials represented by lists.

```
plus = [x,y] ->                                          (2)
            IF null(x) THEN y
            ELSE IF null(y) THEN x
            ELSE car(x)+car(y) . cdr(x)+cdr(y)
```

In this definition, the plus in cdr(x)+cdr(y) is a recursive invocation of the function being defined. The type of plus in car(x)+car(y) is determined by the context of the definition. If its type is the type given in (1), the type of the function (2) is

$$\{\#int * \#int -> \#int, \#rat * \#rat -> \#rat\}$$

and the type of plus in the scope of both definition is

```
{int * int -> int, rat * rat -> rat,
 #int * #int -> #int, #rat * #rat -> #rat}
```

Efficient compilation of (2) requires an analysis of every invocation of the function. If the module containing (2) is compiled in incremental mode, as described in Section 3.4, the selection of the function that adds components must be postponed until run-time. In global mode, the selection can be made at compile-time, possibly resulting in multiple copies of the function body [10].

It is difficult to illustrate the capabilities of a high-level programming language in a limited space. We hope these small examples will convey at least the flavor of L1.

5 Conclusion

We have found the concept of a hierarchy of languages to be useful because it has enabled us to separate concerns. Many compilers use intermediate languages internally. We have extended this concept, using several intermediate levels and allowing the programmer controlled access to them.

We have not found the decision to make the highest level language strictly applicative to be a handicap although we need more extensive experience with the system before we can be sure about this. The applicative style of programming with higher-order functions requires a certain amount of practice for those accustomed to a procedural style but it seems to lead to more elegant and intelligible programs.

We have found environments to be useful as a unifying concept in language design. Although there is only one kind of environment internally, Dee provides different syntactic structures for environments at different levels. Programmers have a choice of notations. For example, the module is a high level environment constructor and the LET expression is a low level environment constructor.

By providing type schemes and type inference we have removed the burden of type declarations from the user without sacrificing security. The advantages of this approach have been demonstrated previously by languages such as ML [9] and B [11]. Executable programs can be developed rapidly; refinement can be postponed until experience has been gained from a working version of the program.

We have implemented Dee in LISP. This implementation, which is a prototype, consists of a parser, interpreter, type-checker, optimizer, and compiler. The language accepted by the compiler is a subset of the language L2 described in this paper. The compiler generates code for an abstract stack machine. We hope to develop a production version of TAPE during 1984.

6 References

1. Ashcroft, E.A., and Wadge, W.W.: R for semantics. ACM Transactions on Programming Languages and Systems, 4, 283-294 (1982)
2. Backus, J.: Can programming be liberated from the von Neumann Style? A functional style and its algebra of programs. Comm. ACM, 21, 613-641 (1978)
3. Bauer, F., et al: Description of the Wide Spectrum Language CIP-L. Institut fur Informatik, Technische Universitat Munchen, 1983.
4. Burge, W.H.: Recursive Programming Techniques. Reading, Mass.: Addison-Wesley 1975
5. Burstall, R.M., MacQueen, D.B., and Sannella, D.T.: HOPE: An experimental applicative language. Conference Record of the 1980 LISP Conference, pp. 136-143, The LISP Conference 1980
6. Demers, A.J., and Donahue, J.E.: 'Type-completeness' as a language principle. Seventh Symposium on the principles of Programming Languages, pp. 234-244, ACM 1980
7. Dewar, R.B.K., Schonberg, E., and Schwartz, J.T.: Higher level programming: Introduction to the use of the set theoretic programming language SETL. Courant Institute of Mathematical Sciences, New York University, 1981
8. Gomaa, H., and Scott, D.B.H.: Prototyping as a tool in the specification of user requirements. Proc. 5th International Conference on Software Engineering, pp. 333-342, IEEE 1981
9. Gordon, M., Milner R., Morris, L., Newey M., and Wadsworth, C.: A metalanguage for interactive proof in LCF. Fifth Symposium on the Principles of Programming Languages, pp. 119-130, ACM 1978
10. Grogono, P., and Alagar, V.S.: Combining type inference and generic functions. In preparation.
11. Meertens, L.: Issues in the design of a beginner's programming language. In: Algorithmic Languages (J.W. de Bakker and J.C. van Vliet, eds.), Amsterdam-New York-Oxford: North-Holland 1981
12. Milner, R.: A theory of type polymorphism in programming. JCSS, 17, 348-375 (1978)
13. Mycroft, A.: The theory and practice of transforming call-by-need into call-by-value. In: International Symposium on Programming (B. Robinet, ed.), Lecture Notes in Computer Science, Vol. 83, pp. 269-281. Berlin-Heidelberg-New York: Springer 1980
14. Rain, M.: MARY/2 Reference Manual. Penobscot Research Center, Deer Isle, Maine, 1980
15. Robinson, J.A.: A machine-oriented logic based on the resolution principle. J. ACM., 12, 23-41 (1965)
16. Sandewall, E.: Programming in the interactive environment: the LISP experience. ACM Comp. Surv., 10, 1, 35-71, (1978)
17. Squires, S.L. (Chmn.): Working Papers from the ACM SIGSOFT Rapid Prototyping Workshop. ACM Software Engineering Notes, 7, (1982)
18. Turner D.A.: Programming with infinite data structures. Conference on LISP and Functional Programming, (invited talk), ACM 1982
19. Voda P.J.: Maple: A programming language and operating system. Ninth Symposium on the Principles of Programming Languages, pp. 157-168, ACM 1982

Erfahrungen mit einem MIL - Entwurfswerkzeug

H.D. Rombach, K. Wegener

FB Informatik
Universität Kaiserslautern

Zusammenfassung

Es wird über Erfahrungen bei der Entwicklung und dem praktischen Einsatz eines
Werkzeugs zur Unterstützung einer aus der Literatur bekannten Entwurfssprache
(MIL) berichtet.
An der übernommenen Sprache und der zugrundeliegenden Methode mußten zunächst
umfangreiche Änderungen vorgenommen werden. Die Änderungen bestanden in der
Anpassung sowohl an eine spezielle Einsatzumgebung als auch an heute anerkannte
grundsätzliche Anforderungen an eine Entwurfsmethode und -sprache.
Die Erfahrungen aus dem Einsatz des Werkzeugs werden zum Teil in Form experimentell
gewonnener Meßdaten vermittelt.

1. Einleitung

Die erfolgversprechende Verwendung von Methoden und Sprachen zur Softwareerstellung
setzt deren Unterstützung durch Werkzeuge voraus. Die **Erfahrungen** bei der
Entwicklung eines Werkzeugs für eine existierende Methode und Sprache sowie dessen **praktische Erprobung** werden präsentiert. Die zugrundegelegte Methode und
Sprache **MIL75** [7] (Kap.2.1) ist geeignet für das **Entwerfen statischer Aspekte**
von Software, wie z.B. Strukturierung eines Software-Systems in Bausteine, Definition der Schnittstellen zwischen diesen Bausteinen.
Eine **Mängelanalyse** (Kap.2.2) ergab, daß sowohl fehlende Übereinstimmung mit der
beabsichtigten Einsatzumgebung als auch die teilweise Nichtberücksichtigung heute
unumstrittener Anforderungen an eine Entwurfsmethode eine direkte Umsetzung der
MIL75 in ein Werkzeug nicht ratsam erscheinen ließen. Die Integration der als
notwendig erachteten Änderungen in die MIL75 führte zur **MIL82** (Kap.2.3).
Für diese modifizierte Methode und Sprache wurde ein spezielles Werkzeug (Kap.3)
entwickelt. Die bislang erzielten Erfahrungen aus dem Einsatz des Werkzeugs (Kap.4)
zeigen, daß bei Erfüllung bestimmter Grundanforderungen an das unterstützende
Werkzeug die Verwendung der MIL82 den Softwareerstellungsprozeß positiv beeinflußt.

2. Die Sprache

2.1 Das Original von DeRemer/Kron

Frank DeRemer und Hans H. Kron zeigten in ihrem Artikel [7] die grundsätzlichen Unterschiede zwischen dem Entwerfen großer Programmpakete (`programming-in-the-large`)

in eine Menge kleiner Bausteine (`Moduln`) und dem Implementieren dieser Bausteine (`programming-in-the-small`) auf.
Mit diesen Unterschieden qualitativer Art begründen DeRemer/Kron ihre Forderung nach einer Klasse von Sprachen, mit deren Hilfe das Entwerfen großer Software - Systeme unterstützt und der Entwurf formuliert werden kann. Diese Sprachklasse wird mit dem Begriff `module-interconnection-languages` (MIL) bezeichnet.

DeRemer/Kron formulierten eine Reihe von Anforderungen, die an eine solche Sprachklasse gestellt werden müssen:

Eine MIL ist ein **Hilfsmittel** für die Tätigkeit des **Entwerfens** und für die **Dokumentation** des Ergebnisses dieser Tätigkeit, den Entwurf. Sie unterstützt dabei grundlegende Prinzipien des Software Engineering (Information Hiding, Abstrakte Maschinen usw.) und beschreibt die Struktur eines Systems in überschaubarer und prüfbarer Form. Außerdem werden **Projektmanagement** (z.B. Aufgabenverteilung) und **Prüfungsmaßnahmen** (z.B. Konsistenzerhaltung bei Änderungen) unterstützt.

Im oben genannten Artikel [7] wird ein Prototyp einer solchen Sprache, MIL75, vorgestellt.
MIL75 erlaubt zwei Darstellungsformen, die im wesentlichen den gleichen Informationsgehalt tragen:
- Eine **graphische Repräsentation**, die die Systemzerlegung als Baumstruktur, erweitert durch verschiedene Typen von Zugriffsrechten zwischen den einzelnen Knoten, darstellt
- Eine **sprachliche Repräsentation** in Form sogenannter `System-Beschreibungen` jedes einzelnen Knotens
  Eine Systembeschreibung definiert die lokale Sicht (Zugriffsrechte, Zerlegung) eines Knotens. Sie kann aus der graphischen Repräsentation abgeleitet werden.
Eine detaillierte Beschreibung von MIL75 ist in [7] bzw. in [15] zu finden.

2.2 Änderungen und Erweiterungen
Die wesentlichen Merkmale von MIL75, insbesondere das zugrundeliegende Prinzip des Top - Down - Entwerfens, die duale Repräsentation und die formale Beschreibung der lokalen Sichten der einzelnen Komponenten, entsprechen, zumindest im Ansatz, den grundsätzlichen Anforderungen an eine Entwurfsmethode (Strukturierung in funktional abgeschlossene Bausteine, Dokumentation aller Entwurfsentscheidungen) und wurden in der erweiterten MIL beibehalten.
Die Vorteile der dualen Repräsentation liegen in der Übersichtlichkeit und Verständlichkeit der graphischen Darstellung (zum Entwerfen sowie für Warten/Pflegen) einerseits und in der Exaktheit der sprachlichen Beschreibung (zur Definition der Anforderungen für den nächsten Erstellungsschritt) andererseits.
Die Beschreibung der lokalen Sichten der einzelnen Komponenten (Ein - Ebenen - Beschreibungen, EEBs) im Gegensatz zu einer globalen Beschreibung des Gesamtsystems ermöglicht erst eine sinnvolle Aufteilung der Bearbeitung verschiedener Systemteile auf verschiedene Bearbeiter. Die EEB einer Komponente enthält, neben der Definition ihrer Schnittstellen, die Beschreibung der Anforderungen an die bei der Zerlegung entstandenen Subkomponenten. Diese Anforderungen werden als nichtänderbare Vorgaben für die weitere Bearbeitung in die EEBs der jeweiligen Subkomponenten einkopiert (Abb.2.2). Durch dieses Verfahren können konsistente Schnittstellen zwischen den

einzelnen Komponenten gewährleistet werden.

Der Prototyp MIL75 enthält jedoch einige, zum Teil grundsätzliche Mängel. Diese Mängel sowie zusätzliche Erfordernisse, die aus dem Wunsch der Werkzeugunterstützung sowie der speziellen Einsatzumgebung resultierten, machten ein Überarbeiten von MIL75 notwendig.

Die wichtigsten Änderungen und Erweiterungen werden im folgenden vorgestellt:

a) Zur **besseren Verständlichkeit** werden die Sprachelemente vereinheitlicht. So wird z.B. den Pfeilen zur Darstellung der Zugriffsrechte in der graphischen Repräsentation eine einheitliche Bedeutung (`Benutzt`-Relation) unterlegt. In MIL75 werden sowohl die `Benutzt`-Relation als auch die Umkehrrelation `Bietet an` verwendet.

   Allen graphischen Ausdrucksmitteln wird genau ein Schlüsselwort in der sprachlichen Repräsentation zugeordnet. Dadurch wird eine einfache rechnergestützte Übertragung der graphischen Repräsentation in die sprachliche Form ermöglicht.

b) **Alle Zugriffsrechte werden explizit beschrieben.**

   In MIL75 werden Zugriffe auf Geschwisterkomponenten (`Horizontal Access`) immer, Zugriffe auf Nachkommen (`Vertical Access`) nur in bestimmten Fällen und Zugriffe auf Vorfahren (`Inherited Access`) überhaupt nicht graphisch dargestellt. Die beiden letztgenannten Zugriffe sind deshalb nur implizit aus der Kombination anderer Zugriffsrechte zu erkennen. Die daraus resultierenden Indirektionen erschweren einerseits das Verständnis des Entwurfs und andererseits eine automatische Überprüfung der Korrektheit der Zugriffsrechte. In MIL82 werden alle tatsächlichen vergegebenen Zugriffsrecht graphisch dargestellt.

   Obwohl der `Inherited Access` grundsätzlich im Widerspruch zu einer hierarchischen Systemstrukturierung steht, ist dieser Zugriff in MIL75 imlizit erlaubt. Da ein striktes Verbot dieses Zugriffsrechts in der Praxis eine zu starke Einschränkung darstellen würde, ist der `Inherited Access` auch in MIL82 zulässig, muß jedoch explizit erlaubt werden.

   Zusätzlich werden Einschränkungen der vererbten Leistungen ermöglicht. Diese Maßnahme verhindert das zwangsläufige ungewollte Anwachsen nicht benötigter Leistungen bei Vererbung über mehrere Ebenen (Minimale Schnittstellen).

c) Die **lokale Sicht** einer Systemkomponente wird **vollständig beschrieben**, d.h. zur Bearbeitung einer Komponente sind keine Beschreibungen weiterer Komponenten notwendig. Die vollständige Beschreibung der Schnittstelle ermöglicht eine Beschränkung der Korrektheits- und Konsistenzprüfung auf das lokale Umfeld einer Komponente, da keine Indirektionen auftreten können.

   Eine weitere wichtige Folge dieser Maßnahme ist die Möglichkeit zur unabhängigen (und gleichzeitigen) Bearbeitung verschiedener Komponenten durch verschiedene Mitarbeiter. Diese Möglichkeit ist im Prototyp MIL75 nicht gegeben, da aus der Beschreibung einer Komponente nur hervorgeht, auf welche Komponente sie Zugriff besitzt, nicht aber, welche Leistungen dieser Komponente sie verwenden kann. Allgemein sind somit zur Bearbeitung einer Komponente die Beschreibungen aller anderen erforderlich.

e) Die **Erweiterungen** bestehen aus einer funktionalen (z.Zt. informalen) Beschreibung der Komponente in der sprachlichen Repräsentation (dieser Punkt wurde bereits von DeRemer/Kron als notwendige Ergänzung vorgeschlagen). Außerdem werden zur Unterstützung des Projektmanagements die organisatorischen Angaben von MIL75 (Autor, Datum) um Fertigstellungstermin und Versionsnummer ergänzt.

f) Zur **Anpassung** an das der zu erstellenden Software zugrundeliegende DISTOS-**Strukturkonzept**[11] wird eine zusätzliche Zerlegungsstufe eingeführt (dieser Punkt ist nicht von allgemeiner Bedeutung, sondern typisch für die spezielle Einsatzumgebung des Werkzeugs).
MIL75 sieht eine einstufige Zerlegung eines Systems in eine Menge von Bausteinen (`Moduln`) vor. Im DISTOS-Konzept für verteilte Betriebssysteme besteht ein Gesamtsystem zunächst aus einer Menge funktional abgeschlossener Einheiten der Verteilung, den `Instanzen`. Jede Instanz besteht aus einer Menge von `Moduln` als Einheiten getrennter Übersetzung.
Dementsprechend wird in der ersten Phase ein System bis auf Instanzenebene zerlegt (Systementwerfen). Anschließend wird jede Instanz entsprechend bis zur Modulebene zerlegt (Instanzenentwerfen). Beide Phasen der Zerlegung können durch MIL82 beschrieben werden. Die Beschreibung der Moduln kann durch Pseudocode bzw. eine höhere Programmiersprache (Methoden für das `programming-in-the-small`) erfolgen.

2.3 Die Sprache MIL82

Die in 2.2 angeführten Änderungen und Erweiterungen führten zur Sprache MIL82, die hier nur kurz anhand eines Beispiels vorgestellt werden kann. Eine ausführliche Beschreibung kann [15] und [9] entnommen werden.

Das Beispiel in Abb.2.1 zeigt den Systementwurf eines Systems zur Steuerung einer Paketverteilanlage [8]. Die Schnittstelle dieses Systems zur Außenwelt wurde in den Systemanforderungen festgelegt. Es sind die Leistungen EINGANG und CONTROL zur Verfügung zu stellen; die externe Leistung PLATTE darf benutzt werden.
Im ersten Schritt des Systementwerfens wird PVSTEUER in die Subsysteme VERTEIL, EINGANG und DOK zerlegt und die Zugriffsrechte werden definiert. Die Bereitstellung der von PVSTEUER geforderten Leistungen wird an VERTEIL und EINGANG delegiert (`Vertical Access`). Die vom System importierte Leistung PLATTE wird an DOK vererbt (`Inherited Access`). Anschließend werden die Zugriffsrechte der Geschwisterkomponenten untereinander (`Horizontal Access`) festgelegt. Dieser erste Zerlegungsschritt ist in der Ein - Ebenen - Beschreibung des Systems PVSTEUER (Abb.2.2) unter Ebene 1 vollständig dokumentiert. Die so entstandenen Anforderungsbeschreibungen der einzelnen Subsysteme im `Consists`-Teil werden vom Werkzeug als Vorgabe für die weitere Bearbeitung der einzelnen Komponenten in die EEBs der Ebene 2 einkopiert (Pfeile in Abb.2.2). Diese Vorgaben können von den Bearbeitern der jeweiligen Komponenten nicht lokal geändert werden. Durch diesen Mechanismus wird eine unabhängige Bearbeitung bei Erhaltung konsistenter Schnittstellen gewährleistet.
Im zweiten Schritt werden die beiden Subsysteme VERTEIL und EINGANG nicht weiter zerlegt. Sie realisieren die von ihnen geforderten Leistungen durch Instanzen. Diese Instanzen importieren Leistungen, auf die die ihnen zugeordneten Subsysteme Zugriffsrechte besitzen. Damit ist die Phase `Systementwerfen` für diese Komponenten beendet.
Das Subsystem DOK wird in zwei weitere Subsysteme zerlegt. Die Bereitstellung der

durch die horizontalen Zugriffe auf DOK geforderten Leistungen AUSWERT und DV wird
an die Nachkommen delegiert. PLATTE wird von DOK weiter an DATVERW vererbt. Die
sprachliche Dokumentation der Zerlegung von DOK ist in Abb. 2.2 unter Ebene 2
dargestellt.
Die vollständige Dokumentation des Systementwurfs besteht aus den EEBs des Systems
und aller Subsysteme. Dieses Dokument beschreibt alle Entwurfsentscheidungen und
stellt damit eine wertvolle Hilfe bei späteren Wartungs-/Pflegemaßnahmen dar. Ein
Extrakt dieser sogenannten `Entwurfsdokumentation` bildet die
`Realisierungsdokumentation`. Sie enthält nur die Realisierungseinheiten (hier:
System und Instanzen) mit ihren Schnittstellen. Dieses Dokument dient als Vorgabe
für die dem Systementwerfen folgende Phase des Instanenentwerfens.
Beide Dokumentationen werden von KADDIS erzeugt.

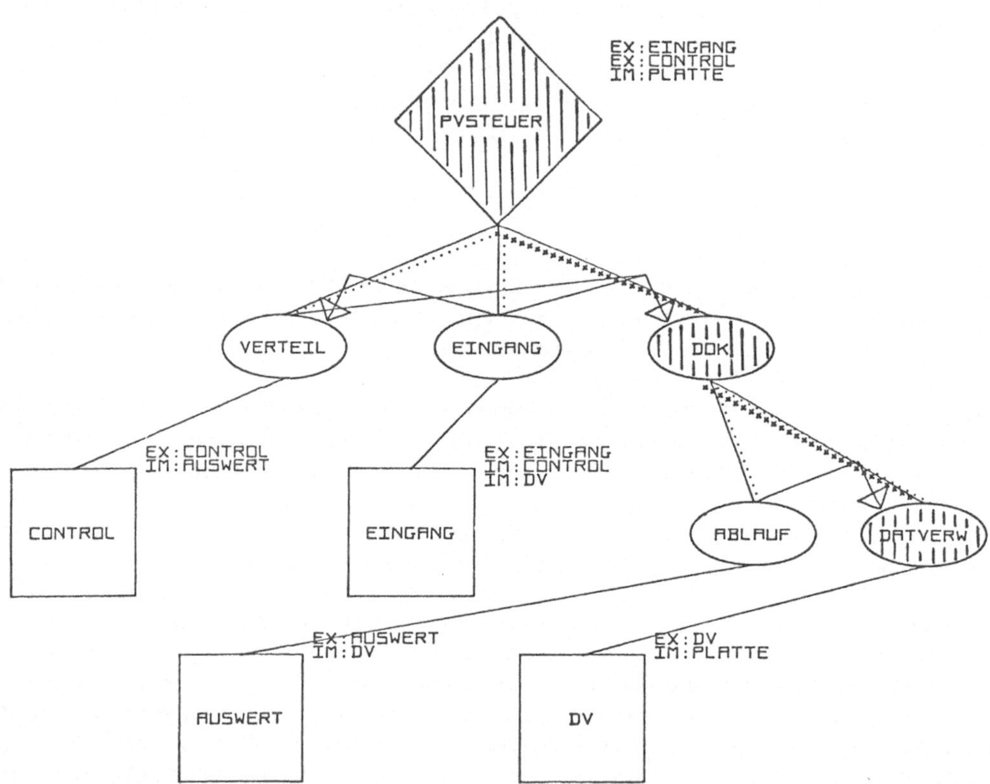

Abb.2.1: Graphische Repräsentation eines Systementwurfs (Entwurfsdokumentation).

```
*************************************        *************************************
*                                   *        *                                   *
*        EBENE  1                    *        *        EBENE  2                    *
*                                   *        *                                   *
*************************************        *************************************


SYSTEM   :    PVSTEUER                       SUBSYSTEM :    DOK

   AUTHOR  :   K.WEGENER                         AUTHOR  :   K.WEGENER
   DEADLINE:   1.10.1983                         DEADLINE:   1.10.1983
   DATE    :   9. 8.1983                         DATE    :   9. 8.1983
   VERSION :   2                                 VERSION :   2
   PROBLEM :   Steuerung einer ( simulierten ) Paketverteil -    PROBLEM :   Dokumentation des Paketablaufs, dazu wird
               anlage; Realisierung der Funktionen :                         eine Instanz Plattenverwaltung "PLATTE"
                  - LIES_KODIERUNG                                           benutzt.
                  - FREIGEBEN
                  - STELLE_WEICHE ( EBENE, KNOTEN,           PROVIDES VERTICAL   :      NOTHING
                                    WEICHENSTELLUNG )        PROVIDES HORIZONTAL :      AUSWERT, DV
                                                             HAS  INHERITED  ACCESS  :  PVSTEUER ( PLATTE )
               Der Paketablauf soll dokumentiert werden, dazu    HAS  HORIZONTAL ACCESS  :  NOTHING
               wird eine Instanz Plattenverwaltung "PLATTE"      HAS  VERTICAL   ACCESS  :  ABLAUF, DATVERW
               importiert.
                                                          CONSISTS OF
               BEMERKUNG : Die Instanz zur Steuerung der
               Verteilstationen kann mehrfach existieren. Bei       NO ROOT INSTANCE
               der Initialisierung erhaelt jede Auspraegung
               der Instanz Informationen darueber, welche          SUBSYSTEM :    ABLAUF
               Verteilstationen sie zu steuern hat und welche          AUTHOR  :   K.WEGENER
               Nachfolger sie besitzt.                                  DEADLINE:   1.10.1983
                                                                       PROBLEM :   Dokumentation des Paketablaufs.
   EXPORT  :   EINGANG, CONTROL                                                    - Aufbereitung von Statistikdaten
   IMPORT  :   PLATTE                                                              - Ausgabe von Schreibbefehlen an die
                                                                                     Dateiverwaltung
CONSISTS OF
                                                                       MUST PROVIDE VERTICAL   :  AUSWERT
   NO ROOT INSTANCE                                                    MUST PROVIDE HORIZONTAL :  NOTHING
                                                                       MAY  ACCESS  INHERITED  :  NOTHING
   SUBSYSTEM :    VERTEIL                                              MAY  ACCESS  HORIZONTAL :  DATVERW ( DV )
      AUTHOR  :   K.WEGENER                         +-----------------------------------------------------+
      DEADLINE:   1.10.1983                         | SUBSYSTEM :    DATVERW                               |
      PROBLEM :   Verwaltung   und  Steuerung  der  Verteil -  |    AUTHOR  :   K.WEGENER                    |
                  stationen. Buchhaltung ueber ankommende und  |    DEADLINE:   1.10.1983                    |
                  ausgehende Pakete. Steuerung der Weiche, dh. |    PROBLEM :   Dateiverwaltung              |
                  Realisierung der Funktion :                  |               - Einrichten einer Ausgabedatei |
                                                               |               - Oeffnen einer Datei        |
                     - STELLE_WEICHE ( EBENE, KNOTEN,          |               - Schreiben in Datei         |
                                       WEICHENSTELLUNG )       |                                            |
                                                               |    MUST PROVIDE VERTICAL   :  DV           |
      MUST PROVIDE VERTICAL   :  CONTROL                       |    MUST PROVIDE HORIZONTAL :  DV           |
      MUST PROVIDE HORIZONTAL :  CONTROL                       |    MAY  ACCESS  INHERITED  :  DOK ( PLATTE )|
      MAY  ACCESS  INHERITED  :  NOTHING                       |    MAY  ACCESS  HORIZONTAL :  NOTHING      |
      MAY  ACCESS  HORIZONTAL :  DOK ( AUSWERT )               +-----------------------------------------------------+

   SUBSYSTEM :    EINGANG
      AUTHOR  :   K.WEGENER                         *************************************
      DEADLINE:   1.10.1983                         *                                   *
      PROBLEM :   Verwaltung  und  Steuerung  der  Eingangs -  *        EBENE  3        *
                  station der Paketverteilanlage, Realisierung *                        *
                  der Funktionen :                             *************************************

                     - LIES_KODIERUNG
                     - FREIGEBEN                   SUBSYSTEM :    DATVERW

                  Ausserdem initialisieren einer Datei, die       AUTHOR  :   K.WEGENER
                  das Protokoll des Paketablaufs aufnimmt.         DEADLINE:   1.10.1983
                                                                  DATE    :   9. 8.1983
      MUST PROVIDE VERTICAL   :  EINGANG                          VERSION :   2
      MUST PROVIDE HORIZONTAL :  NOTHING                          PROBLEM :   Dateiverwaltung
      MAY  ACCESS  INHERITED  :  NOTHING                                      - Einrichten einer Ausgabedatei
      MAY  ACCESS  HORIZONTAL :  VERTEIL ( CONTROL ), DOK ( DV )              - Oeffnen einer Datei
+-----------------------------------------------------+                       - Schreiben in Datei
| SUBSYSTEM :    DOK                                   |
|    AUTHOR  :   K.WEGENER                             |       PROVIDES VERTICAL   :'    DV
|    DEADLINE:   1.10.1983                             |       PROVIDES HORIZONTAL :     DV
|    PROBLEM :   Dokumentation des Paketablaufs, dazu wird |   HAS  INHERITED  ACCESS  :  DOK ( PLATTE )
|                eine Instanz Plattenverwaltung "PLATTE"   |   HAS  HORIZONTAL ACCESS  :  NOTHING
|                benutzt.                              |       HAS  VERTICAL   ACCESS  :  NOTHING
|                                                     |
|    MUST PROVIDE VERTICAL   :  NOTHING               |    CONSISTS OF
|    MUST PROVIDE HORIZONTAL :  AUSWERT, DV           |
|    MAY  ACCESS  INHERITED  :  PVSTEUER ( PLATTE )   |       LEAF INSTANCE : DV
|    MAY  ACCESS  HORIZONTAL :  NOTHING               |          AUTHOR  :   K.WEGENER
+-----------------------------------------------------+          DEADLINE:   1.10.1983
                                                                 PROBLEM :   Dateiverwaltung
                                                                             - Einrichten einer Ausgabedatei
                                                                             - Oeffnen einer Datei
                                                                             - Schreiben in Datei

                                                                 MUST EXPORT  :  DV
                                                                 MAY  IMPORT  :  PLATTE
```

Abb.2.2: Sprachliche Repräsentation des schraffierten Teils des Systementwurfs aus
         Abb.2.1

3. Das Werkzeug

Die graphische Repräsentation von MIL82 eignet sich durch ihre Natürlichkeit und
Übersichtlichkeit besonders zur direkten Unterstützung beim Entwerfen. Sie kann
manuell ohne großen Aufwand während des Entwerfens angefertigt werden.
Die Überprüfung der Entwürfe, die Erstellung der sprachlichen Repräsentation und die
Verwaltung der dabei anfallenden Produkte wird durch das **Werkzeug KADDIS**
unterstützt. Dabei dient die graphische Repräsentation als Eingabe und wird mit
Hilfe eines Abfragesystems in die sprachliche Repräsentation von MIL82 übertragen.
Die in der graphischen Form fehlenden Informationen (organisatorische Angaben,
Aufgabenbeschreibung) werden dabei ergänzt.
Das Abfragesystem prüft jede Eingabe sofort auf ihre Zulässigkeit. Dadurch können
Fehler, die auf eine fehlerhafte Benutzung der Methode zurückzuführen sind,
frühzeitig weitgehend ausgeschlossen werden.
Mit den eingegebenen Informationen können nun zweckangepaßte sprachliche
Dokumentationen automatisch erstellt und ausgedruckt werden. Zusätzlich können
graphische Darstellungen von Entwürfen zu Kontrollzwecken über einen Plotter
ausgegeben werden.

Bei der Realisierung des Werkzeugs wurde besonderen Wert auf eine komfortable
Benutzerschnittstelle gelegt. Die einzelnen Funktionskomponenten des Werkzeugs
KADDIS sind ausschließlich über hierarchische Menüs zugänglich. Der Aufbau der Menüs
ist abhängig von dem Verantwortungsbereich des jeweiligen Benutzers, d.h. jedem
Benutzer sind nur solche Funktionen zugänglich, zu deren Benutzung er berechtigt
ist. Die Hierarchie der Menüs entspricht der statischen Systemstruktur von KADDIS
(Abb.3.1).
Beim Abfragesystem wurde besonderer Wert auf leichte Bedienbarkeit gelegt. Alle
Fragen werden umgangssprachlich (mit Erläuterungen) formuliert und mit dem
zugehörigen Schlüsselwort der sprachlichen Repräsentation gekennzeichnet. Dies
ermöglicht einerseits eine Benutzung des Werkzeugs ohne lange Einarbeitungszeit für
Benutzer, die noch nicht mit dem System vertraut sind und andererseits eine
effiziente Bedienung für erfahrene Anwender. Die Antworten auf die Fragen sind
soweit möglich bereits voreingestellt. Dem Benutzer wird eine Auswahl aller
zulässigen Antworten angeboten, aus der er die gewünschten wählen kann. Alle neuen
Eingaben werden auf ihre Zulässigkeit überprüft. Durch die Voreinstellungen werden
Schreibfehler bei der Eingabe minimal gehalten und Fehler, die aus der Verletzung
der bereits definierten Zugriffsrechte resultieren, sofort abgefangen. Logische
Fehler, die nicht durch das Werkzeug erkannt werden können, sind durch einen
Vergleich der graphischen Ausgabe mit der Vorlage erkennbar.
Zur Eingabe von Text, z.B. der Aufgabenbeschreibung, steht ein integrierter
bildschirmorientierter Editor zur Verfügung.
Das Werkzeug ist für Mehrbenutzerbetrieb ausgelegt, es können sowohl verschiedene
Systeme, als auch disjunkte Teilbäume eines Systems durch verschiedene Benutzer
gleichzeitig bearbeitet werden. Dabei hat jeder Benutzer nur Zugriff auf
Komponenten, bei denen er als `Autor` eingetragen ist.

Die gesamte Produktverwaltung wird ausschließlich vom Werkzeug durch ein
integriertes **Bibliotheks-System** organisiert. Alle Produktinformationen sind dem
berechtigten Benutzer über die entsprechenden logischen Komponentennamen zugänglich.
Dateinamen werden intern erzeugt und sind nicht nach außen bekannt. Damit wird zum

Zugriff der ˘offizielle˘ Weg über die Menüs erzwungen und unerlaubte Manipulationen an Daten bzw. unberechtigte Zugriffe werden verhindert.

Das Bibliotheks - System wurde unter dem Aspekt einer möglichen Verteilung des Werkzeugs auf mehrere Rechner entworfen. Es besteht aus einer zentralen System-Bibliothek und beliebig vielen, im Aufbau identischen, privaten Benutzer - Bibliotheken (Abb.3.1).

Die System - Bibliothek enthält neben den Systemanforderungen nur konsistente System(-teil)e. Der direkte Zugriff ist nur durch autorisierte Benutzer über die zentrale Systemverwaltung möglich.

Die Bearbeitung eines Systems bzw. von Systemteilen erfolgt ausschließlich in der jeweiligen Benutzer - Bibliothek. Diese Bibliotheken werden von KADDIS angelegt und sind nur jeweils einem Benutzer zugänglich.

Die Anforderungen an die von einem Benutzer zu bearbeitende Komponente werden bei Bedarf (insbesondere nach Änderungen) von KADDIS aus der System-Bibliothek in die jeweilige Benutzer-Bibliothek kopiert. Nach Erstellung einer oder mehrerer Komponenten kann der Antrag zur Übernahme in die System - Bibliothek gestellt werden. Das Kopieren erfolgt nach einer Analyse wiederum unter Kontrolle von KADDIS. Dieser Mechanismus gewährleistet die Konsistenz der Schnittstellen, insbesondere bei Änderungen im Mehrbenutzerbetrieb.

KADDIS ist auf einem Minirechner Texas Instruments TI990/10 in (zur Systemimplementierungssprache erweitertem) PASCAL realisiert. Um die ca. 110KByte Code im nur 64KByte großen logischen Adressraum unterbringen zu können, wurden Overlays benutzt.

Eine detaillierte Beschreibung des Werkzeugs KADDIS ist in [15] enthalten.

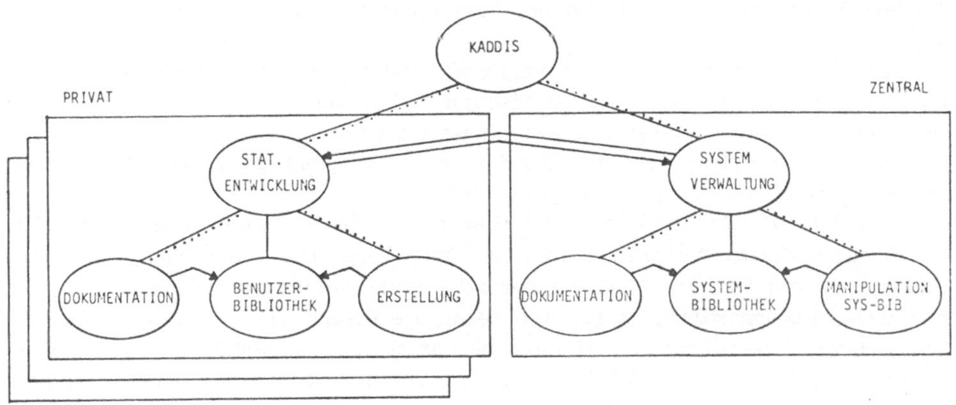

Abb. 3.1: Statische Systemstruktur von KADDIS

<u>**4.**</u> <u>Erfahrungen</u> <u>aus</u> <u>dem</u> <u>praktischen</u> <u>Einsatz</u> <u>von</u> <u>KADDIS</u>

Mit der Verwendung eines Werkzeugs zur Unterstützung einer Entwurfsmethode sollen folgende **Ziele** erreicht werden:

a) **Verbesserung der Qualität erstellter Software–Produkte**
Die Qualität eines Software–Produkts kann quantitativ durch die Zahl auftretender Fehler (Abweichungen gegenüber geforderten Leistungen) der Software nach Inbetriebnahme pro Zeiteinheit (Fehlerrate) oder durch die mittlere Zeit zwischen 2 Fehlern (MTTF) charakterisiert werden.

b) **Verringerung des Erstellungsaufwands**
Der Erstellungsaufwand ist charakterisiert durch den Aufwand bis zur Inbetriebnahme der Software.

c) **Verringerung des Wartungs– und Pflegeaufwands**
Der Wartungsaufwand ist charakterisiert durch die Zahl der Fehler nach Inbetriebnahme pro Zeiteinheit (Fehlerrate) sowie den mittleren Aufwand zur Behebung eines Fehlers. Der Pflegeaufwand ist charakterisiert durch den mittleren Aufwand zur Durchführung einer Anpassung an eine Umgebungsveränderung oder Weiterentwicklung.

Das isolierte Erreichen eines der Ziele zu Lasten mindestens eines anderen (geringer Erstellungsaufwand zu Lasten der Qualität und des Wartungsaufwands, gute Qualität zu Lasten des Erstellungsaufwands, geringer Wartungsaufwand zu Lasten des Erstellungsaufwand) ist relativ einfach zu erreichen, jedoch wenig sinnvoll.
Im Vordergrund steht, den Gesamtaufwand über die Lebenszeit eines Software–Produkts zu minimieren sowie einen geeigneten Zeitpunkt für die Inbetriebnahme zu finden, ab dem Fehlerrate und Behebungsaufwand pro Fehler auf ein tolerierbares Maß abgesunken sind.
Das Verhältnis zwischen durchschnittlichem Aufwand vor Inbetriebnahme (Erstellen) und nach Inbetriebnahme (Warten und Pflegen) liegt nach [16] bei ungefähr 1 zu 2. Zusammen mit der Tatsache, daß die Behebungskosten eines Fehlers stark ansteigen je später er entdeckt wird [5], läßt dies den Schluß zu, daß heute beim Erstellen zu Lasten des Wartens und Pflegens gespart wird.
Dies heißt, daß ein Schlüssel zur Erreichung der Ziele a)-c) darin liegt, durch gute werkzeuggestützte Methoden sowohl den Anteil der Erstellung am Gesamtaufwand als auch den Anteil früherer Phasen innerhalb des Erstellens zu erhöhen.
Durch dieses Vorgehen sollte es möglich sein, die Erkennung einer größeren Zahl von Fehlern noch vor Inbetriebnahme mit weitaus geringerem Aufwand zu gewährleisten. Trotz der dadurch möglichen Erhöhung des absoluten Erstellungsaufwandes müßte der über die gesamte Lebenszeit eines Software–Produkts anfallende Aufwand durch die Erleichterung der Behebung von Fehlern absolut gesenkt werden können.

<u>4.1 Meßergebnisse</u>
Im nachfolgenden wird anhand experimentell gewonnener Daten gezeigt, inwieweit die Ziele a)-c) erreicht werden konnten. Die Meßdaten wurden bei der Erstellung von 6 Mehrbenutzerbetriebssystemen (Funktionsumfang ungefähr dem SOLO-Betriebssystems [6] entsprechend) und 6 Steuerungen von Paketverteilanlagen [8] gewonnen. Diese

Software-Systeme wurden von Studenten im Rahmen von Diplomarbeiten unter Verwendung von MIL82 mit Werkzeugunterstützung erstellt.
Die Meßergebnisse werden den aus der Literatur bekannten Zahlen [3,4,16] gegenübergestellt.

Meßergebnisse bezüglich Qualität (Ziel a)):
Die Meßergebnisse über Zahl der Fehler nach Inbetriebnahme und durchschnittlichen Aufwand zur Behebung liegen z.Zt. noch nicht vor.
Allerdings lassen die Zuordnung des Auftretens von Fehlern zu Erstellungsphasen in Tabelle 4.2 (mehr als 50% vor dem Implementieren) und die geringeren Auswirkungen der Fehler auf andere Systemteile in Tabelle 4.3 die Vermutung zu, daß eine Verbesserung des Verhaltens auch nach Inbetriebnahme zu erwarten ist. Diese Erwartung wird gestützt durch Vorhersagemodelle, die die Fehlerrate nach Inbetriebnahme durch den Verlauf der Fehlerrate während der Erstellung und vor allem durch den (nach Tabelle 4.3 gering gehaltenen) Anteil globaler Fehler (Fehler, deren Behebung sich auf mehrere Bausteine fortpflanzt) an den Gesamtfehlern während der Erstellung abschätzen [10].

Meßergebnisse bezüglich Erstellungsaufwand (Ziel b)
Wie bereits ausgeführt, ist es nicht so entscheidend, den Aufwand der Erstellung absolut zu verringern, vielmehr kann durch eine bessere Verteilung des Aufwands auf die einzelnen Phasen ein Beitrag zu a) und c) geleistet werden.
Es gibt mehrere Anzeichen, daß die erzielte Verteilung (Tabelle 4.1) nicht nur subjektiv besser als die von Boehm [4] und Zelkowitz [16] als Durchschnitt ermittelte erscheint, sondern auch tatsächlich zur Bewältigung des Erstellungsproblems in natürlicher Weise beiträgt. In [4] wurden für größenmäßig vergleichbare Softwaresysteme aus dem Raumfahrtbereich folgende Ergebnisse präsentiert: 64% der während der gesamten Lebensdauer entdeckten Fehler waren Entwurfsfehler. Während der Erstellung selbst wurden davon 55% (absolut: 35,2%), dagegen von den 36% Implementierungsfehlern 91% (absolut: 32,8%) entdeckt und behoben. Wie aus Tabelle 4.2 ersichtlich ist, waren 52,2% der Fehler auf jeden Fall Entwurfsfehler, da sie während des Entwerfens auftraten. Von den 47,8% während des Implementierens aufgetretenen Fehler hatten, wie aus Tabelle 4.3 ersichtlich ist, 14,7% Auswirkungen auf Entwürfe (absolut 7%). Damit gelang es also, den Anteil während der Erstellung erkannter Entwurfsfehler gegenüber den in der Literatur enthaltenen Zahlen auf 59,2% (=52,2% + 7,0%) zu steigern.
Da die Zahl logischer Fehler in der Implementierungsphase stark absank, kann geschlossen werden, daß tatsächlich ein größerer Anteil von Entwurfsfehlern während der Erstellung gefunden werden konnte und dieses Ergebnis nicht durch einen höheren Anteil logischer Fehler an der Gesamtzahl von Fehlern vorgetäuscht wird.
Nur 4,7% aller während der Implementierung gefundener Fehler erforderten Korrekturen an Instanzen- bzw. Systementwürfen. Aus dem in Klammern angegebenen geringen durchschnittlichen Behebungsaufwand in Stunden pro Fehler (Tabelle 4.3) kann zusätzlich ersehen werden, daß selbst die geringe Restzahl globaler Fehler im allgemeinen keine grundsätzliche Neubearbeitung von Entwürfen zur Folge hatte.

Quellen / Phasen	KADDIS-Experimente	/BOE73/, /ZEL79/
Analysieren	–	}
Systementwerfen	21,55% }	
Instanzenentwerfen	17,35% } 62,75%	} 35%
Modulentwerfen	23,85% }	
Implementieren + Integrieren	37,25%	65%

Tabelle 4.1: Phasenspezifischer Anteil am Erstellungsaufwand
(–: war nicht Gegenstand der Experimente)

Quelle / Phasen	KADDIS-Experimente
Analysieren	–
Systementwerfen	6,4% (4,05 h)
Instanzenentwerfen	9% (2,52 h)
Modulentwerfen	36,8% (1,38 h)
Implementieren + Integrieren	47,8% (0,38 h)

Tabelle 4.2: Phasenspezifischer Anteil an der Menge entdeckter Fehler mit
mittlerem Aufwand pro Fehlertyp in Stunden
(–: war nicht Gegenstand der Experimente)

Lokalisierung \ Auswirkung	lokal	Analysieren	System-entwerf.	Inst.-entwerf.	Modul-entwerf.	Implem.+ Integ.
Analysieren	–	–	–	–	–	–
Systementwerfen	100% (4,05h)	–	O	X	X	X
Instanzenentwerfen	37,5% (1,1225h)	–	56,25% (3,44h)	6,25% (2,625h)	X	X
Modulentwerfen	40% (0,7038h)	–	9,1% (2,32h)	33,1% (2,15h)	17,8% (0,9898h)	X
Implementieren + Integrieren	69,6% (0,2385h)	–	1,3% (1,1h)	3,4% (1,19h)	10% (0,5728h)	15,7% (0,66h)

<u>Tabelle 4.3</u>: Aufschlüsselung der Fehler aus Tabelle 4.2 entsprechend ihren maximalen Auswirkungen auf benachbarte Dokumentationen derselben Phase oder Dokumentationen vorausgehender Phasen mit mittlerem Aufwand pro Fehlertyp in Stunden
Die Spalte `lokal` enthält Fehler, die in der Dokumentation, in der sie auftraten, auch behoben werden konnten.

(– : war nicht Gegenstand der Experimente,
 X : nicht sinnvoll zu belegen)

<u>Meßergebnisse</u> <u>bezüglich</u> <u>Wartungs-/Pflegeaufwand (Ziel c))</u>
Hierzu liegen die Meßergebnisse noch nicht vor; allerdings können aufgrund des Verlaufs der Erstellung (Tabelle 4.2/4.3) dieselben positiven Entwicklungen angenommen werden.

4.2 Bewertung

Bei den experimentell festgestellten positiven Abweichungen gegenüber aus der Literatur bekannten Ergebnissen stellt sich die Frage, inwieweit dies auf
   – unterschiedliche Meßobjekte,
   – die zugrundegelegte Entwurfsmethode MIL82,
   – die Verwendung des Entwurfswerkzeugs
zurückzuführen ist.

Es kann davon ausgegangen werden, daß die Unterschiedlichkeit der Meßobjekte (insbesondere wenn man zusätzlich die Erfahrung der Bearbeiter berücksichtigt) die positiven Abweichungen nicht allein erklären kann.
Gesichert scheint, daß der werkzeugunterstützte Einsatz einer den Problemen eines Tätigkeitsbereichs (hier Entwerfen) angemessenen Methode die Softwareerstellung im Sinne von Kap.4.1 positiv beeinflußt.

Interessant ist nun die Frage, welcher **Anteil an der Verbesserung** dem alleinigen
Einsatz der Methode MIL82 und welcher Anteil dem diese Methode unterstützenden
Werkzeug KADDIS zukommt.
Zur Beantwortung dieser Frage sind die im Rahmen eines Software-Praktikums
gewonnenen Erfahrungen und Meßdaten bei Erstellung eines Systems unter Verwendung
der MIL82 **mit** und **ohne** Werkzeugunterstützung von Interesse. Die im Rahmen des
Praktikums erzielten Ergebnisse können allerdings wegen des geringeren
Aufgabenumfangs und geringerer Motivation der Studenten zur Sorgfalt bei der
Datenerhebung nur mit Einschränkungen benutzt werden. Die dabei festgestellten
Ergebnisse lassen sich wie folgt zusammenfassen:

a) Die Fehlerrate war zu Beginn für beide Gruppen vergleichbar mit den Ergebnissen
   in Kap.4.1 (System-,Instanzenentwerfen in Tabelle 4.2).
b) Beginnend mit den ersten größeren Änderungen (i.a. beim Modulentwerfen)
   überstieg die Fehlerrate bei den Studenten ohne Werkzeugunterstützung die
   Fehlerrate derjenigen mit Werkzeugunterstützung.
c) Wenn man den Behebungsaufwand bei Auftreten eines Fehlers aufteilt in Lokalisierungsaufwand (Zeit bis festgelegt ist, wo was zu ändern ist) und Kor-
   rekturaufwand (lokales Durchführen der festgelegten Änderungen), so ergab
   sich für den Lokalisierungsaufwand bei Gruppen mit und ohne Werkzeugunterstützung ein Verhältnis von ungefähr 1:2.

Aus a) kann der Schluß gezogen werden, daß die Verwendung der MIL82 und nicht das
Werkzeug grundsätzlich die Ursache für die in Kap. 4.1 beschriebenen positiven
Auswirkungen ist. Ohne Werkzeugunterstützung können die positiven Möglichkeiten
allerdings auf Dauer nur unzureichend genutzt werden. Insbesondere die aufwendige
Aktualisierung der Dokumente bei Änderungen hat ohne Werkzeugunterstützung entweder,
wie durch b) dokumentiert wird, zu Inkonsistenzen (und damit zu neuen Fehlern) oder
zur Unterlassung der Aktualisierung geführt. Beide Auswirkungen manuellen
Methodeneinsatzes tragen zum Ergebnis c) bei. Für eine prozentuale Aufteilung der
erzielten Verbesserungen zwischen Methode und Werkzeug wären weitere aufwendige
Untersuchungen derselben Software-Produkte mit und ohne Werkzeugunterstützung
notwendig.

<u>5. Zusammenfassung</u>

Der Softwareerstellungsprozeß kann durch werkzeuggestützten Einsatz dem jeweiligen
Tätigkeitsbereich (hier Entwerfen) angepaßter Methoden verbessert werden. Die
Verbesserungen treten bereits bei kleinen bis mittleren Projekten, die hier die
Grundlage der Erfahrungen bilden, offensichtlich auf. Dabei konnte im vorliegenden
Fall der Nutzen des MIL82-Werkzeugs durch Beachtung folgender vermutlich all-
gemeingültiger **Grundregeln** optimiert werden:

- **Leicht erlernbare Werkzeugbenutzung** (z.B. Menütechnik)
- **Leicht verständliche Benutzungshilfen** (z.B. Help-Funktion)
- **Interaktive Eingabe** in einer für die Methode und Benutzerklasse natürlichen
  Form (z.B. graphisch)
- **Minimale Eingabe,** d.h. dem Werkzeug bereits bekannte Informationen werden nicht
  redundant abgefragt

- **Änderungen** müssen **lokal** durchgeführt werden können, ihre etwaigen Auswirkungen soweit wie möglich vom Werkzeug selbst durchgeführt werden
- Die Menge von Informationen muß gezielt abrufbar sein, d.h. man muß **dedizierte** Dokumente (mit der gewünschten Menge von Bausteinen, interessierenden Aspekten als Parameter) erstellen können
- Jede Eingabe wird nur akzeptiert bei **Konsistenz** mit den bereits eingegebenen Informationen
- Bei Abschluß eines Entwurfsschrittes (Systementwerfen, Instanzenentwerfen, Modulentwerfen) wird die Menge eingegebener Informationen auf **Minimalität** und **Vollständigkeit** überprüft

Das vorgestellte Werkzeug wurde für die beschriebenen Experimente bewußt eingeschränkt auf die Beschreibung statischer Aspekte. Dies erlaubt es, die Veränderungen bei der Softwareerstellung nicht nur festzustellen, sondern auch auf die systematische Behandlung dieses einen Aspekts zurückzuführen. In vier Werkzeugen [1,2,12,14] wird eine MIL mit anderen Methoden und Sprachen kombiniert. Von diesen Ansätzen sind jedoch keine quantitativen Erfahrungen bekannt.

Für den nichtexperimentellen Einsatz ist eine Ergänzung des vorgestellten Entwurfswerkzeugs um Werkzeuge zur Bearbeitung dynamischer (Kontrollfluß, Datenfluß) und funktionaler (Funktion einzelner Bausteine) Systemaspekte in Bearbeitung und teilweise abgeschlossen [13]. Die Schnittstelle zwischen diesen Teilen sowie geplanten Werkzeugen zur Unterstützung von Vor- und Nach-Entwurfsphasen bildet die in Kap. 3 beschriebene zentrale System-Bibliothek.

Um weitere Erfahrungen über den Nutzen von Erstellungswerkzeugen zu sammeln, müssen weitere Experimente der hier beschriebenen Art durchgeführt werden, zum einen mit der Unterstützung anderer Methoden, zum anderen durch Erprobung desselben Werkzeugs in anderer Umgebung. Einer breiten Erprobung des vorgestellten Werkzeugs KADDIS steht z.Zt. noch die Implementierung auf Rechnern der Firma Texas Instruments entgegen. Es ist jedoch geplant, das vorgestellte Werkzeug innerhalb der nächsten 2 Jahre auf Motorola 68000-Systeme zu portieren.

Literaturverzeichnis

1. Archibald, J.L.: The External Structure: Experience with an Automated Module
    Interconnection Language. The Journal of Systems and Software 2, No.2, S. 147-
    157, June 1981
2. Balzert, H.: Die Programmiersprache PLASMA78. Dissertation, FB Informatik,
    Universität Kaiserslautern, 1979
3. Boehm, B.W.: Software and its Impact, A Quantitative Accessment. Datamation,
    Vol. 19, No. 5, S. 48-59, 1973
4. Boehm, B.W.: Some Experience with Automated Aids to the Design of Large-Scale
    Reliable Software. Proc. Int. Conf. on Reliable Software, IEEE-Cat. No.75CH0940-
    7CSR, S. 105-113, Los Angeles, 1975
5. Boehm, B.W.: Software Engineering Education: Some Industry Needs, in A.J.
    Wassermann, P. Freeman (Ed.): Software Engineering Education, Needs and
    Objectives. Proc. of an Interface Workshop, S.13-19, Springer-Verlag, New York,
    1976
6. Brinch Hansen, P.: The Architecture of Concurrent Programs. Prentice Hall, 1977
7. DeRemer, F. Kron, H.H.: Programming-in-the-Large versus Programming in-the-
    Small. IEEE Transactions on Software Engineering, Vol.SE-2, No.2, S. 80-86, June
    1976
8. Hommel, G.: Vergleich verschiedener Spezifikationsverfahren am Beispiel einer
    Paketverteilanlage. Reihe PDV-Berichte, KfK-PDV 186 Teil 1,
    Kernforschungszentrum Karlsruhe, August 1980
9. Mangerich, M.: Syntax-Beschreibung einer Sprache zur Dokumentation statischer
    Softwareaspekte. Projektarbeit, FB Informatik, Universität Kaiserslautern, WS
    81/82
10. Mohanty, S.N.: Models and Measurements for Quality Assessment of Software. ACM
    Computing Surveys, Vol.11, No.3. S. 251-275, September 1979
11. Nehmer, J.: DISTOS - Eine Konstruktionsmethodik für verteilte Betriebssysteme.
    DISTOS-Projekt-Zwischenbericht, April 1982
12. Penedo, M.H. et al.: The Use of a Module Interconnection Language in the SARA
    System Design Methodology. Proc. 4. Intern. Conf. on Software Engineering,
    München, 1979
13. Rombach, H.D.: Ein Werkzeug zum Entwerfen von Software für verteilte Systeme.
    Interner Bericht 46/81, FB Informatik, Universität Kaiserslautern, Dezember 1981
14. Tichy, W.F.: Software Development Control Based on Module Interconnection. Proc.
    4. Intern. Conf. on Software Engineering, München, 1979
15. Wegener, K.: KADDIS - Ein Werkzeug für das Entwerfen statischer Aspekte
    verteilter Systemsoftware. Diplomarbeit, FB Informatik, Universität
    Kaiserslautern, 1981
16. Zelkowitz, M.V. et al.: Principles of Software Engineering and Design. Prentice-
    Hall, 1979

<u>C I D R E</u>

Eine interaktive <u>Software-Entwurfs-</u> und

<u>Entwicklungsumgebung</u> <u>mit</u> <u>Zielsprache</u> <u>COBOL</u>

Mechthild Budde
Christoph Knabe
Werner Simonsmeier

PSI - Gesellschaft für Prozesssteuerungs-
und Informationssysteme GmbH

<u>Abstract</u>

Es wird eine auf dem baum-orientierten interaktiven
Entwurfswerkzeug BOIE basierende
Programmentwicklungsumgebung beschrieben, die Entwurf,
Algorithmischen Entwurf, Codierung, Test und Dokumentation
grosser in COBOL zu realisierender Softwaresysteme leitet
und unterstützt.

A software engineering environment is described which is
based on the tree-oriented interactive design tool BOIE.
This environment supports design, algorithmic design,
coding, testing, and documentation of large COBOL programs.

<u>Inhalt:</u>

Stand: 15 Dec 83

1.0 Zielstellung

Die Entwurfs- und Programmierumgebung CIDRE (*) <CID83> wurde besonders mit Zielrichtung auf grosse, industrielle Projekte entwickelt, die aufgrund von Marktanforderungen in COBOL realisiert werden müssen. Es handelt sich dabei nicht um eine Sammlung von spezialisierten Werkzeugen, sondern um die Realisierung eines allgemeinen Konzeptes für Systementwurf und -implementierung.

Von CIDRE werden die Phasen der Software-Entwicklung vom Systementwurf (Zerlegung in Moduln) über Modulentwurf, Algorithmischen Entwurf bis zu Codierung und Test unterstützt. Besonderer Wert wird auf die "Programmierung im Grossen", d. h. auf die Lösung der mit der Integration vieler Moduln verbundenen Probleme gelegt.

Da ein wesentlicher Teil der Beziehungen in einem Softwareentwurf hierarchisch ist, wurde das PSI-Produkt BOIE (**) <BOIE> zugrunde gelegt. Die damit mögliche Baumdarstellung eines Softwaresystems reflektiert die verschiedenen "besteht aus" - Beziehungen, wohingegen "benutzt" - Beziehungen durch BOIE-Verweise dargestellt werden.

CIDRE bietet dem Systementwickler die Möglichkeit der schrittweisen Verfeinerung von der obersten Entwurfsebene bis zur Codierung. Jede Verfeinerungsentscheidung wird durch die Untergliederung eines bereits bestehenden Knotens im Baum getroffen. Die Beschränkung auf die formal zulässigen Verfeinerungen wird durch eine vorgegebene Baumgrammatik gewährleistet.

Das CIDRE-Entwurfssystem ermöglicht und fördert die Verwendung moderner Informatik-Konzepte der modularen und strukturierten Programmierung mit ANSI-COBOL als Zielsprache. Es werden unterstützt:
- Gliederung eines Software-Systems in seine Komponenten und Moduln
- Schichtung der Moduln in Steuerung, Aktivitäten, Dienstleistungen
- konsistente "benutzt"-Beziehungen der Moduln
- Abstrakte Datentypen als Moduln
- Verwaltung der Modulschnittstellen unter Gewährleistung der Beschränkungen von Eingangs-, Durchgangs- und Ausgangsparametern
- Vereinbarung symbolischer Konstanten mit Dimensionierungswirkung
- Benutzerdefinierte Datentypen
- Verwaltung von Ausnahmen und deren Behandlung/Meldung

(*) CIDRE = COBOL-oriented Interactive Design and Realization
            Environment
(**) BOIE = Baum-Orientiertes Interaktives Entwurfswerkzeug

Diese Konzepte werden auf einfache Weise im Entwurfsbaum dargestellt, dieser zur Dokumentation druckaufbereitet bzw. durch den Codegenerator in äquivalente COBOL-Konstrukte überführt. Die Generierung des Codes ist bei COBOL besonders wichtig, da die Realisierung obiger Konzepte in COBOL so schreibaufwendig ist und so viel Disziplin verlangt, dass derartige Programmierrichtlinien normalerweise nicht durchsetzbar sind.

CIDRE ist in PASCAL geschrieben und ebenso wie BOIE auf VAX/VMS verfügbar. CIDRE generiert Code für frei formatiertes ANSI-COBOL mit VMS-spezifischen Dateinamen.

ABGRENZUNG

Die hinter CIDRE stehenden Methoden sind weitgehend anerkannt, wenn auch nicht breit in die industrielle Praxis eingeführt. Die Modularisierungs- und Datentypkonzepte finden sich in klarer Form in Modula-2, die Verwaltung von Ausnahmen ähnelt der in Ada, ähnliche Gliederungen eines Softwaresystems wurden in grösseren Projekten, z.T. mit Werkzeugen, verwaltet.

An Programmierumgebungen sind im deutschen Sprachraum besonders PET ⟨PET⟩ und DELTA ⟨DEL83⟩ bekannt. Neben komfortablen Editier- und Verwaltungsmöglichkeiten unterstützen PET und DELTA, was die Programmentwicklung betrifft, hauptsächlich die "Programmierung im Kleinen" (durch IF-, CASE-, WHILE-Konstrukte und COBOL-Syntaxführung). Im Gegensatz zu PET, dessen Syntaxführung direkt an COBOL ausgerichtet ist, wird der Benutzer von CIDRE beim Entwurf durch die Baumgrammatik problemadäquat geführt, und der so erstellte Baum wird anschliessend in COBOL-Code umgewandelt. Auch gegenüber DELTA als Werkzeugsammlung für standardmässige Aufgaben ist CIDRE stärker auf Entwurf und Entwicklung von Lösungen für neue, komplexe Aufgaben ausgerichtet.

Im folgenden sollen für die einzelnen Phasen der Systementwicklung ⟨SIM82⟩ die zugrundeliegenden Methoden und ihre Unterstützung durch CIDRE dargestellt werden.

2.0 Systementwurf (Zerlegung in Moduln)

Im Softwareentwurf sollen die wesentlichen Methoden für die Lösung der im Pflichtenheft beschriebenen Aufgaben gefunden und dokumentiert werden. Hauptproblem ist dabei die Reduzierung der auf einmal zu bewältigenden Komplexität. Dazu dienen je nach Ebene verschiedene Zerlegungen, die in CIDRE als Baumstruktur abgebildet werden.

Der __Systementwurf__ hat das Ziel, aus der informellen Problembeschreibung des Pflichtenhefts Funktionsklassen zu ermitteln und diese ihrerseits in Teile so zu zerlegen, dass die Entwicklung eines Teils weitgehend unabhängig von anderen erfolgen kann.

Die Funktionsklassen nennen wir __Komponenten__. Komponenten können z.B. sein: Datenbankverwaltung, Benutzerhauptdialog, Auskunftsfunktionen, Stücklistenprozessor. Sie bearbeiten einen Aufgabenkomplex des Gesamtsystems, der weitgehend unabhängig von anderen Komponenten funktionsfähig ist. (Es liegt nahe, Komponenten als Tasks zu realisieren; dies ist jedoch nicht in jedem Fall sinnvoll und möglich. Die Entscheidung über die Task-Aufteilung sollte letztlich von anderen Kriterien, die i. allg. wesentlich von der Basismaschine abhängen, beeinflusst werden.)

Die Komponenten zerlegen wir in __Moduln__, so dass klar abgegrenzte Teilaufgaben entstehen. Grob gesehen besteht ein Modul aus Datenstrukturen und darauf operierenden Funktionen, jedoch besitzen Moduln je nach Abstraktionsebene verschiedene Ausprägungen: Moduln, die eine Teilaufgabe einer Komponente erledigen, werden nach "unten" gegen die Basismaschine und die Realisierung der Datenstrukturen abgegrenzt und "oben" durch Steuermoduln in einen ablaufmässigen Zusammenhang mit anderen Teilaufgaben gebracht.

Wesentlich für die Beziehungen der Moduln untereinander ist die "benutzt"-Struktur. Für zwei verschiedene Moduln A und B sagen wir, Modul A __benutzt__ Modul B, wenn von einer Stelle in Modul A eine Funktion aus Modul B aufgerufen wird. Um Rekursionen auszuschliessen, muss die "benutzt indirekt"-Relation zwischen den Moduln (die transitive Hülle der "benutzt"-Relation) irreflexiv sein. Damit ergibt sich eine Hierarchie (Halbordnung) der Module. Die von der Halbordnung bestimmten Ebenen werden sinnvollerweise in drei Schichten zusammengefasst.

Die Moduln der obersten Ebene bilden die __Steuerschicht__. Sie werden von keinen anderen Moduln benutzt, benutzen aber Moduln der zweiten Ebene, die mit Moduln weiterer Ebenen in der __Aktivitätenschicht__ zusammengefasst sind. Die Moduln der Aktivitätenschicht sollen die eigentlichen Funktionen der Komponente realisieren. Sie benutzen ihrerseits Moduln der untersten Ebenen, die in der __Dienstleistungsschicht__ zusammengefasst sind. Moduln der Dienstleistungsschicht sollen die basismaschinen- und datenstruktur-abhängigen Funktionen enthalten. Sie müssen also Zugriffe auf Dateien und abstrakte Datenstrukturen zur Verfügung stellen.

Zusätzlich unterteilen wir die Dienstleistungsschicht in __lokale Dienstleistungen__, die nur für eine Komponente zur Verfügung stehen, und __globale Dienstleistungen__, die für mehrere Komponenten zur Verfügung stehen (z.B. Datenbankzugriffe).

Ähnliche Zerlegungen finden sich z.B. auch bei <KOS76>, <KIM79>, <HRU81>.

<u>BAUMVERWALTUNG MIT BOIE</u>

Zur Darstellung des Entwurfs werden Bäume verwendet, die mit BOIE editiert werden können. Jeder Baumknoten kann verschiedene Informationen tragen. Diese sind: 1. Knotenname, 2. Knotentyp, 3. Attribut, 4. Text und 5. Verweise auf andere Knoten. Knotenname und Attribut sind vom Benutzer frei wählbare Zeichenketten. Als Text kann eine beliebige, mit einem Texteditor erstellte Datei einem Knoten zugeordnet werden. Der Knotentyp bestimmt jeweils, wie die anderen Knoteninformationen zu interpretieren sind. In den folgenden graphischen Darstellungen von Teilbäumen erscheinen die Typangaben jeweils in Grossbuchstaben, Namen und Attribute mit Kleinbuchstaben und Verweise als Pfeile.

Im BOIE-Baum lässt sich im Gesamtentwurf die Gliederung eines Softwaresystems folgendermassen darstellen:

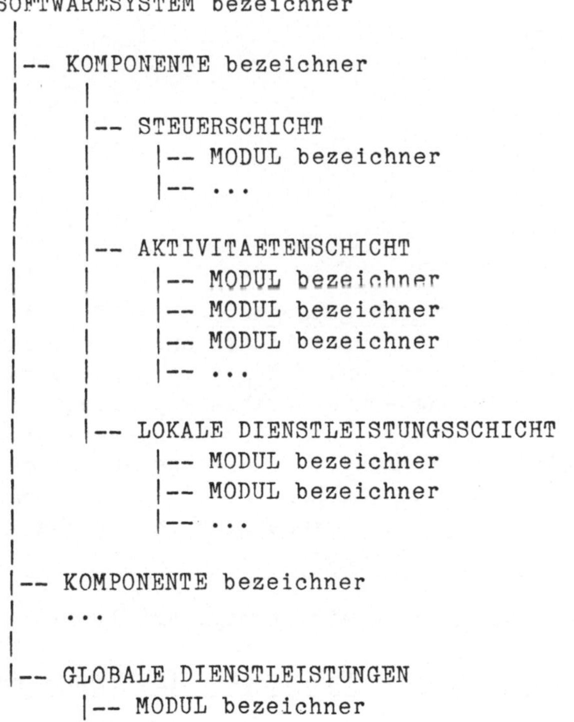

```
SOFTWARESYSTEM bezeichner
|
|-- KOMPONENTE bezeichner
|     |
|     |-- STEUERSCHICHT
|     |    |-- MODUL bezeichner
|     |    |-- ...
|     |
|     |-- AKTIVITAETENSCHICHT
|     |    |-- MODUL bezeichner
|     |    |-- MODUL bezeichner
|     |    |-- MODUL bezeichner
|     |    |-- ...
|     |
|     |-- LOKALE DIENSTLEISTUNGSSCHICHT
|          |-- MODUL bezeichner
|          |-- MODUL bezeichner
|          |-- ...
|
|-- KOMPONENTE bezeichner
|     ...
|
|-- GLOBALE DIENSTLEISTUNGEN
       |-- MODUL bezeichner
       |-- MODUL bezeichner
```

Die "bezeichner" als Namen für Gliederungen vom Typ KOMPONENTE bzw. MODUL sind frei wählbar.

3.0 Modulentwurf

Beim Modulentwurf werden innerhalb jedes Moduls die Daten und die auf ihnen operierenden Funktionen beschrieben. Damit kann das Konzept der Abstrakten Datentypen realisiert werden.

Für ein Modul werden die möglichen Ausnahmefälle vereinbart, die bei Benutzung dieses Moduls auftreten können. Dies beinhaltet eine Benennung und Klassifizierung der Ausnahme sowie den dazugehörigen Meldungstext. Auf Ausnahmefälle, die beim Aufruf einer exportierbaren Funktion auftreten können, wird von der Funktionsdefinition aus verwiesen.

Die modulweiten Daten werden mit Hilfe von einfachen (BOOL, INT, FIXED, CHAR, STRING) oder zusammengesetzten (RECORD, ARRAY) vordefinierten Typen bzw. aus diesen vom Benutzer definierten Typen vereinbart. Zur Typ- und Datendefinition können auch benutzerdefinierte, symbolische Konstanten mit Dimensionierungswirkung auf STRING-Längen und ARRAY-Grössen verwendet werden.

Für die Funktionen werden festgelegt:
- Eingangsparameter,
- Durchgangsparameter,
- Ausgangsparameter,
- mögliche Ausnahmefälle,
- Ergebnis,
- Effekt.

Als Eingangs-, Durchgangs- und Ausgangsparameter sind die Datendefinitionen der entsprechenden Parameterlisten anzugeben, auf die möglichen Ausnahmefälle wird verwiesen, unter Ergebnis wird verbal beschrieben, welche Werte die Ausgangs- und Durchgangsparameter in Abhängigkeit von den Werten der Eingangs- und Durchgangsparameter annehmen, und unter Effekt wird die Wirkung, die die Ausführung der Funktion auf modulweite Daten oder nach aussen hin hat, beschrieben, z.B. Maske auf Bildschirm ausgeben, Änderung von globalen Zustandswerten oder Dateien.

Die Aufrufschnittstelle zwischen zwei Moduln wird festgelegt durch:

1. die Definition der exportierbaren Funktionen im benutzten Modul und
2. einen Eintrag in der Importliste des benutzenden Moduls, welcher den benutzten Modul benennt und auf die Definitionsknoten der importierten Funktionen verweist.

In BOIE wird der Entwurf eines Moduls z. B. durch folgenden Teilbaum
dargestellt:

```
MODUL schlangenverwaltung
 |(Knotentext enthält eine allgemeine Aufgabenbeschreibung des Moduls)
 |
 |---AUSNAHMENLISTE
 |    |-- schlange leer: FEHLER <------------------------------------+
 |    |-- schlange fast voll: WARNUNG <----------------------------+ |
 |    |-- schlange voll: FEHLER <----------------------------------+ |
 |    |                                                          | |
 |---KONSTANTENLISTE                                             | |
 |    |-- maxlaenge: CONSTINT ..<--+                             | |
 |    |                           |                             | |
 |---TYPENLISTE                    |                             | |
 |    |-- Element: RECORDTYP <-----|------+-<------------+       | |
 |    |              |-- ...       |      |              |       | |
 |    |              |-- ...       |      |              |       | |
 |    |                            |      |              |       | |
 |---DATENLISTE                    |      |              |       | |
 |    |-- tabelle: ARRAY-----------+      |              |       | |
 |    |              |--elem: EIGENER TYP->+              |       | |
 |    |                                                  |       | |
 |    |-- fuellstand: INTEGER ...                        |       | |
 |    |                                                  |       | |
 |-- IMPORTLISTE                                         |       | |
 |    -> ... <FUNKTION-Knoten>                           |       | |
 |    -> ... ...                                         |       | |
 |                                                       |       | |
 |-- FUNKTION initialisiere schlange                     |       | |
 |    |-- EFFEKT loescht alle Eintraege der Schlange      |       | |
 |        und setzt deren Fuellstand auf 0.              |       | |
 |                                                       |       | |
 |-- FUNKTION trage ein----------------------------------------+ |
 |    |-- INPARLISTE  (*Eingangsparameter*)               |       | |
 |    |    |-- eintrag: EIGENER TYP-------------------->-+       | |
 |    |                                                  |       | |
 |    |-- EFFEKT traegt "eintrag" in der Schlange ein.   |       | |
 |                                                       |       | |
 |-- FUNKTION entnehme aeltestes---------------------|----------->-+
 |    |                                              |
 |    |-- OUTPARLISTE (*Ausgangsparameter*)          |
 |    |    |-- aeltestes: EIGENER TYP----------------->-+
 |    |
 |    |-- ERGEBNIS liefert das älteste Element aus der Schlange (FIFO)
 |    |
 |    |-- EFFEKT Das gelesene älteste Element wird der Schlange
 |    |          entnommen (gelöscht).
 |    ...
```

4.0 Algorithmischer Entwurf

Im Algorithmischen Entwurf wird die statische Beschreibung der Funktionen durch eine algorithmische Beschreibung des Funktionsablaufs ergänzt. Ebenso werden die für die algorithmische Beschreibung notwendigen Detaillierungen der modulweiten Daten sowie die evtl. für einzelne Funktionen nötigen funktionslokalen Daten beschrieben.

Der Funktionsalgorithmus wird in einem freien Pseudocode unter Verwendung der im Entwurf eingeführten Datennamen (modulweite Daten und Parameter) formuliert. Er wird als Text zum RUMPF-Tochterknoten der Funktion plaziert. An Konstruktions- bzw. Zerlegungsprinzipien sind empfohlen:

- Verfeinerung (Notation: Hinschreiben des Verfeinerungsnamens)
- Prozeduraufruf (Prozedurname plus -in Klammern- die aktuellen
                  Parameter)
- Reihung (mache dies; mache das)
- Alternative (IF gültig THEN mache dies ELSE mache das FI)
- Fallauswahl (CASE abc OF a: tu dies,
                        b: tu das
                        OTHERWISE: tu etwas anderes
              ESAC)
- abweisende Schleife (WHILE gültig DO irgendwas OD)
- nicht abweisende Schleife (DO irgendwas UNTIL gültig OD)
- Zählschleife (FOR n TIMES DO irgendwas OD
            oder: FOR i:=n To m DO irgendwas OD)

Da man den Algorithmus möglichst problemnah formulieren möchte, wird der Pseudocode nicht automatisch umgesetzt. Dennoch wird durch die Bereitstellung aller notwendigen Datendeklarationen viel COBOL-Formulierungsaufwand eingespart. Im Modulbaum wird die algorithmische Beschreibung im Text des FUNKTION-Tochterknotens vom Typ RUMPF untergebracht.

5.0 Quellprogrammerstellung

5.1 Codierung

In der Codierungsphase ist der Algorithmische Entwurf in COBOL-Anweisungen umzusetzen. Diese sind zusätzlich an die FUNKTIONs-RUMPF-Knoten als Texte anzuhängen. Ausserdem können für Verfeinerungen COBOL-Anweisungen in weitere Knoten vom Typ SECTION eingetragen werden. In die RUMPF/SECTION-Knoten können alle in der PROCEDURE DIVISION zulässigen COBOL-Anweisungen eingetragen werden. Daneben sind Makros für den Aufruf einer importierten Funktion und für das Verlassen des Moduls über einen bestimmten Ausnahmeausgang zulässig.

5.2 Codegenerierung

Aus dem Entwurfsbaum kann zu jedem Entwicklungszeitpunkt Quelltext generiert werden, der nach Durchlaufen eines Präprozessors fehlerfrei kompiliert werden kann. Dabei wird jeder MODUL in eine Kompilationseinheit (COBOL: PROGRAM) umgesetzt.

Der Codegenerator setzt die im Baum dargestellten Konzepte (wie Datentypen, ADT, Ausnahmenvereinbarung usw.) in äquivalente COBOL-Konstrukte um. Diese Umsetzung wäre im Prinzip auch manuell möglich und geht in der Tat auf einen Codier-Vorschlag der FG Softwaretechnik an der TU Berlin (betr. ADT) und darauf aufbauende COBOL-Codierrichtlinien <COD81> zurück, die zunächst in einem grösseren Projekt (6 MJ) erprobt und danach einer gründlichen Revision unterzogen wurden. Jedoch wäre eine manuelle Umsetzung sehr schreibaufwendig und böte die Gefahr von Inkonsistenzen, so dass sie weder rationell noch durchsetzbar wäre.

Wichtigstes Hilfsmittel für die Umsetzung des Datentypkonzepts und der Schnittstellenverwaltung sind COPY-Dateien, in die die Datentyp- bzw. Parameterlistendefinitionen hineingeneriert werden und COPY-Anweisungen auf diese Dateien, die in die Quelltexte der beteiligten Moduln generiert werden und damit die Gleichheit der Datenstrukturen gewährleisten. Diese COPY-Anweisungen sind an den COBOL-Standard angelehnt, müssen aber, da sie auch geschachtelt auftreten können und dabei die COBOL-Levelnummern entsprechend angepasst werden müssen, von dem CIDRE-Präprozessor aufgelöst werden.

Das Konzept der Moduln als Zusammenfassung mehrerer auf denselben Datenstrukturen operierender Funktionen wird realisiert durch Übergabe eines Funktionscodes an ein aufgerufenes Modul und einen davon abhängigen Sprungverteiler innerhalb dessen, der den Rumpf der entsprechenden Funktion aufruft.

Ein aus einem MODUL-Teilbaum generiertes COBOL-Program hat folgenden
Aufbau:

```
IDENTIFICATION DIVISION.
PROGRAM-ID.    a.         (*MODUL-Name*)
* <Dokumentationstext: Beschreibung der Aufgaben des Moduls und der
* enthaltenen Funktionen>
DATA DIVISION.
  <Deklarationen modulweiter Daten>
* Import-Schnittstelle  MODUL x:
  COPY <Statische Schnittstelle zu x>
  COPY <Allgemeine Parameter    zu x>
  COPY <Maximaler Parameterbereich der Funktionen von MODUL x>
  COPY <Parameter für FUNKTION 1    von x>
     ...
  COPY <Parameter für FUNKTION m    von x>
* Import-Schnittstelle  MODUL y:
  ...
* Export-Schnittstelle  (MODUL a):
  COPY <Statische Schnittstelle zu a>
  COPY <Maximaler Parameterbereich der Funktionen von MODUL a>
  COPY <Parameter für FUNKTION 1    von a>
     ...
  COPY <Parameter für FUNKTION n    von a>
  ...
LINKAGE SECTION.
  COPY <Allgemeine Parameter   zu a>
  COPY <Maximaler Parameterbereich der Funktionen von MODUL a>
PROCEDURE DIVISION
    USING Allgemeine Parameter,
          Maximaler Parameterbereich der Funktionen von MODUL a.

  <Funktionsaufrufverteiler mit Übergabemechanismus für
   IN-, TRANS- und OUT-Parameter>
     EXIT PROGRAM.
/
<Funktionsname_1> SECTION.
BEGIN-<Funktionsname_1>.
* <Dokumentationstext: algorithmischer Entwurf der Funktion>
  <COBOL-Anweisungen des Funktionsrumpfs>
END-<Funktionsname_1>.
  ...
/
<Funktionsname_n> SECTION.
BEGIN-<Funktionsname_n>.
  ...
END-<Funktionsname_n>.
END PROGRAM.
```

Die Exportschnittstelle eines Moduls besteht aus mindestens 4 Teilen:

- Statische Schnittstelle,
- Allgemeine Parameter,
- Maximaler Parameterbereich,
- jeweils ein Parameterblock für jede Funktion, gegliedert in IN-, TRANS- und OUT-Parameter.

Die Statische Schnittstelle enthält die Namen aller Funktionen und die Namen aller möglichen Ausnahmen, die der Modul nach oben reichen kann. Um Namenskonflikte zwischen den verschiedenen Importschnittstellen in einem Modul zu vermeiden, werden die importierten Moduln jeweils durch ein eindeutiges, vom Benutzer bestimmbares Kürzel identifiziert (im folgenden: "Kürzel").

Den Ausnahmen werden Codes zugeordnet, die aus dem Modulkürzel und einer laufenden Nummer bestehen. Unter diesen Codes als Schlüssel werden die Knotenattribute der Ausnahmenvereinbarungen in einer Meldungstextdatei eingetragen, wo sie bei Ausnahmefällen für eine Meldungsausgabe zur Verfügung stehen.

Beispiel Statische Schnittstelle:

```
   Modul Schlangenverwaltung:
   *Funktionen:
   01  Kürzel-initialisiere-schlange      PIC 99     VALUE 01.
   01  Kürzel-trage-ein                   PIC 99     VALUE 02.
   01  Kürzel-entnehme-aeltestes          PIC 99     VALUE 03.
   *Ausnahmefälle:
   01  Kürzel-Schlangenverwaltung-OK      PIC X(8) VALUE "Kürzel00".
   01  Kürzel-schlange-leer               PIC X(8) VALUE "Kürzel01".
   01  Kürzel-schlange-fast-voll          PIC X(8) VALUE "Kürzel02".
   01  Kürzel-schlange-voll               PIC X(8) VALUE "Kürzel03".
   *END Statische Schnittstelle Schlangenverwaltung-----------------
```

Die Allgemeinen Parameter sind der Funktionscode, der zur Aufrufzeit den Code für die aktuelle Funktion enthält, der Ausnahmecode, der bei Rückkehr in das aufrufende Programm eine in der Statischen Schnittstelle genannte Ausnahme enthalten kann und die Meldungsvariable, in der variable Information zur zugehörigen Meldung übergeben werden kann.

Beispiel Allgemeine Parameter für Modul Schlangenverwaltung:

```
   01 Kürzel-INFO.
      02 Kürzel-FUNKTIONSCODE       PIC 99.
      02 Kürzel-AUSNAHMECODE        PIC X(8).
      02 Kürzel-MELDUNGSVARIABLE    PIC X(30).
```

Der Maximale Parameterbereich ist so dimensioniert, dass er genausoviel Speicherbereich belegt, wie der längste Parameterbereich einer Funktion. Diesem Bereich werden zwecks Platzersparnis alle Parameterbereiche der Funktionen überlagert.

Die <u>Parameterblöcke</u> enthalten die Ein-, Durch- und Ausgangsparameter einer Funktion.

Beispiel Parameterblock der FUNKTION entnehme-aeltestes (mit einer konkretisierten Untergliederung für den Datentyp 'Element'):

```
01 PAR-Kürzel-FKT02.
   02 IN-entnehme-aeltestes      PIC X.           (*Dummy-Bereich*)
   02 OUT-entnehme-aeltestes.
      03 aeltestes.
         04 Nachricht    PIC X(80).
         04 Datum        PIC X(6).
         04 Nr           PIC 999.
```

6.0 <u>Übersetzen, Binden, Testen</u>

Die CIDRE-Kommandos für Modulübersetzung, Modulfreigabe und Binden orientieren sich an der KOMPONENTEn/MODUL-Gliederung des Softwaresystems und rekurrieren auf VMS-Kommandos. Für alle Moduln können ausserdem Testtreiber erzeugt werden, mit denen ihr Verhalten interaktiv getestet werden kann. Aus Platzgründen ist eine genauere Darstellung hier nicht möglich.

7.0 <u>Zusammenfassung</u>

Gegenüber anderen auf COBOL zielende Programmierumgebungen zeichnet CIDRE sich dadurch aus, dass es die Software-Entwicklung nach einem einheitlichen Konzept von Systementwurf über Modulentwurf, Algorithmischen Entwurf bis zu Codierung und Test unterstützt. Die Betonung ist dabei auf die sich bei der "Programmierung im Grossen" ergebenden Probleme (insbesondere Schnittstellenverwaltung) gelegt.

8.0 Literatur

<CID83> CIDRE. Benutzerhandbuch.
  Entwurf und COBOL-Programmentwicklung mit BOIE, PSI Berlin 1983
<BOIE> Winkler P., BOIE - Ein interaktives Entwurfswerkzeug,
        GI 11. Jahrestagung 1979
  Winkler P., Erste Erfahrungen mit dem interaktiven
    Entwurfswerkzeug BOIE,
    Fachtagung Prozessrechner 1981, Informatik-Fachberichte Bd. 39
  Hass P., Das BOIE-System im praktischen Einsatz, IKD '82 Berlin
<PET>   PET/MAESTRO - Kurzbeschreibung,
  SOFTLAB/PHILIPS Form-Nr. W2401-04-06
<DEL83> DELTA Referenz-Handbuch COBOL MAN-109,
  SODECON AG, Schwerzenbach 1983
<SIM82> Simonsmeier W., Reduzierung von Komplexität: Kernpunkt jeder
  Softwareentwicklung, IKD '82 Berlin
<KOS76> Koster C.H.A., Visibility and Types,
  ACM SIGPLAN Notices II, 76 Special Issue
<KIM79> Kimm R./Koch W./Simonsmeier W./Tontsch F., Einführung in
  Software Engineering, de Gruyter, Berlin-New York 1979
<HRU81> Hruschka, Peter, Ein Projektmodell und Werkzeuge zu dessen
  Unterstützung, GI 11. Jahrestagung 1981
<COD81> COBOL-Codierrichtlinien, PSI Berlin 1981

Ein Testsystem fuer Echtzeitprogramme

Roger Schoenberger

Zentrallabor Landis & Gyr Zug

Abstract

We describe a system that facilitates debugging of programs written
in the real-time programming language Portal. The System allows programs to run unaltered and without any additional code on the target
machine; thus there is no change in their run-time behaviour, unless
they are interrupted manually or by a preset trigger. At this point
they can be analysed interactively at the level of the source language; subsequently their execution may be resumed. The paper explains
the principles and functions of the system and discusses the expe-
riences gained in actual use. Even though the system has been well
received and has proven very useful, improvements are still possible;
some ideas for future test systems are presented.

Einfuehrung

Noch im Jahre 1980 hat R. L. Glass [1] den Mangel an guten Testhilfs-
mitteln fuer Echtzeitprogramme beklagt: Falls ueberhaupt hoehere
Sprachen eingesetzt werden (was im Interesse der Zuverlaessigkeit
sein sollte), dann sind die vorhandenen Testhilfen trotzdem nicht auf
diese Sprachen orientiert, sondern auf das Maschinenniveau. Das ist
vor allem dadurch bedingt, dass Echtzeitprogramme meist auf speziali-
sierter Hardware ablaufen, und nicht auf der Maschine, auf der sie
entwickelt werden, weshalb der Zugriff auf Quellentext und Symbolta-
bellen erschwert ist.

Im folgenden wird ueber die Erfahrungen mit den Werkzeugen um die
Sprache Portal [2], [3] berichtet, die zu einem Teil die in [1] gewuenschten uebertreffen, indem sie den vollen Komfort auf der Zielmaschine bieten, ohne an diese bezueglich Hardware und Software gros-

se Anforderungen zu stellen. Portal ist verwandt mit Sprachen wie Concurrent Pascal [5] und Modula [6] und wurde im Zentrallabor der Firma Landis & Gyr ab 1975 entwickelt und seit 1977 eingesetzt. Das hier speziell betrachtete Testwerkzeug PDS (Portal Debug System) steht fuer ein MC68000-System seit Ende 1981 zur Verfuegung, waehrend eine erste eingeschraenkte Version fuer PDP-11-Systeme schon 1979 vorhanden war.

Die Testkonfiguration

Die betrachtete Konfiguration besteht aus einer Programmentwicklungs-maschine (VAX-11 oder PDP-11) und der Zielmaschine (MC68000) mit angehaengtem Terminal (z.B. VT100).

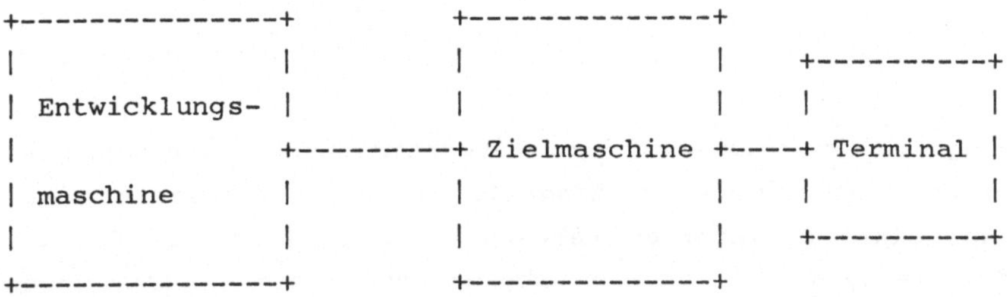

Die Verbindung zwischen Entwicklungsmaschine und Zielmaschine wird durch eine serielle Verbindung gewaehrleistet. Es genuegt, auf der Zielmaschine zwei Terminalschnittstellen und die Software zu ihrer Bedienung zu haben, um Portal-Programme zu entwickeln und zu testen, da Editor, Compiler und das Testsystem PDS auf der Entwicklungsma-schine laufen. Die Programme brauchen fuer die Verwendung von PDS nicht besonders uebersetzt zu werden und erfordern keinen Overhead an Speicherplatz oder Laufzeit. Das ist besonders wichtig bei Echtzeit-programmen, die oft empfindlich sind in Bezug auf Aenderungen in den zeitlichen Verhaeltnissen und den zur Verfuegung stehenden Speicher-platz voll ausnutzen. Es ist damit auch garantiert, dass jedes Pro-duktionsprogramm direkt mit PDS getestet werden kann und nicht nur ein reduziertes Testprogramm, das nach dem Auftreten eines Fehlers erst noch neu uebersetzt werden muss.

Der Benutzer arbeitet am Terminal in vier verschiedenen Modi:

(1) Programm-Entwicklungs-Modus:
    In diesem Modus kann der Benutzer arbeiten, wie wenn das Terminal
    direkt an der Entwicklungsmaschine angehaengt waere, also insbe-
    sondere Programme editieren und uebersetzen.

(2) Programm-Lade-Modus:
    Damit kann ein auf der Entwicklungsmaschine uebersetztes Programm
    in die Zielmaschine geladen und gestartet werden.

(3) Programm-Lauf-Modus:
    Das uebersetzte Programm laeuft auf der Zielmaschine, mit even-
    tuellem Dialog via Terminal.

(4) Programm-Inspektions-Modus:
    In diesem Modus kann der Zustand des Programms untersucht und
    eventuell ein Haltepunkt auf einer Zeile des Programms definiert
    werden.

Der Uebergang vom Programm-Lauf- zum Programm-Inspektions-Modus kann
erfolgen durch einen manuellen Eingriff an der Zielmaschine, durch
Auflaufen auf einen definierten Haltepunkt oder durch die Detektion
eines Laufzeitfehlers; die andern Uebergaenge erfolgen durch Befehle
via Terminal. Insbesondere ist das Weiterfahren vom momentanen Zustand des unterbrochenen Progamms aus moeglich, wobei aber im Falle
eines Laufzeitfehlers der dafuer verantwortliche Prozess nicht wei-
terlaufen kann.

Im Programm-Entwicklungs-Modus ist die Zielmaschine transparent, d.h.
ein kleines Stueck Software auf der Zielmaschine sorgt fuer die direkte Weitergabe der Zeichen vom Terminal an die Entwicklungsmaschine
und umgekehrt, ausser bei einem speziellen Kontrollzeichen, das fuer
die Modusumschaltung reserviert ist. Der gleiche Effekt koennte na-
tuerlich dadurch erzielt werden, dass man das Terminal direkt an die
Entwicklungsmaschine haengt. Die Konfiguration wurde deshalb so ge-
waehlt, weil Anschluesse am Entwicklungssystem knapp sind und meist
an der Zielmaschine ohnehin ein Terminal notwendig ist.

Im Programm-Lade-Modus wird mittels eines speziellen Protokolls der
Programmcode von der Entwicklungsmaschine auf die Zielmaschine uebertragen. Der Code kann dort direkt in den Hauptspeicher geladen oder,
falls vorhanden, auf einem Massenspeicher fuer spaeteres wiederholtes
Laden zwischengespeichert werden.

Im Programm-Lauf-Modus wird die Verbindung zwischen Ziel- und Entwicklungsmaschine nicht benutzt und PDS bleibt inaktiv. Die Entwicklungsmaschine braucht in diesem Fall gar nicht angeschlossen zu sein,
was besonders dann interessant ist, wenn das Programm vom lokalen
Massenspeicher geladen wird. Prinzipiell wuerde die Konfiguration
dynamisches Testen erlauben, d. h. die Ueberwachung des laufenden
Programms, was aber eine betraechtliche Verlangsamung bedingen wuerde
und deshalb nicht in Betracht gezogen wurde.

Im Programm-Inspektions-Modus wird die Verbindung zwischen Entwick-
lungs- und Zielmaschine doppelt ausgenutzt, naemlich fuer den Benut-
zerdialog zwischen PDS und dem Terminal und fuer die Uebermittlung
von Information ueber den Programmzustand und die Haltepunkte zwischen PDS und seinem Gegenstueck auf der Zielmaschine. Dieses bean-
sprucht etwa 1.4 K Bytes Code, wovon etwas mehr als die Haelfte
allein fuer das Abfangen der Laufzeitfehler noetig ist. PDS holt sich
die Information ueber Programmstruktur sowie Typen und Adressen von
Variablen aus speziellen (vom Compiler erzeugten) Files auf der Entwicklungsmaschine, die dynamische Programminformation (Werte von Variablen, Laufzeitstruktur von Prozessen und gerufenen Routinen) bei
Bedarf durch Austausch von Meldungen mit der Zielmaschine.

Inspektion des Programmzustands

Der Benutzer kann den ganzen Zustand seines Programms auf dem Niveau
seines Quellentexts sichtbar machen. Das heisst bezueglich Portal,
dass man die Strukturierungsmittel Modul, Prozess und Routine, die
Synchronisationsmittel Monitor und Signal, sowie die Variablen an
ihrem Namen und der Zeile ihrer Deklaration erkennt. Die Zustandsmel-
dung erfolgt bei einem Prozess in der Form "wartend auf Signal",
"wartend auf Monitor" bzw. "laufend auf Prioritaet p", bei einem Monitor in der Form "frei" bzw. "besetzt", bei einem Signal in der Form
"erwartet" bzw. "nicht erwartet", bei einer Routine durch Angabe der
Zeilennummer, wo der Kontrollfluss in der betrachteten Aktivierung

steht, und bei einer Variablen durch Angabe des Werts gemaess dem deklarierten Typ.

Beim Eintritt in den Inspektions-Modus wird automatisch der gerade unterbrochene Prozess angegeben mit umgebendem Modul, Deklarations-zeile, gegenwaertiger Prioritaet, zuletzt aufgerufener Routine und der Zeile, worin er unterbrochen wurde. Im Falle eines Laufzeitfehlers hat man zusammen mit den sofort zugaenglichen Werten der lokalen Variablen oft schon genug Information, um den Fehler verstehen zu koennen. Sonst kann auch der Zustand jedes andern Prozesses abgefragt werden, die Ketten von Routinen-Aufrufen sowie die zu Signalen und Monitoren gehoerenden Prozess-Warteschlangen koennen durchgegangen und die Werte aller zu Moduln oder aufgerufenen Routinen gehoerigen Variablen koennen sichtbar gemacht werden.

Die Benutzerschnittstelle beruht auf der Idee von Fenstern, die allerdings nur konzeptionell existieren und nicht auf einem Bild-schirm erscheinen, da jedes gewoehnliche ASCII-Terminal (insbesondere ein druckendes) verwendbar sein soll. Es gibt die Fenster-Typen Modul, Prozess, Routine, Monitor, Signal, Variable. Ein Fenster eines bestimmten Typs zeigt jeweils auf ein Objekt der entsprechenden Art im zu testenden Programm. Es gibt Befehle, um solche Fenster aufzusetzen, zu verschieben, oder um Information ueber die durch sie bezeichneten Objekte auszugeben. Als Beispiel fuer Setzbefehle seien genannt der Uebergang von einem Prozess zu der zuletzt gerufenen Routine, von einer Routine zur ersten Variablen, von einer Variablen zum umgebenden Modul, von einem Modul zu einer bestimmten Variablen. Verschiebebefehle erlauben zum Beispiel den Uebergang von einer Routine zur aufrufenden, von einer Variablen zur naechsten.

Die durch einen Befehl bewirkte Ausgabe ist bewusst gering gehalten (wenige Zeilen), um den Benutzer nicht mit Information zu ueberfluten. Dafuer kann man sich mit einem Tastendruck leicht fortbewegen, indem eine leere Befehlszeile - je nach dem zuletzt angewaehlten Fenster - einen sinnvollen Setz- bzw. Verschiebebefehl und anschliessend einen Ausgabebefehl bewirkt. So ist es leicht, Warteschlangen und Aufrufse-quenzen durchzugehen oder strukturierte Variablen anzusehen, bei denen der Benutzer die interessanten Teile mit Bewegungen ansteuert, da sie nicht als Ganzes erscheinen.

Erfahrungen mit dem Testsystem

Das vorgestellte Testsystem hat sich als ausserordentlich nuetzliches Instrument erwiesen, u.a. bei der Entwicklung eines Filesystems, eines syntax-gesteuerten Editors und eines 30'000-Zeilen-Programms fuer eine Fernwirktechnik-Zentrale. Im folgenden sollen aber einige aufgedeckte Schwaechen und von den Benutzern geaeusserte Wuensche diskutiert werden.

Die Benutzerschnittstelle macht besonders Anfaengern gewisse Schwierigkeiten, da die Fenstertechnik ohne die Verwendung von Bitmap-Display und Maus offenbar zu abstrakt ist und die Modi mit den notwendigen Uebergaengen zu wenig klar und systematisch dargestellt sind, was zum grossen Teil auf technische Randbedingungen zurueckzufuehren ist, d. h. auf die Benutzung vorgegebener Hardware. Etwas Muehe hat man auch, wenn man gewisse Werte in einem bestimmten Zusammenhang sehen will, der nicht durch die normale Bewegungsart unterstuetzt wird, etwa beim Ueberpruefen von Listenstrukturen, weil dann der Uebergang von Element zu Element immer wieder von Hand vorgenommen werden muss. Hier waere die Moeglichkeit benutzerdefinierter Bewegungen bzw. Befehlssequenzen hilfreich; es soll deshalb ermoeglicht werden, dass PDS auch Befehle aus einer vorher als Text-File zusammengestellten Sequenz akzeptieren kann.

Die groesste Einschraenkung der Bequemlichkeit ist die Notwendigkeit des Zugriffs auf ein gueltiges Listing, da alle Referenzen auf Stellen im Code via Zeilennummern funktionieren. Da man oft nicht ein aktuelles Listing auf Papier zur Verfuegung hat, muss man ein entsprechendes File auf der Entwicklungsmaschine suchen (was insbesondere nach Teilkompilationen schwierig sein kann) und die gewuenschten Zeilen mit einem Texteditor ansehen. Zudem ist die Angabe von Zeilennummern zu wenig fein, besonders wenn mehrere Anweisungen auf einer Zeile stehen. Analog wie bei den Listings stellt sich auch bei den von PDS benoetigten Strukturfiles das Problem, die zu einem bestimmten Programm passenden zu finden, da sie ja nicht mit dem Programm auf die Zielmaschine uebertragen werden.

PDS erlaubt nur, Variablen anzusehen, nicht aber, ihnen einen Wert zuzuweisen. Diese Einschraenkung ist nicht durch Implementationsprobleme bedingt, sondern soll undiszipliniertes Testen verhindern. Meist wird diese Moeglichkeit nur gewuenscht, um lange Kompilationszeiten zu umgehen, selten ist sie ein wirkliches Beduerfnis wie im

Fall, wo man fehlerhafte Zustaende erzeugen will, um die Fehlertoleranz des Programms zu pruefen. Eine Implementationseinschraenkung verhindert es ferner, die durch sogenannte With- und Using-Anweisungen eingefuehrten temporaeren Variablen anzusehen. Diese (fuer Portal spezifische) Schwierigkeit ist verwandt mit dem allgemeinen Problem von optimierenden Compilern, wo der Ort einer Variablen waehrend ihrer Lebensdauer aendern kann, insbesondere bei Verwendung von Registern.

Im Moment kann zu jedem Zeitpunkt nur ein einziger Haltepunkt aktiv sein; wenn man aber Verzweigungen im Programm untersuchen will, ist das eine wesentliche Einschraenkung. Diese wird allerdings in naechster Zeit aufgehoben, wobei gleichzeitig die Moeglichkeit geschaffen wird, mehrere Fenster von jedem Typ zu haben. Ein anderer Wunsch betrifft von Bedingungen abhaengige Haltepunkte; solche, die nur gelten sollen, wenn ein bestimmter Prozess darauf auflaeuft, sind inzwischen moeglich, allerdings koennen dabei unbeteiligte Prozesse leicht verzoegert werden. Echt dynamisches Testen, wie etwa Tracing, wird erstaunlicherweise selten verlangt, und auch dann meist nur darum, weil es in andern Testsystemen vorhanden ist, wo es aber nicht ohne Eingriff in den Code und damit in die Laufzeit geht.

Vorstellungen ueber ein zukuenftiges Testsystem

Aus den Erfahrungen mit PDS lassen sich drei Problemkreise herausfiltern, die beim Entwurf eines neuen Testsystems wesentlich sind, naemlich die Abfragesprache, die Echtzeitueberwachung und die integrierte Programminformation. Die ersten beiden werden in [7] behandelt - ausgehend von einer Uebersicht ueber die vorhandene Literatur. Der dritte wird mit den integrierten Programmierumgebungen angegangen ([8], [9], [10]) , wo Editor, Compiler und Debugger eine Einheit bilden, allerdings nicht fuer grosse Programme und nicht fuer Tests in Echtzeit.

Mit einer _Abfragesprache_ moechte man es dem Anwender erlauben, aus den von einem Testsystem zur Verfuegung gestellten elementaren Funktionen Programme herzustellen, die es erlauben, gezielte Testablaeufe zu definieren. Diese Ablaeufe sollen durch beliebige Bedingungen gesteuert werden und die gewuenschte Information in der gewuenschten Form festhalten koennen. Man muss allerdings beachten, dass die Existenz der Sprache allein noch nicht genuegt, um alle Testfaelle zu automatisieren, denn dazu muss man auch alle auf die Zielmaschine wirkenden Signale erzeugen koennen, was ohne besondere Hardware nicht moeglich ist.

Mit einer <u>Echtzeitueberwachung</u> moechte man zum Beispiel Synchronisationsablaeufe untersuchen und Laufzeiten bestimmter Programmteile messen. Dies muss ohne Verzoegerung des laufenden Programms geschehen, d. h. man will einen intelligenten Logic Analyzer haben. Dies ist, wenn ueberhaupt, nur mit hochspezialisierter schneller Hardware loesbar (vgl. [11], [12], [13], [14]).

<u>Integrierte Programminformation</u> heisst, dass das Testsystem die volle Information ueber das zu testende Programm geben muss. Hinweise auf Teile des Programms gehen dann nicht mehr via Zeilennummern, sondern direkt durch ihre Darstellung am Terminal. Ferner muessen Suchprozesse durch das Programm angeboten werden, im Sinne eines auf die Sprache angepassten Cross-Reference-Systems. Ein solches ist zwar fuer Portal vorhanden [4], jedoch nicht mit dem Testsystem integriert.

Zum Schluss sei als Beispiel noch ein Testfall erwaehnt, in dem alle drei Problemkreise angesprochen werden. Dabei geht es um eine bestimmte Variable (die man zuerst mit der Abfragesprache spezifiziert), von der man wissen will, wann (Echtzeitueberwachung) und wo (Programminformation) sie modifiziert wird.

Schlussbemerkungen

Es sei noch einmal herausgestellt, was PDS im Vergleich zu anderen bekannten Testsystemen leistet, naemlich die Moeglichkeit, ein Programm direkt auf der Zielmaschine, gemaess den Konzepten einer hoeheren Sprache auszutesten, ohne dass dieses Programm in irgend einer Weise vorher besonders behandelt werden muss. Der dazu notwendige Hardware-Aufwand ist minimal. Da Echtzeitprogramme auch beim Testen ungestoert ablaufen sollen, solange sie nicht manuell angehalten werden oder auf einen Haltepunkt auflaufen, muss allerdings auf Moeglichkeiten wie Tracing verzichtet werden.

Der Autor dankt R. Schild und A. Businger fuer ihre Hilfe bei der Abfassung des Manuskripts sowie A. K. Gorrengourt, H. Oswald und J. M. Zingg fuer ihre Beitraege zur Implementation von PDS.

Literaturverzeichnis

[1] Glass, R.L.: Real-time: The "lost world" of software debugging and testing. CACM 23, no. 5, pp. 264-271 (1980).

[2] Businger, A.: Portal Sprachbeschreibung. Zug: Landis & Gyr 1983.

[3] Schild, R.: PORTAL - a PASCAL-based real-time programming language. In: Algorithmic Languages (de Bakker, van Vliet eds.), Proc. IFIP Congress 1981, pp. 49-58. Amsterdam: North-Holland 1981.

[4] Voelkle, F.: Portal crossref description. Ecole Polytechnique Federale de Lausanne, Chaire d'Informatique Theorique, Rapport no. 19, 1981.

[5] Brinch Hansen, P.: The programming language Concurrent Pascal. IEEE Tr. Software Engineering, vol. 1, pp. 37-65 (1977).

[6] Wirth, N.: Modula: A language for modular multiprogramming. Software-Practice and Experience, vol. 7, pp. 3-35 (1977).

[7] Plattner, B., Nievergelt, J.: Monitoring program execution: A Survey. Computer, vol. 14, no. 11, pp. 76-93 (1981).

[8] Medina-Mora, R., Feiler, P.H.: An incremental programming environment. IEEE Tr. Software Engineering, vol. SE-7, no. 5, pp. 472-482 (1981).

[9] Teitelbaum, T., Reps, T.: The Cornell Program Synthesizer: A syntax-directed programming environment. CACM 24, no. 9, pp. 563-573 (1981).

[10] Fritzson, P.: A systematic approach to advanced debugging through incremental compilation. In: ACM SIGSOFT/ SIGPLAN software engineering symposium on high-level debugging, ACM SIGPLAN Notices, vol. 18, no. 8, pp. 130-139 (1983).

[11] Gentleman, W. M., Hoeksma, H.: Hardware assisted high level debugging. In: ACM SIGSOFT/SIGPLAN software engineering symposium on high-level debugging, ACM SIGPLAN Notices, vol. 18, no. 8, pp. 140-144 (1983).

[12] Hill, C. R.: A real-time microprocessor debugging technique. In: ACM SIGSOFT/SIGPLAN software engineering symposium on high-level debugging, ACM SIGPLAN Notices, vol. 18, no. 8, pp. 145-148 (1983).

[13] Witschorik, C. A.: The real-time debugging monitor for the Bell System 1A processor. Software-Practice and Experience, vol. 13, pp. 727-743 (1983).

[14] Macke, D. P., Ashley, P. C.: Symbolic testing: its philosophy and application in the testing of a real-time distributed system. Proc. first annual Phoenix conf. in computers and communications, pp. 178-181 (1982).

Programmieren mit graphischen Mitteln:
Die Überwachung der Ausführung von GRADE-
Programmen am graphischen Bildschirm[1]

H.E.Sengler

URW Unternehmensberatung, Hamburg

Abstract

The language GRADE is an attempt to utilize graphic descriptions
directly for programming. An implementation of such a language must
not only offer means to edit, compile and output graphical programs
but also to test and debug them. Because of the conceptual difference
between the (two dimensional) source code and the (essentially one
dimensional) object code this should be done on source level, i.e.
graphically too.

The concept of such a debug system is presented. It uses the graphics
entered by the programmer and within these displays the progress of
execution, so the programmer can actually "watch his program work".
This makes it easy for him to check its actual function against the
one desired during design. For ease of use, the system allows various
degrees of refinement in display, both in terms of execution time and
program locations. The implementation is done with very little
overhead in code (allowing fast execution in non-display mode) but
with a detailed description file and, for faster access to it, with an
additional index file.

---

[1] Die diesem Bericht zugrunde liegenden Arbeiten wurden mit
Mitteln des Bundesministers für Forschung und Technologie
(Förderungskennzeichen 083 02145) gefördert. Die Verant=
wortung für den Inhalt liegt allein beim Autor.

1. Einleitung

Die Programmiersprache GRADE /1/ ist ein Versuch, graphische Darstel=
lungen direkt zur Programmierung einzusetzen, d.h. nicht nur als Ent=
wicklungs-, Dokumentations- oder Test-Hilfsmittel. In einem Projekt
bei der Fa. URW Unternehmensberatung, Hamburg, gefördert durch das
Bundesministerium für Forschung und Technologie, BMFT(GMD), wurde eine
Pilotversion eines GRADE-Systems entwickelt, mit dem die Sprache rea=
lisiert wird. Das System umfaßt einen Editor zum Erstellen und Ändern
von Programmen am graphischen Bildschirm, einen Compiler zum Überset=
zen des graphischen Programms in ausführbaren Code sowie ein
"Überwacher" genanntes Programm, das die Ausführung eines übersetzten
GRADE-Programms kontrolliert und auf Wunsch am graphischen Bildschirm
darstellt. Dieser Aufsatz befaßt sich mit den Konstruktionszielen, die
dem Überwacher zugrunde liegen, beschreibt die dem Programmierer damit
angebotenen Leistungen und erläutert die bei seiner Realisierung
verwendeten Konzepte und Methoden.

Das Pilot- GRADE-System wurde auf einer DEC-LSI 11/23 in PASCAL
realisiert. Es wurden Bildschirme des Typs DEC-VT100 (12 Zoll) mit
einem Graphik-Zusatz eingesetzt, der eine Auflösung von 480*640 Punk=
ten bietet. Für einen Produktionseinsatz des Systems ist jedoch sowohl
ein Rechner mit größerem Adreßraum als auch ein größerer und schnelle=
rer Bildschirm (mit speziellen Funktionen wie Blinken) notwendig, um
sowohl bezüglich der Verarbeitungsgeschwindigkeit als auch der opti=
schen Darstellbarkeit für den Benutzer ansprechende Resultate zu
erzielen.

2. Motivation und Entwurfsziele

Die Sprache GRADE will dem Programmierer vermitteln, daß das Erstellen
eines Programms der Konstruktion einer Maschine gleichkommt[1]. Die

---

[1] Entsprechend einer Forderung von N.Wirth /2/, Programmieren
nicht als Instruieren sondern als Konstruieren einer Maschine
aufzufassen.

GRADE-Sprache bildet dabei einen Vorrat an (im wesentlichen graphi=
schen) Konstruktionselementen, die in einer Konstruktionszeichung nach
den Regeln der Sprache zu der Beschreibung einer (rein sequentiell
arbeitenden) Maschine zusammengesetzt werden können.

Eine solche Konstruktionszeichung hat etwa folgendes Aussehen:

U R W   GRADE-SRVhcp V1.2   1983-12-13 16:35
        Element: ZUERI.WORDCOUNT;P

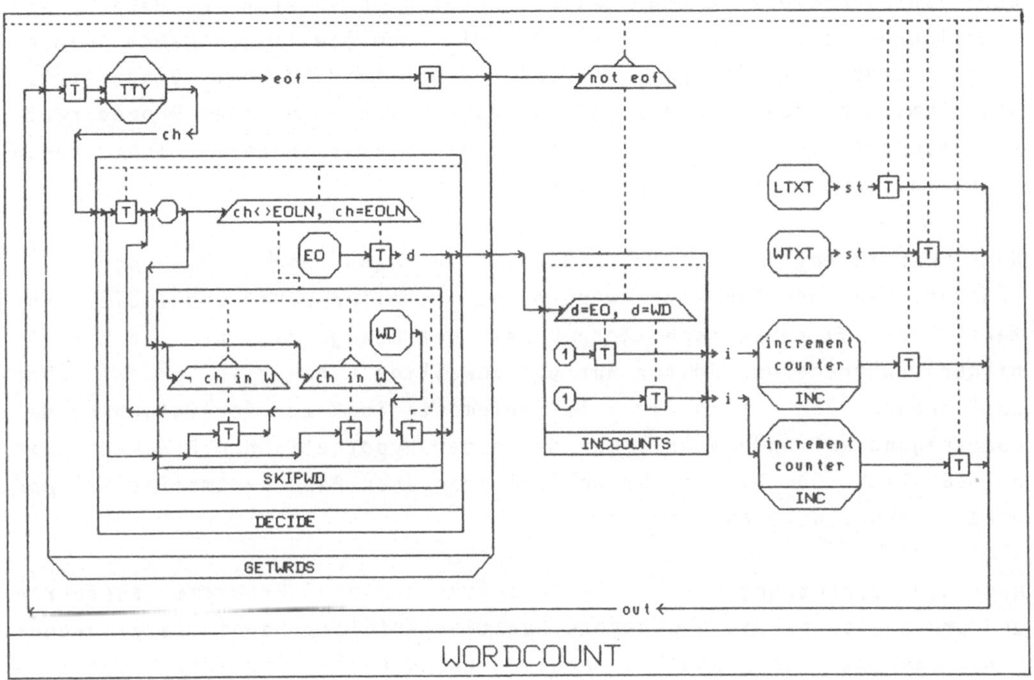

        type   ch=char; eof=bool; d=(EO,WD); out=equiv i=int, st=string end;
        const W(charset)=['A'..'Z','0'..'9','_']; LTXT(st)='lines: '; WTXT(st)='words: '

(Im Rahmen dieses Aufsatzes muß auf eine detaillierte Erläuterung der
Sprache GRADE verzichtet werden. Eine kurze Beschreibung der Bedeutun=
gen der wichtigsten Symbole findet sich im Anhang hinter dem Litera=
turverzeichnis. Der interessierte Leser sei ferner auf die Definition
der Sprache in /3/ verwiesen. Es sei noch erwähnt, daß hier und in den
folgenden Zeichnungen Speicher nicht als Kreise sondern als Achtecke
dargestellt sind.)

Der Programmierer stellt eine Konstruktionszeichnung (evtl. an Hand
von Skizzen auf Papier) direkt am graphischen Terminal her. Ein
sprachorientierter Editor stellt ihm die Symbole der GRADE-Sprache zur

Verfügung und prüft ihre syntaktisch korrekte Verwendung. Der graphi=
sche Bildschirm kann jedoch wegen seiner beschränkten Größe nicht das
gesamte Programm in einem Bild darstellen. Der Programmierer erstellt
sein Programm daher als Menge von benannten Einzelbildern, die eine
hierarchische Programmstruktur bilden.

Jedes Einzelbild ist dabei ein "Prozessor" oder "Speicher" im Sinne
der Sprache GRADE (in etwa der "Prozedur" bzw. der "Class" vergleich=
bar). Jedes Einzelbild kann beliebig häufig in anderen Bildern durch
Einzeichnen eines Referenzsymbols mit dem jeweiligen Namen "einge=
setzt" werden. (Im Beispiel ist INC zweimal in WORDCOUNT eingesetzt.)
Die Semantik des "Einsetzens" ist dabei nicht die eines Prozedurauf=
rufs sondern die der Makro-Ersetzung. Das Einsetzen darf nicht (auch
nicht indirekt) rekursiv erfolgen.

Nach Fertigstellung aller Einzelbilder kann ein GRADE-Programm in
ausführbaren Code übersetzt werden. Der Compiler prüft dabei die syn=
taktische und semantische Korrektheit der Bezüge zwischen den Einzel=
bildern (während der Editor nur das jeweilige Einzelbild prüft). Der
ausführbare Code ist in der Pilotimplementation -zur Vereinfachung der
Übertragung auf andere Anlagen- der einer hypothetischen Stack-Maschi=
ne (ähnlich dem P-Code für den übertragbaren PASCAL-Compiler/4/) und
wird interpretativ ausgeführt.

Nach der Übersetzung kann der Programmierer sein Programm ausführen
und prüfen, ob es die gewünschte Funktion erfüllt. Dabei ist zu beden=
ken, daß der konzeptuelle Abstand zwischen der (zweidimensionalen)
graphischen Programmkonstruktion und dem (linearen) ausführbaren Code
noch größer ist als bei den üblichen höheren Programmiersprachen, in
denen Programme ebenfalls eine im wesentlichen lineare Struktur besit=
zen. Informationen über die Programmausführung, die sich auf den aus=
geführten Code beziehen, sind daher vom Programmierer nur schwer in
Beziehung zu der ursprünglichen graphischen Darstellung zu bringen.

Es wurde daher als notwendig erachtet, schon in die Grunkonzeption des
GRADE-Systems ein Überwachungsprogramm einzubeziehen, das es dem Pro=
grammierer erlaubt, die Ausführung seines Programms an Hand derjenigen
graphischen Darstellungen zu beobachten, die er selbst in das System
eingegeben hat. Dieses Überwachungsprogramm sollte die Idee des Pro=
gramms als einer konstruierten Maschine aufgreifen und dem Programmie=
rer die Ausführung seines Programms in Form einer Animation zeigen,

die das "Arbeiten" der von ihm konstruierten Maschine graphisch dar=
stellt.

Die Informationen, die eine solche Darstellung erfordert, entsprechen
im wesentlichen denen, die auch übliche höhersprachliche Trace- oder
Debug- Programme anbieten. Die Darstellung der Informationen in Form
einer Animation, in der das konstruierte Programm erkennbar "läuft",
macht es dem Programmierer jedoch leichter, die Funktion des Programms
zu beobachten und dabei Abweichungen von der angestrebten Funktion zu
erkennen. Durch das Ausnutzen der vom Programmierer eingegebenen Dar=
stellung wird zudem das Ziel erreicht, den Programmierer sowohl beim
Erstellen seines Programms als auch bei der Dokumentation (graphische
Hardcopy) und beim Testen mit der gleichen Sprache arbeiten zu lassen.

Zur Realisierung eines derartigen Überwachungsprogramms boten sich
zwei Verfahren an:

  (1) Eine interpretative Ausführung der gespeicherten
       Konstruktionszeichungen.
  (2) Eine Rückabbildung des ausgeführten Codes in die
       Konstruktionszeichungen des Programmierers.

Eine interpretative Ausführung bietet zwei Vorteile: Sie läßt sich zum
einen leichter realisieren, da alle graphischen Informationen direkt
zugänglich sind, sie entlastet auch den Compiler von der Erzeugung von
Zusatzinformationen für die Rückabbildung. Sie erlaubt zum anderen das
Ändern des Programms während der Programmausführung, d.h. ein schnel=
les Reagieren des Programmierers auf erkannte Fehler.

Die Rückabbildung ist aufwendiger, sie erlaubt auch kein direktes
Eingreifen in das ausgeführte Programm, da damit ein erneuter Überset=
zungsvorgang notwendig wird. Ihr einer Vorteil ist jedoch, daß derje=
nige Code ausgewertet und geprüft wird, der auch bei einem Anwendungs=
einsatz des Programms zur Ausfuehrung kommt, so daß also auch Fehler
erkannt werden, die vom Compiler oder vom Laufzeitsystem des ausge=
führten Programms hervorgerufen werden. Ihr zweiter Vorteil ist die
mögliche höhere Ausführungsgeschwindigkeit, die z.B. für das Über=
springen von bereits ausgetesteten, aber rechenzeitaufwendigen Pro=
grammteilen notwendig ist.

Da mit der GRADE-Pilotimplementation gezeigt werden sollte, daß diese graphische Sprache sich in vergleichbar effektiven Code wie PASCAL übersetzen läßt und sie daher auch in der Produktion einsetzbar ist, wurde für das Überwachungsprogramm der zweite Weg, die Rückabbildung, gewählt.

3. Leistungen der graphischen Darstellung

Die Darstellung der Programmausführung besitzt für den Programmierer einen räumlichen und einen zeitlichen Aspekt. Der räumliche Aspekt betrifft die Frage, welche Ausschnitte eines Programms in welchem Detaillierungsgrad dargestellt werden, der zeitliche Aspekt betrifft den Abstand zwischen zwei aufeinanderfolgenden Darstellungen der Pro= grammausführung, also die Feinheit der Zerlegung der Programmausfüh= rung in Einzelschritte. Beide Aspekte sind gut mit einer Lupenfunktion zu vergleichen, die der Programmierer anwenden können muß, um gezielt bestimmte Programmteile zu beobachten, andere jedoch nur in groben Zügen zu sehen oder sogar zu ignorieren.

3.1 Der räumliche Aspekt

Dem Programmierer sollte sein Programm als Gesamtkonstruktion bewußt sein, d.h. als eine hierarchische Struktur der erstellten Einzel= bilder. Ein entsprechendes Gesamtbild darzustellen ist jedoch aus zwei Gründen nicht möglich. Zum einen ist der Rechenaufwand sehr hoch, der nötig ist, aus den beim Editieren erzeugten Einzelbildern ein optisch ansprechendes Gesamtbild zu erzeugen, in dem der Programmierer auch die von ihm erzeugte Struktur wiedererkennt. Zum anderen ist die Auf= lösung selbst hochwertiger Graphikbildschirme zu gering, um bei größe= ren Programmen noch eine Erkennbarkeit der Details zu gewährleisten.

Um die Gesamtstruktur zu überblicken, wird dem Programmierer daher eine Darstellung angeboten, in der nur die Namen der Einzelbilder sowie ihre Schachtelung ineinander dargestellt sind. Diese (reine Text-) Darstellung dient zum einen der Auswahl von Einzelbildern, die genauer untersucht werden sollen, zum anderen der Angabe von Parame= tern, die für jedes Bild die Art der zeitlichen Auflösung seiner Dar= stellung definieren (s.u.).

```
Beispiel:        WORDCOUNT;P            (Wurzelprozessor)
                  GETWRDS;S            (Speicher in WORDCOUNT)
                   DECIDE;P            (Prozessor in GETWRDS)
                    SKIPWD;P           (Prozessor in DECIDE)
                INCCOUNTS;P            (Prozessor in WORDCOUNT)
                   INC;S (1)           (Speicher in WORDCOUNT)
                   INC;S (2)           (Speicher in WORDCOUNT)
```

Die Auswahl eines Bildes erlaubt es dann, dieses Bild zu "vergrößern",
d.h. die zugehörige graphische Darstellung des Bildes auf dem Bild=
schirm erscheinen zu lassen. Durch entsprechende Kommandos kann der
Programmierer dann auch in der Programmhierarchie "wandern", d.h. ein
inneres Bild (von WORDCOUNT z.B. GETWRDS) oder ein äußeres Bild aus=
wählen.

Auf einer dritten Verfeinerungsebene schließlich kann sich der Pro=
grammierer die Inhalte der Speicher-Komponenten eines Bildes zeigen
lassen. Er kann dazu mit einem Cursor eine Komponente anwählen und
sich deren Inhalt ausgeben lassen. Das entspricht der Ausgabe von
Variablenwerten durch ein höhersprachliches Debug-Programm. Die Ausga=
be von Daten erfolgt entsprechend des jeweiligen Datentyps, in der
Pilotimplementation jedoch nur fuer einfache Datentypen. Der Program=
mierer kann nach dem Anwählen einer Komponente zudem auch andere Arten
angeben, in der deren Inhalt dargestellt werden soll.

3.2 Der zeitliche Aspekt

Der zeitliche Aspekt ist die Auflösung der Programmausführung in Ein=
zelschritte. Vier Verfeinerungsebenen werden hier angeboten:

  (0) Ein Einzelschritt ist die Ausführung des gesamten
      Programms. Dabei erfolgt keine Darstellung der Aus=
      führung, die Ausführungsgeschwindigkeit ist iden=
      tisch mit der Ausführung ohne Überwachung. Im Falle
      eines Fehlers wird das Programm jedoch angehalten und
      der Programmierer erhält die Möglichkeit, dessen
      momentanen Zustand (räumlich) zu inspizieren.

  (1) Ein Einzelschritt ist die Ausführung eines Bildes.
      Dabei wird bei jedem ersten Ansprechen eines Bildes

dessen Name ausgegeben, jedoch keine weitere Infor=
mation.

(2) Ein Einzelschritt ist die Aktivierung eines Prozessors
(das entspricht der Ausführung einer Anweisung).
Dabei wird das jeweilige Bild dargestellt und der
aktivierte Prozessor darin durch Aufleuchten der Akti=
vierungsleitung zu ihm gekennzeichnet. Wiederholtes
Aktivieren des gleichen Prozessors in einem Bild wird
durch einen zugeordneten Zähler angezeigt.

(3) Ein Einzelschritt ist die Aktivierung eines Daten=
transports (das entspricht dem Zugriff auf eine Va=
riable oder einer Parameterversorgung). Zusätzlich
zur Aktivierung wird hier die jeweils benutzte Daten=
leitung durch Aufleuchten gekennzeichnet und das
transportierte Datum ausgegeben. Wiederholtes Trans=
portieren auf einer Datenleitung wird ebenfalls durch
einen Zähler angezeigt.

Wählt der Programmierer zur Ausführung die Ebene 0, so ist ihm keine
Verfeinerung (d.h. genauere Darstellung der Ausführung) bei einzelnen
Elementen möglich. Er kann jedoch das Programm unterbrechen und dann
eine andere Verfeinerungsebene wählen.

Wählt der Programmierer für die Ausführung eine der Ebenen 1 bis 3, so
kann er die Elemente der Programmstruktur einzeln mit Parametern ver=
sehen, die festlegen, welche Verfeinerungsebene jeweils für sie zu
wählen ist. Auf diese Weise kann er Elemente von der Darstellung aus=
schließen (Ebene 0), nur ihren Namen angeben lassen (1) oder ihre
Ausführung graphisch in den jeweiligen Bildern darstellen lassen (2
und 3). Auch hierbei kann der Programmierer die Ausführung unterbre=
chen und das Programm inspizieren oder Parameter ändern. Auch ein
schrittweises Ausführen ist möglich, wobei die Bedeutung eines Einzel=
schritts durch die gültige Verfeinerungsebene definiert wird.

Beispiele:

Eine Ausführung könnte auf Ebene 1 folgendermaßen aussehen:

```
            WORDCOUNT;P
             GETWRDS;S
     *         DECIDE;P
              SKIPWD;P
           INCCOUNTS;P
           INC;S (1)
           INC;S (2)
```

Der Stern links der Namen zeigt das jeweils ausgeführte Bild an, im
Beispiel ist es also der Prozessor DECIDE.

Auf Ebene 2 würde z.B. in DECIDE die Aktivierung der Prozessoren fol=
gendermaßen dargestellt:

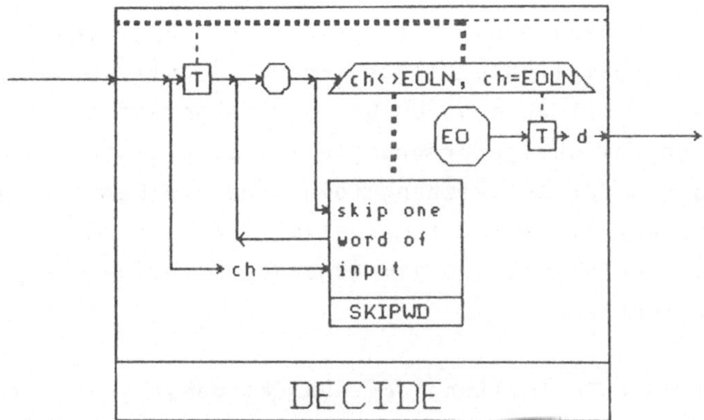

Auf Ebene 3 würden zusätzlich zur Aktivierung von Prozessoren die
Datentransporte dargestellt:

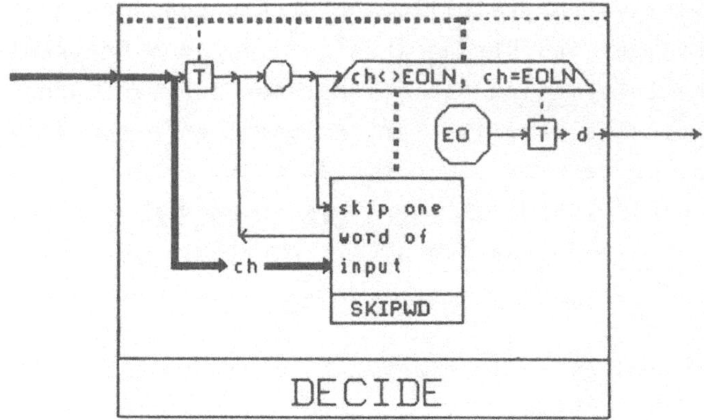

4. Methoden und Konzepte der Realisierung

Zwei Zielsetzungen bestimmten die Wahl der Methoden und Konzepte für die Realisierung des Überwachers:

Zum einen sollte der Objektcode möglichst frei von Zusätzen für die Überwachung bleiben. Damit sollte erreicht werden, daß für den Test und für die Anwendung eines Programms nur eine, überwachbare, Version des Objektcode benutzt wird, und nicht aus Effizienzgründen bei der Anwendung eine andere, nicht mehr überwachbare Version zum Einsatz kommt.

Zum anderen sollte die Ausführungsgeschwindigkeit eines Programms dem Detaillierungsgrad seiner Darstellung entsprechen. Die Ausführungsge= schwindigkeit des Codes von nicht darzustellenden Bildern (Ebene 0) sollte durch die Überwachung möglichst nicht beeinträchtigt werden, durch Namen darzustellende Bilder (Ebene 1) sollten nur mit geringer Verzögerung ausgeführt werden, um bereits ausgetestete oder für eine bestimmte Frage unwichtige Programmteile schnell überspringen zu kön= nen. Darstellungen der Aktivierungsfolge und der Datentransporte (Ebe= nen 2 und 3) dagegen müssen mit wesentlich verlangsamter Ausführungs= geschwindigkeit erfolgen, um vom Auge des Programmierers leicht ver= folgt werden zu können.

Das erste Ziel, die Freihaltung des Objektcodes von Daten für den Überwacher, kann durch die bekannte Methode des Ablegens der Überwa= cherinformationen in einer eigenen Datei, zusätzlich zum Objektcode, verwirklicht werden. In einer derartigen Datei befinden sich i.A. die Symbole des Quellcodes, ihre zugehörigen Adressen im Objektcode sowie evtl. Informationen über Art und Typ der Symbole. Das reicht für die an das GRADE-Pilotsystem gestellten Anforderungen jedoch nicht aus, da ja zu Darstellung der Ausführung in einem Bild des Programms die ge= samte graphische Information des Bildaufbaus zur Verfügung stehen muß. Es ist auch nicht sinnvoll, hierfür lediglich einen Verweis auf die Datei abzulegen, in der das vom Programmierer erzeugte Bild gespei= chert ist. Dieses Bild dürfte damit ja nicht mehr verändert oder ge= löscht werden, um die Überwachungsmöglichkeiten nicht zu beeinträchti= gen.

Im GRADE-System wird daher in einer Zusatz-Datei, hier "Display Datei" genannt, durch den Compiler die gesamte Bild- und damit Struktur-

Information eines übersetzten Programms abgelegt. Der Compiler über=
setzt ein Programm in einem Durchgang (one pass). Er erzeugt die
Display Datei, indem er den eingelesenen Quellcode, der auch die Bild=
informationen enthält, einfach in die Display Datei kopiert und dabei
die bei der Codeerzeugung berechneten Adressen von Datenbereichen oder
Codeabschnitten einfügt. Auf diese Weise entsteht eine Datei, die alle
(auch für etwaige spätere Ausbaustufen) notwendigen Informationen für
eine graphische Ausführungsdarstellung enthält. Da die Bildinformation
in ihr im wesentlichen wie im Quellcode abgelegt ist, läßt sie sich
auch gut mit schon vorhandenen Algorithmen und Routinen der Bilddar=
stellung bearbeiten.

Die Display Datei erfüllt schon einige der Anforderungen an den Über=
wacher. Die Verbindung zwischen ihr und dem ausführbaren Code kann
hergestellt werden, indem in der Display Datei nach den vom Compiler
dort abgelegten Adressen gesucht wird. Der momentane Zustand eines
(unterbrochenen) Programms kann auf folgende Weise dargestellt werden:

An Hand der aktuellen Codeadresse wird das zugehörige Bild gesucht und
mit Hilfe der dort gespeicherten Datenadressen sein momentaner Zustand
ausgegeben. Über die statische Programmschachtelung (ebenfalls der
Display Datei entnehmbar) und die dynamische Aufrufschachtelung
(Keller der Rücksprungadressen) lassen sich auch die zum Unterbre=
chungszeitpunkt "aktiven" Bilder auffinden und auf die gleiche Weise
darstellen. Die Display Datei erlaubt zudem ein schrittweises Vorgehen
in den Verfeinerungsstufen 2 (Aktivierungsfolge) und 3 (Datentrans=
porte). Dabei wird durch das Überwachungsprogramm jeweils an den (oder
die) folgenden Aufsetzpunkt(e) im Code ein Unterbrechungsbefehl ge=
setzt und nach Erreichen die zugehörige Stelle in der graphischen
Darstellung markiert. Die dazu notwendige Analyse der Display Datei
erfordert auf langsamen Rechnern so viel Zeit, daß keine zusätzliche
Verlangsamung der Ausführung notwendig ist, auf schnellen Rechnern
sollte sie jedoch vorgesehen werden, um die Ausführungsgeschwindigkeit
der optischen Aufnahmefähigkeit des Programmierers anzupassen.

Die Display Datei allein ist jedoch in zweierlei Hinsicht für die
Überwachung ungeeignet. Zum einen erfordert das Suchen nach einem zu
einer Programmadresse gehörigen Bild bei großen Programmen u.U. sehr
viel Zeit. Zum anderen wird auch die schnelle Ausführung von Bildern
(ohne Darstellung oder mit Darstellung nur des Namens) nicht unter=
stützt. Hierfür wurden zwei zusätzliche Maßnahmen ergriffen.

Zum einen werden vom Compiler an den Stellen des Objektcodes, die den Einstieg in ein neues Bild oder das Verlassen eines Bildes bedeuten, spezielle Befehle abgelegt. Diese Befehle besitzen keine Parameter und sind die einzige Ergänzung des Objektcodes um Überwacher-spezifische Daten. Sie sind wirkungslos, wenn keine Überwachung erfolgt und führen bei eingeschalteter Überwachung zu einer Programmunterbrechung.

Zum anderen wird vom Compiler zusätzlich zur Display Datei eine Index Datei angelegt, die Querverweise zwischen dem Code und der Display Datei enthält. In ihr sind in aufsteigender Reihenfolge diejenigen Codeadressen eingetragen, die einen Einstieg in ein neues Bild bedeu= ten. Zu diesen Adressen ist ein Index in den zugehörigen Teil der Display Datei abgelegt, der Name des jeweiligen Bildes, die Anfangs= adresse der Bildinformation in der Display Datei sowie die vom Pro= grammierer angegebene, für die Darstellung des Bildes zu verwendende Verfeinerungsstufe.

Über die Index Datei kann der Überwacher nun schnell auf die Display Datei zugreifen, sie erlaubt ihm zudem die Ausgabe der Namen von Bil= dern ohne die Display Datei überhaupt anzusprechen. Der Zugriff auf die Index Datei ist schnell, da in ihr eine binäre Suche nach der Programmadresse möglich ist und sie wegen ihrer geringen Größe ganz oder zu großen Teilen im Speicher gehalten werden kann.

5. Einschränkungen und Anwendbarkeit für Textsprachen

Das insoweit beschriebene Verfahren geht von einem Compiler aus, der direkt ausführbaren, d.h. schon gebundenen und absolut adressierten Code erzeugt. Das ist der Fall in der Pilotimplementation. Das Verfah= ren läßt sich jedoch auch für ein getrenntes Übersetzen und Binden anwenden. Dabei kann der Compiler dann nur Display Dateien mit relati= ven Adressen erzeugen, erst beim Binden wird dazu die Index Datei angelegt.

Das beschriebene Verfahren berücksichtigt zudem weder Overlay-Techni= ken noch die Optimierung von Code. Auf die Behandlung von Overlay-Techniken wurde in der Erwartung verzichtet, daß die großen Adress= räume, die heute bereits in Mikroprozessoren angeboten werden, diese Technik langfristig überflüssig machen. Das Problem der möglichen Ungültigkeit der Darstellung bei optimiertem Code entspricht dem übli=

cher höherer Sprachen, Lösungsmöglichkeiten dafür werden z.B. in /5/
diskutiert.

Die Anwendbarkeit des Verfahrens für übliche höhere Textsprachen ist
im Prinzip gegeben, jedoch treten insbesondere bezüglich der Darstel=
lung Probleme auf, die durch die speziellen Eigenschaften der Sprache
GRADE vermieden werden:

(1)   Die Programme der Sprache GRADE besitzen eine statische
        Struktur, die eine eindeutige Zuordnung von Codeab=
        schnitten zu Quellprogrammabschnitten erlaubt. Für Spra=
        chen, die eine dynamische Änderung der Programmstruktur
        erlauben (Rekursion, Pointer), müßten die Darstellungs=
        methoden erweitert werden.

(2)   Die darzustellenden Bilder sind in GRADE durch den Pro=
        grammierer definiert, während in Textsprachen Ausschnit=
        te durch den Überwacher gewählt werden müßten, da Routi=
        nen länger als eine Bildschirmseite seien können. Hierzu
        wäre eine spezielle Verschiebe- oder Auswahlfunktion
        notwendig.

(3)   Sprünge oder Zugriffe zu Variablen können in Textpro=
        grammen zu häufigen Wechseln des Bildausschnitts auch
        innerhalb einer Routine führen und die Darstellung op=
        tisch schwer verfolgbar machen. Hier könnten Fenster-
        Techniken eingesetzt werden, die z.B. gleichzeitig zum
        einen die Deklaration von Variablen und zum anderen die
        Anweisungen einer Routine zeigen.

Literatur

1. Sengler, H.E.: Programmieren mit graphischen Mitteln: Die Sprache
   GRADE und ihre Implementation, in: H.Woessner(Hrsg.): Programmier=
   sprachen und Programmentwicklung, Informatik Fachberichte 53,
   Springer,Berlin 1982, S.67-92

2. Wirth, N.: Programming Languages: What to Demand and How to Assess
   Them, Report 17, ETH Zuerich, Institut fuer Informatik, Maerz 1976

3. Sengler, H.E.: Ein Modell des Verstehens von Programmen und seine
   Anwendung beim Entwurf der Programmiersprache GRADE, Dissertation
   Univ. Hamburg, (in Veroeffentlichung, vorauss. Jan.84)

4. Nori, K.V., Amman, U., Jensen, K., Naegeli, H.H.: The PASCAL
   P-Compiler: Implementation Notes, Report 10, ETH Zuerich,
   Institut fuer Informatik, Dezember 1974

5. Hennessy, J.: Symbolic Debugging of Optimized Code, ACM Transactions on Progr. Languages and Systems, Vol 4(82)3, S.323-344

Anhang

Überblick über die Konstruktionselemente in GRADE:

⟶ d ⟶   Datenleitung, kann Daten vom Typ d transportieren.

                        Aktivierungsleitung, überträgt einen Aktivierungs=
                        impuls (sequentielle Aktivierung) von links nach
                        rechts, nacheinander an die unten angeschlossenen
                        Prozessoren.

□   Prozessor allgemein (Operation/Prozedur)

T   Transportprozessor (Zuweisung)

⟨E1, E2,...,En⟩   Verzweigung (guarded command IF)

⟨E1, E2,...,En⟩   Wiederholung (guarded command DO)

⬡   Speicher allgemein (Variable/Class)

①   Speicher (Variable) mit Vorbesetzung 1

Objektorientierte Systementwicklung:
Einfluss auf die Projektorganisation

Barbara Mergler

Institut für Informatik
der Universität Zürich

Zusammenfassung

Es wird gezeigt, auf welche Art eine objektorientierte Systementwicklung die Projektorganisation von Softwaresystemen beeinflussen kann. Dazu teilen wir die in einem Softwaresystem existierenden Objekte in vier Hierarchiestufen ein. Die drei unteren Ebenen entsprechen allgemein verwendbaren Objekten (z.B. Zeichen, FIFO-Strukturen, Datenbanken). Die vierte Stufe bilden Objekte, die speziell für einzelne Applikationen notwendig sind (z.B. Inventarliste, Belegungsplan). Eine ähnliche Klassifizierung finden wir bei der Gliederung von Komponenten, welche für die industrielle Einzelfertigung verwendet werden.

Das objektorientierte Vorgehen in der Systementwicklung ermöglicht die Änderung der Organisationsstruktur einer Softwareabteilung, weil eine neue Gliederung der Aufgaben vorgenommen werden kann. Die Aufgabenteilung erfolgt nicht mehr entsprechend der Projekthierarchie von oben nach unten, sondern die Aufgaben werden so zugewiesen, dass einzelne Gruppen für bestimmte autonome Teile eines Softwaresystems verantwortlich sind. So wird ein besserer Einsatz des Personals und anderer Ressourcen erreicht.

Da die vorgeschlagene Projektorganistion mit dem Organisationsaufbau für die industrielle Einzelfertigung grosse Ähnlichkeit hat, können wir die Planungs-, Führungs und Kontrollmechanismen aus diesem betriebswirtschaftlichen Bereich auf die Softwareproduktion übertragen.

1. Einleitung

Probleme, die heute häufig im Zusammenhang mit der Systementwicklung von EDV-Projekten genannt werden, sind z.B. Terminschwierigkeiten, unstrukturiertes Vorgehen bei der Projektabwicklung, Unzuverlässigkeit der Software, Probleme bei der Wartung etc. All diese angesprochenen Schwierigkeiten stehen in engem Zusammenhang mit der Projektorganisation. Dabei hat die Art und Weise der Programmentwicklung bedeutenden Einfluss auf die Organisation solcher Software-Projekte. Unter *Systementwicklung* versteht man allgemein die Gestaltung eines Softwaresystems. Wir meinen hier vor allem die *Programmerstellung*.

Das Ziel dieser Arbeit ist es, die Auswirkungen eines objektorientierten Vorgehens in der Systementwicklung auf die Projektorganisation darzustellen. Dazu werden wir Teile eines Softwaresystems (z.B. Programmteile, Unterprogramme) mit den gleichen Organisationsmethoden in Verbindung bringen, die auch bei Produkten Anwendung finden, die in industrieller Einzelfertigung hergestellt werden. Bei der Organisation "objektorientierter Softwaresysteme" können bewährte Methoden aus der Industriebetriebswirtschaftslehre (IBWL) auf die Planung und Herstellung von Softwaresystemen übertragen werden.

Wir beginnen mit der Erklärung, was unter objektorientiertem Vorgehen, bzw. dem objektorientierten Ansatz in der Systementwicklung zu verstehen ist. Die Definition und Entstehung des Objekt-Begriffes wird in Abschnitt 2 beschrieben. Eine mögliche Klassifizierung der Objekte, die in Softwaresystemen existieren, versuchen wir in Abschnitt 3 vorzunehmen. In Abschnitt 4 werden die heute übliche Projektorganisation und die von uns vorgeschlagene, objektorientierte Projektorganisation erläutert und einander gegenübergestellt.

2. Entstehung und bisherige Entwicklung des objektorientierten Ansatzes

Die grundlegende Idee zu einem objektorientierten Aufbau von Software stammt aus der Programmiersprache SIMULA 67 [Dah-68]. SIMULA 67 wurde für Simulationszwecke entwickelt und stellt eine Erweiterung der Sprache ALGOL 60 [Nau-63] dar. Ausgang für die Ideen in SIMULA 67 war die Überlegung, dass eine Simulation komplexe Einheiten (Prozesse) umfasst, die aus Datenstrukturen und Algorithmen bestehen. Zur Arbeitserleichterung führte man deshalb eine Verknüpfung dieser Daten und Algorithmen ein. Es wurde dafür der Begriff *Klasse* geprägt. Klassen ermöglichen, dass man diese komplexen Einheiten global verwenden kann, ohne sich auf die Bestandteile beziehen zu müssen. Ausser Klasse findet man in SIMULA auch den Begriff Objekt. Als *Objekte* werden die tatsächlichen Verwirklichungen einer Klasse bezeichnet. Die Begriffe Klasse und Objekt gehen weiter zurück auf die Bezeichnungen *Block* und *Blockeinheit* in ALGOL 60, sowie auf *Record Klasse* und *Record*, die von Hoare und Wirth [Hoa-68/Wir-66] eingeführt wurden. Ebenfalls neu war in SIMULA 67 das Konzept der Koroutinen bzw. der quasi-parallelen Verarbeitung von zwei oder mehreren Klassen.

Das Klassenkonzept von SIMULA 67 wird als Ursprung der *Datenabstraktion bzw. Datenkapseln* [Gut-77] oder des *information hiding* [Par-72] angesehen. Verschiedene Programmiersprachen haben diese Mechanismen als *Modul-Konzept* übernommen. Beispiele dafür sind Modula-2 [Wir-82] und Euclid [Lam-77] (*module*), Ada [Ada-82] (*package*), CLU [Lis-81] (*cluster*), ALPHARD [Wul-76] (*form*). Die Grundidee dieses Konzeptes ist, dass ein Modul eine Datenstruktur und eine Anzahl Operationen zur Bearbeitung dieser Datenstruktur zusammenfasst. Ausserdem sollen die internen Details des Moduls nach aussen verborgen bleiben. Diese Prinzipien werden von den einzelnen Sprachen unterschiedlich stark unterstützt. Euclid und Ada z.B. erlauben im Gegensatz zu Modula-2, dass ein Modul selbst als Typ verwendet werden darf. Somit können zur Laufzeit mehrere Exemplare dieses Moduls kreiert werden. Ein wichtiger Bestandteil des Modulkonzeptes ist die Schnittstelle zwischen den Modulen, d.h. wie zwischen den Modulen der Datenaustausch geregelt wird. Dazu wurden, je nach Sprache, unterschiedliche Lösungen eingeführt.

Bei den Konzepten und dem Entwurf einer Programmiersprache werden konkrete Ziele verfolgt, und es wird ein bestimmtes Anwendungsgebiet ins Auge gefasst. SIMULA 67 soll Simulationen unterstützen, ALPHARD und CLU sind experimentielle Sprachen. Ada und auch Modula-2 werden als *general-purpose-languages* vorgestellt. Allgemein gesprochen steht es jedem Programmierer offen, mit welcher Sprache er arbeiten will. Probleme werden leichter und sinnvoller gelöst, wenn dazu eine Sprache gewählt wird, die der Problemstellung möglichst viel Unterstützung gewährt.

Alle bisher angesprochenen Konzepte versucht man beim objektorientierten Ansatz zu integrieren. Mittlerweile ist die objektorientierte Programmierung bereits zu einem Schlagwort geworden. Leider findet man selten eine präzise Definition [Sto-83]. Wir geben hier keine neue Definition, wollen aber kurz aufzeigen, wie es zu dem Begriff *objektorientierte Programmierung* bzw. *objektorientierter Ansatz* gekommen ist.

In der Informatik wird vieles als Objekt bezeichnet. Deshalb hat man meistens nur eine vage Vorstellung von der genauen Bedeutung des eigentlich Gemeinten. Es ist einfacher und fördert meistens das Verständnis, einen neuen Denkansatz mit etwas Ähnlichem, Vertrautem in Verbindung zu bringen. So lag bei den *Objekten* das *Modul* als Verbindungsglied nahe. Es scheint jedoch nicht sinnvoll, zu fragen, wo jetzt genau der Unterschied liegt. Vielmehr sollen die Prinzipien der objektorientierten Programmierung seperat betrachtet werden. Die Entwicklung dieser Denkweise lässt sich seit über 10 Jahren verfolgen [Byte-81/War-79/Gol-77]. Selbstverständlich haben dabei auch andere Sprachentwicklungen mit ihren Konzepten Einfluss ausgeübt, ebenso wie die Forschung auf dem Gebiet der Computerarchitektur (z.B. Intel-iapx432 [Org-83]) und der Betriebssysteme (z.B. Hydra [Wul-81]). Heute versucht man sogar, andere Programmiersprachen auf ihre Tauglichkeit zum objektorientierten Programmieren zu beurteilen. Man kann mit vielen Sprachen, mehr oder weniger gut, die Prinzipien des objektorientierten Ansatzes nachvollziehen [Sto-83/Ren-82].

Als Basis des objektorientierten Programmierens kann man sicher Smalltalk nennen. Der Begriff *objektorientiert* tauchte dort zum ersten mal auf. Im Gegensatz zu SIMULA 67, oder anderen teilweise objektorientierten Sprachen, ist Smalltalk-80 ein komplettes objektorientiertes Programmiersystem, d.h. eine objektorientierte Programmiersprache und eine objektorientierte Programmierumgebung sind vorhanden.

Da Smalltalk-80 bisher das objektorientierte Entwickeln von Softwaresystemen am konsequentesten unterstützt, sollen kurz die Prinzipien von Smalltalk-80 als Beispiel erläutert werden. (Die Syntax der Beispiele entspricht nicht derjenigen von Smalltalk.) In der Einleitung des Buches Smalltalk-80 [Gol-83] findet man folgende Bemerkung: "Smalltalk basiert auf einigen wenigen Konzepten. Diese Konzepte können durch die Definition von 5 Worten vorgestellt werden, die zugleich das Smalltalk-Vokabular darstellen: *Objekt, Botschaft, Klasse, Exemplar, Methode.* Diese 5 Begriffe werden durch gegenseitige Bezugnahme definiert. Deshalb scheint es, als ob der Leser zuerst alles wissen muss, bevor er irgendetwas versteht."[1] Dieses Zitat klärt die Hauptschwierigkeit von Smalltalk: Womit soll man beginnen?

---

1. "Smalltalk is based on a small number of concepts .... These concepts are presented by defining the five words ... that make up the vocabulary of Smalltalk - object, message, class, instance, and method. These five words are defined in terms of each other, so it is almost as though the reader must know everything before knowing anything."

- *Objekte*

Unter einem *Objekt* kann man sich eine Gruppierung von Informationen vorstellen, zusammen mit der Beschreibung, wie diese Informationen behandelt werden sollen. Ein Objekt enthält somit z.B. Daten und Funktionen, die auf diese Daten angewendet werden können. Beispiele für Objekte sind Zahl, Zahlen, Zeichen, Zeichenketten, Warteschlangen, graphische Zeichnungen, Programme etc. Welche Operationen auf ein Objekt angewendet werden können, hängt von der Art des Objektes ab. Beispielsweise werden auf das Objekt Zahl die arithmetischen Verknüpfungen als Operationen angewendet. Für Zeichenketten ist das Vergleichen, Verlängern, Ändern etc. denkbar. Für den Typ FIFO (Warteschlange, first-in-first-out Struktur) muss ein Element hinzugefügt oder entfernt werden können. Ausserdem soll die Abfrage möglich sein, wieviele Elemente gerade in der Schlange gespeichert sind.

- *Methode*

Ähnlich der heute üblichen Bezeichnung Prozedur oder Funktion, wird für die Objekte der Begriff *Methode* verwendet. Eine Methode ist die Beschreibung wie eine Operation, die für ein bestimmtes Objekt definiert ist, ausgeführt wird. Ein Objekt besteht somit aus Informationen (z.B. Daten) und den Methoden, um diese Informationen (z.B. Daten) zu verarbeiten. Mit den Prozeduren und Funktionen haben die Methoden gemeinsam, dass sie aus einer Sequenz von Anweisungen bestehen, die von einem Prozessor verarbeitet werden. Im Gegensatz zu Prozeduren oder Funktionen aus herkömmlichen Programmiersprachen, kann aber eine Methode nicht direkt irgendeine andere Methode aufrufen, um von dieser aufgerufenen Methode das Weiterarbeiten zu verlangen. Methoden sind nur über ein Objekt ansprechbar und nicht als selbständige Einheit. Ein Objekt muss immer von aussen betrachtet werden. Man kann Objekte nur als Ganzes verwenden, nicht Einzelteile davon.

- *Botschaft*

Ein Objekt wird durch eine *Botschaft*[2] angesprochen. Die Botschaften haben eine zentrale Stellung in Smalltalk, da sie die einzige Möglichkeit für eine Kommunikation zwischen den Objekten untereinander bilden (bzw. auch zwischen dem Verwender und den Objekten). Ausschliesslich dem (Objekt-)Programmierer ist es möglich, für ein Objekt festzulegen, wie dieses Objekt auf bestimmte Botschaften reagieren soll, nicht dem Verwender eines Objektes. Eine Botschaft besteht aus

   — dem Namen des Empfängers (dh. eines Objektes),

   — einem oder mehreren Selektoren, die bestimmen, welche Methoden auf das Objekt
      angewendet werden sollen (d.h. Angabe des Methodennamens),

   — u.U. noch Argumenten für die Methoden.

---

2. Welche deutsche Übersetzung für *message* (bzw. die Wörter *instance* oder *incarnation*) verwendet werden soll, wird z.Z. noch heftig diskutiert. Wir entschieden uns für *Botschaft* (bzw. *Exemplar* und *Erzeugung*), da unserer Meinung nach dieser Begriff der eigentlichen Bedeutung am besten entspricht.

Das Senden einer Botschaft an ein bestimmtes Objekt aktiviert eine Methode, die für dieses Objekt definiert ist. Die *Aktivierung* einer Methode hat eine ähnliche Wirkung wie ein Prozeduraufruf (bzw. Funktionsaufruf). Bei einem Prozeduraufruf wird allein durch die Nennung des Namens der Prozedur bestimmt, welche Aktionen ausgeführt werden sollen. Deshalb ist nur eine Prozedur zu einem bestimmten Namen zulässig. Im Gegensatz dazu kann die gleiche Botschaft (d.h. der gleiche Selektor) an verschiedene Objekte gerichtet werden. Erst zusammen mit der Bezeichnung des Empfängerobjektes wird eindeutig, welche Methoden aktiviert werden sollen, d.h. gleiche Botschaften (Selektoren) können verschieden interpretiert werden.

So hat z.B. die Botschaft **add** beim Senden an das Objekt **Zahlen**[3] die Bedeutung, dass eine Zahl mit einer anderen Zahl summiert werden soll. Beim Senden der gleichen Botschaft **add** an das Objekt **Warteschlange**, muss der Warteschlange ein Element hinzugefügt werden. Die Methoden, die auf diese beiden Objekte (**Zahl** bzw. **Warteschlange**) angewendet werden, sind trotz gleicher Botschaft sicher verschieden. Nicht der Sender einer Botschaft entscheidet, welche Aktionen durch die Botschaft veranlasst werden, sondern der Empfänger. Die Botschaft **add** an das Objekt Warteschlange könnte z.B. folgendermassen aussehen: **Warteschlange add ElementNeu**. Damit wird das **ElementNeu** genannte Objekt an die Datenstruktur **Warteschlange** (ebenfalls ein Objekt) hinzugefügt.

Da durch den Aufruf einer Prozedur sofort bestimmt wird, welche Operationen ausgeführt werden, liegt die Kontrolle über die durchzuführenden Aktionen bei der aufrufenden Stelle. Mit dem Senden einer Botschaft wird die Kontrolle an das in der Botschaft bezeichnete Objekt übergeben. Die Interpretation der Botschaft wird ganz dem Empfängerobjekt überlassen. [Ren-82] bezeichnet diesen Gedanken der "Kontrollaufgabe" als *call-by-desire*.

● *Klasse / Exemplar*

Es wäre sehr unpraktisch, wenn tatsächlich jedes einzelne Objekt samt seinen Methoden beschrieben werden müsste, z.B. jede einzelne ganze Zahl mit allen ihren arithmetischen Operationen (d.h. den Methoden). Deshalb wird bestimmten Objekten eine sogenannte *Klasse* übergeordnet. Die Klasse ist eine logische Beschreibung von einer Gruppe einzelner, ähnlicher Objekte, die als *Exemplare* dieser Klasse bezeichnet werden. Mit der Beschreibung einer Klasse existieren noch keine einzelnen Objekte aus dieser Klasse, erst durch eine Erzeugung werden Objekte gebildet (siehe dazu weiter unten: Erzeugung). Mit der *Klassenbeschreibung* wird ein Schema zur Bildung von Objekten dieser Klasse deklariert.

---

3. Die Operation ˝3 plus 4˝ wäre in Smalltalk-Notation 3 + 4. Das Beispiel mit **add** wurde nur zur Verdeutlichung gewählt.

Die Klassenbeschreibung enthält

— den Namen der Klasse,

— den internen Aufbau der Objekte dieser Klasse (Variablen der Klasse bzw. der Exemplare),

— eine Beschreibung aller Methoden, die auf Objekte dieser Klasse angewendet werden können.

Nehmen wir als Beispiel die Klasse Datum. Hier gibt es, ebenso wie bei den ganzen Zahlen, eine grosse Anzahl einzelner Objekte, die man beschreiben müsste.

```
Name              Datum
Interner Aufbau   tag        <nat.Zahl | 1..31>
                  monat      <nat.Zahl | 1..12>
                  jahr       <nat.Zahl>
Methoden          neuesDatum <Datum,Diff>        (Datum plus/minus Tage)
                  tagesDiff <Datum1,Datum2>      (Anzahl Tage zwischen zwei Daten)
                  wochentag <Datum>              (Wochentagsbezeichnung eines Datums)
                  heute                          (heutiges Datum)
                  etc.
```

Abb.1 Beschreibung der Klasse Datum

Jedes einzelne Datum ist ein Exemplar aus dieser Klasse. Alle Exemplare arbeiten mit denselben Methoden und den gleichen Variablen, wobei aber jedes Exemplar seine private Ausprägung der Variablen besitzt[4].

Nach unserer Definition eines Objektes, ist eine Klasse auch selbst ein Objekt, weil sie ja sowohl aus der Beschreibung von Methoden besteht als auch aus den Informationen, auf die diese Methoden angewendet werden. Da eine Klasse eine Menge ähnlicher Objekte beschreibt, und da eine Klasse selbst ebenfalls ein Objekt ist, kann eine Klasse auch mehreren Klassen übergeordnet sein. In diesem Fall sind die Exemplare einer Klasse wieder Klassen und es werden Methoden beschrieben, die auf diese Klassen angewendet werden können.

Diese Gliederung der Objekte entspricht einem strengen hierarchischen Aufbau. Jeder Klasse ist immer nur einer Klasse (ihre Superklasse) übergeordnet. Eine Klasse erbt von ihrer Superklasse jeweils die Methodenbeschreibungen. Die oberste Stufe bildet die Klasse mit dem Namen object.

---

4. *Gleiche* Variablen bedeutet nicht *dieselben* Variablen. Als Illustration dient folgendes Beispiel: Zwei Fahrzeughalter fahren das *gleiche* Auto, 2 rote VW-Käfer, jedes Auto hat aber eine andere (seine eigene) Fahrzeugnummer. Bei *demselben* Auto, würde es sich um ein einziges Auto (ein-und-dasselbe) handeln. Andererseits benutzen beide Fahrzeughalter *dieselbe* Methode zum Starten der PKWs. Die Methode existiert also nur einmal, und jeder der sie benutzen will, kann sie verwenden.

Die Klasse **object** ist wie viele andere Objektbeschreibungen ebenfalls Bestandteil des Smalltalk-80 Systems. Diese Klasse **object** entspricht der Wurzel des Baumes. Alle anderen Klassen werden von dieser Wurzel abgeleitet und erben die dort beschriebenen Methoden.

Das Konzept der Vererbung findet man im Klassenkonzept von SIMULA 67 in ähnlicher Form. In Smalltalk-72 existiert der hierarchische Zusammenhang der einzelnen Klassen über mehrere Stufen noch nicht. In dieser Smalltalk Version sind Klassen auch keine Objekte. Erst in Smalltalk-74 wurden Klassenbeschreibungen als Objekte eingeführt. Aus dem Klassenkonzept von SIMULA 67 wurde die Möglichkeit übernommen, Klassen und Superklassen nicht nur im Teilmenge - Gesamtmenge Zusammenhang zu sehen (analytisches Vorgehen), sondern eine Klasse kann auch zusätzliche Eigenschaften gegenüber ihrer Superklasse besitzen (synthetische Beziehung). Die zentrale Betrachtung, dass alle Elemente eines Systems aus Objekten bestehen, wurde mit Smalltalk-76 möglich, indem dort zwischen den Klassen eine Beziehung hergestellt werden kann [Kras—83].

Klassenname	**Käfer**
Superklasse	**VW**
Variablen der Exemplare	**baujahr, ps, fahrgestellnummer**
Botschaften und Methoden	
methode1 **methode2** **methode3**	

Abb.2 Beispiel für ein Klassenschema

Die Abbildung 2 zeigt das Muster eines Klassenschemas. In der Abbildung 3 wird ein hierarchisches System dargestellt. Alle Rechtecke entsprechen Klassen. Die Exemplare einer Klasse sind als Ovale eingezeichnet.

● *Erzeugung*

Das Bilden eines Exemplares kann z.B. durch das Senden einer bestimmten Botschaft an eine Klasse erfolgen. Diesen Vorgang nennen wir die *Erzeugung* eines Objektes. Dabei werden alle Eigenschaften der Klasse an dieses Exemplar vererbt (z.B. Datenstrukturen und Methoden). Die meisten Klassen in Smalltalk erzeugen beim Erhalten der Botschaft **new** ein neues Exemplar. Es existieren aber auch Klassen, die als Antwort auf andere Botschaften ein neues Exemplar bilden. Die Klasse Datum antwortet z.B. auf die Botschaft **heute** mit der Kreation eines Exemplares, welches das heutige Datum repräsentiert.

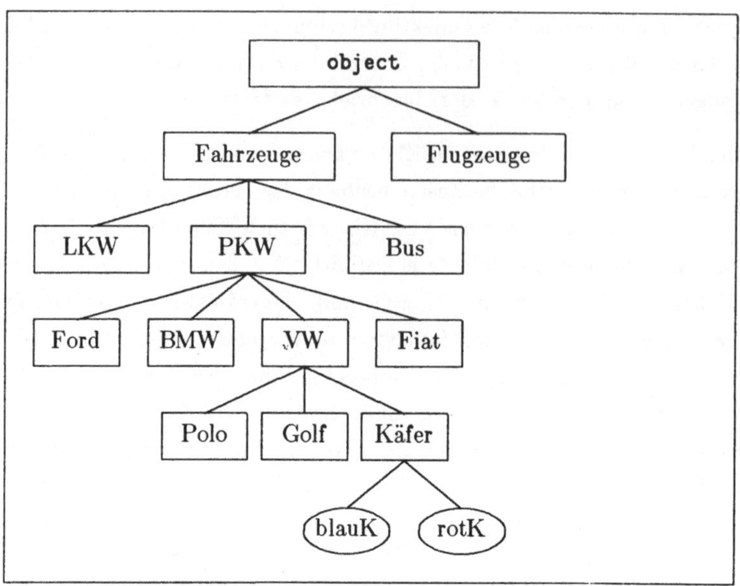

Abb.3 Aufbau einer Klassenhierarchie

3. Objekte als Komponenten eines Software-Systems

Nach einer Einführung in die Theorie der objektorientierten Software beschäftigen wir uns nun mit der Anwendung von Objekten und bilden eine Klassifizierung der Objekte, die als Komponenten in einem Softwaresystem vorkommen.

● *Elementarobjekte*

Auf der untersten Stufe der Objekthierarchie finden wir Objekte, die nicht mehr aus anderen Objekten aufgebaut sind. Diese Objekte haben keine Subklassen-Beziehung, sondern nur Verbindungen zu ihrer Superklasse. Beispiele dafür sind ganze und reelle Zahlen, Zeichen, logische Werte etc. Solche Objekte nennen wir *Elementarobjekte.* In einer objektorientierten Programmiersprache sind derartige Elementarobjekte durch die Sprache vorgegeben. Die Methoden, welche auf die Elementarobjekte angewendet werden können, sind ebenfalls durch die Programmiersprache gegeben (z.B. Vergleiche, arithmetische Operationen auf Zahlen, logische Operationen auf logische Werte etc.).

● *Standardobjekte*

Die nächste (zweite) Stufe umfasst die von uns als *Standardobjekte* bezeichneten Objekte. Standardobjekte sind einfache, allgemein anwendbare Objekte. Sie werden als Bestandteil in vielen höheren Objekten verwendet. Beispiele sind LIFO-Strukturen (Stack, Keller), FIFO-Strukturen (Queue, Warteschlange), Baumstrukturen, Tabellen, Zeichenketten, Dateien auf einfacher Stufe (sequentielle, dirckte, index-sequentielle), Tagesdatum. Zu allen Standardobjekten sind natürlich die dazugehörenden Methoden definiert. Ein Beispiel für ein Standardobjekt, das vielleicht weniger als solches erkannt wird, ist ein Feld auf einem Bildschirm (aus der Klasse **Bildschirm**). Dieses Feld empfängt über eine Botschaft die auszugebenden Werte und besorgt dann die Darstellungsaufbereitung (editing) und die Ausgabe auf den Bildschirm. Andere Objekte aus der Klasse **Bildschirm** sind z.B. die Standardobjekte **Fenster, Maus, Eingabe, Cursor** etc. Durch diese Objekte, zusammen mit den entsprechenden Botschaften, wird die gesamte Steuerung der Terminalinteraktionen ausgeführt, inklusiv der Verarbeitung von Editierbefehlen wie z.B. Zeichenlöschen, Cursorbewegungen.

Dieses Beispiel zu einem Standardobjekt zeigt, dass der Begriff eines Objektes sehr konsistent und allgemein verwendet wird: Jede Informationseinheit in einem System ist ein Objekt, und nur ein Objekt kann ein anderes Objekt produzieren. (Das Objekt **Eingabefeld** produziert beispielsweise ein Objekt **reelle Zahl**, das den eingetippten Wert repräsentiert.)

Die Standardobjekte stehen als allgemein anwendbare, häufig benötigte, technische Objekte zur Verfügung. Die Funktionalität der Standardobjekte bezieht sich nicht auf eine explizite Applikation. Standardobjekte werden als technische Objekte bezeichnet, da sie als Hilfsmittel für die Konstruktion anderer Objekte verwendet werden. Zur Entwicklung von Standardobjekten sind keine Kenntnisse über die Zusammenhänge in einem komplexen Softwaresystem notwendig. Die Prinzipien eines Stacks können beispielsweise völlig unabhängig vom Typ und Inhalt seiner Elemente implementiert werden. Das Resultat ist dann das Standardobjekt **Keller**, das später für bestimmte Applikationen individuell verwendet werden kann.

Im Gegenstz zu diesem neutralen Verwendungsbereich der Standardobjekte sind für eine bestimmte Applikation Objekte erforderlich, die ganz spezielle Anforderungen erfüllen. Diese Objekte sind dann anwendungsbezogene Objekte und haben nicht mehr den universellen Charakter der Standardobjekte. Die Komplexität der Standardobjekte variiert stark. Trotzdem ist auch beim Betrachten sehr komplexer Standardobjekte der Sprung von den Standardobjekten zu den anwendungsbezogenen Objekten gross.

- *Strukturobjekte*

Infolge der Lücke zwischen Standardobjekten und anwendungsbezogenen Objekten führen wir für die abstrakte Datenorganistion höherer Ordnung eine Stufe zwischen den Standardobjekten und den anwendungsbezogenen Objekten ein. Diese Objekte bezeichnen wir als *Strukturobjekte*. Zu ihnen gehören vor allem Datenbanken. Der Übergang zwischen Standardobjekten und Strukturobjekten ist fliessend. So ist z.B. eine komplexe Hashtabelle durchaus im Grenzbereich dieser zwei Hierarchiestufen von Objekten anzusiedeln, während eine verteilte Datenbank sicher zu den komplexesten Strukturobjekten überhaupt zu zählen ist.

Ein weiteres Merkmal der Strukturobjekte ist, dass sie kaum mehr als Elemente von einer Programmiersprache zur Verfügung gestellt werden. Bei einfacheren Standardobjekten kann dies durchaus der Fall sein[5].

- *applikatorische Objekte*

Das Kriterium für die Zurechnung eines Objektes zu den Standard- bzw. Strukturobjekten, ist die Möglichkeit der allgemeinen Anwendbarkeit. Objekte mit dem geringsten Allgemeinverwendungsgrad werden *applikatorische Objekte* genannt und sind jeweils auf ein spezifisches Anwendungsbedürfnis ausgerichtet. Wir reihen die applikatorischen Objekte in die oberste Stufe unserer Hierarchiebildung ein. Die Reichweite applikatorischer Objekte erstreckt sich von einfachen bis zu komplexesten Objekten. Beispiel für ein sehr einfaches applikatorisches Objekt ist eine sequentielle Datei von Messwerten. Im Unterschied zum Standardobjekt "sequentielle Datei", das die Betriebssystem-Sicht einer sequentiellen Datei repräsentiert, ist unter einer sequentiellen Datei als applikatorisches Objekt eine ganz bestimmte Datei gemeint, z.B. unsere Datei von Messwerten. Die Definition einer applikatorischen sequentiellen Datei kann auch Konsistenzprüfungen enthalten, beispielsweise Validitätsprüfungen einzelner Datensatzfelder, Prüfsummentests, Sequenztests etc. Der Datenstrom in einer sequentiellen Datei, die als Standardobjekt auftritt, ist ein anonymer Fluss von Daten. Dagegen werden bei einer applikatorischen sequentiellen Datei konkrete Datenobjekte übertragen (z.B. einzelne Messwerte).

Beispiel für ein kommerzielles, komplexeres applikatorisches Objekt ist **Umsatzliste**, das Umsätze nach Region, Vertreter und Artikeln sortiert und diese Umsätze samt Gruppenbruch- und Gesamtsummen protokolliert. Das Objekt **Umsatzliste** wird dann z.B. über folgende Methoden gesteuert:

```
NeueRegion <Regionenbezeichnung>
NeuerVertreter <Vertreterbezeichnung>
Artikel <Artikel- und Umsatzdaten>
EndeUmsatzliste <>
```

Auch ein Programm im herkömmlichen Sinne ist ein applikatorisches Objekt, denn es stellt nichts anderes dar als eine Zusammenfassung von Funktionen (Methoden) auf bestimmte Datenstrukturen. In solch einem Programm bzw. in einem kompletten Softwaresystem finden wir aus allen vier Hierarchiestufen Objekte (siehe Abb.4), wobei die einfacheren Objekte auch als Bestandteile der komplexeren Objekte verwendet werden.

Die Elementar- Standard- und Strukturobjekte werden im Gegensatz zu den applikatorischen Objekten zusammenfassend auch als *Normobjekte* bezeichnet, da sie als Bausteine für die Erstellung der applikatorischen Objekte dienen.

---

5. Zu den Sprachelementen von Smalltalk-80 z.B. gehört ein weites Angebot an verschiedenen Datenstrukturen, die wir hier als Standardobjekte bezeichnen.

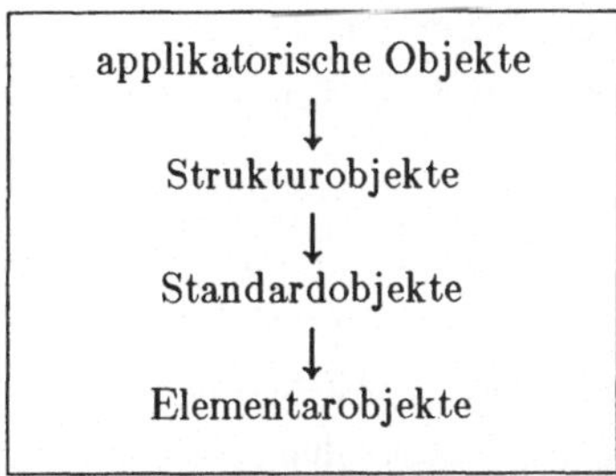

Abb.4 Zusammenstellung der Objekt - Hierarchie

4. Objektorientierte Projektorganisation

Bei der heute üblichen EDV-Projektorganisation wird ganz grob zwischen der Organisationsabteilung und der Softwareabteilung unterschieden. In der Organisationsabteilung ist informatisch-technisches wie auch anwendungsbezogenes Fachwissen vertreten. Sie erarbeitet mit dem Anwender zusammen den Ist- und Sollzustand einer betrieblichen Organisationseinheit, die durch EDV-Mittel unterstützt werden soll. Als Resultat wird durch die Organisationsabteilung das Pflichtenheft erstellt. Die Softwareabteilung übernimmt die Realisierung der Softwarekomponenten des geforderten Sollzustandes. Dies umfasst u.a. Detailanalysen, Datenbank-Entwurf, Programmierung und Tests. Häufig stehen der Softwareabteilung spezialisierte Teams aus Stabsstellen für besondere Aufgaben zur Seite (System-Gruppe, Datenbank-Gruppe, Netzwerk-Gruppe). Die freigegebenen Software-Komponenten werden meistens wieder durch die Organisationsabteilung in den Betrieb eingeführt. Wir haben die Hardware-Seite bewusst nicht berücksichtigt, denn im hier betrachteten Zusammenhang interessieren Auswahlverfahren sowie die Installations- und Betriebsproblematik wenig.

In einer konventionellen Organisation erfolgt die Arbeitsteilung in der Projekthierarchie bis hinunter auf die Programmstufe. Die Aufgaben werden gemäss den spezifizierten Funktionen zugewiesen. Dazu wird ein Projekt in verschiedene Arbeitskreise aufgeteilt. Jeder Arbeitskreis entspricht dabei einer Teilaufgabe aus dem Gesamtsystem. Das Projekt **Laborbefunde** kann beispielsweise in die Arbeitskreise **statistische Auswertungen, Ausgabesteuerung** und **Erfassung** gegliedert werden. Jeder Arbeitskreis bildet ein "Unterprojekt", für das ein bestimmtes Programmierteam zuständig ist. Es erfolgen weitere Aufteilungen der Arbeitskreise bis hin zu einzelnen Programmteilen. So können z.B. die Aufgaben **Druckersteuerung** und **Bildschirmausgabe** des Arbeitskreises **Ausgabesteuerung** an zwei Programmierteams vergeben werden. Ein Programm wird nahezu vollständig durch das Programmierteam erstellt. Ausnahmen können z.B. Datenbanken oder Systemänderungen, die das Betriebssystem betreffen, sein. Eine arbeitsteilige Entwicklung auf der Programmstufe ist wegen der gegenseitig notwendigen Kommunikation nur schwer realisierbar. Ausserdem ist ein mehrfaches Programmieren bestimmter Unterfunktionen in den einzelnen Programmierteams nicht auszuschliessen. Der Programmierer einer bestimmten Funktion aus einem speziellen Team (z.B. der **Bildschirmausgabe**) weiss nicht, was ein anderer Programmierer aus einem anderen Team (z.B. **Erfassung**) programmiert. Wenn beide für ihre Lösung eine verkettete Liste benötigen, müssen die Prinzipien der verketteten Liste zweimal implementiert werden.

Auch in der im folgenden vorgeschlagenen, durch den objektorientierten Ansatz beeinflussten Projektorganisation behält die oben beschriebene *Organisationsabteilung* ihre angestammten Aufgaben bei. Sie bleibt die Kontaktstelle zwischen dem Anwender (der Fachabteilung) und der Informatik. Das durch die Organisationsabteilung erarbeitete Verfahren für einen bestimmten betrieblichen Ablauf stützt sich auf das externe Erscheinungsbild (Benutzerschnittstelle) einer EDV-Lösung ab.

Die genaue, möglichst formale Spezifikation des externen Erscheinungsbildes ist für die Softwareabteilung Grundlage der Projektrealisierung. Basierend auf dem objektorientierten Ansatz können wir die *Softwareabteilung* nun unseren Zwecken entsprechend umgestalten.

- *Die Systementwurfsgruppe*

Gewissermassen die zentrale Gruppe der Softwareabteilung ist die *Systementwurfsgruppe*. Diese Gruppe erhält von der Organisationsabteilung den Auftrag zur Realisierung eines genau umschriebenen Softwareprojektes. Basierend auf dieser Umschreibung hat die Systementwurfsgruppe die applikatorischen Objekte zu entwerfen (z.B. Objekte für Datenbestände, Bildschirmlayouts, Listenbilder etc.). In der Systementwurfsgruppe werden erfahrene, hochqualifizierte Informatiker beschäftigt, da die Qualität des Gesamtsystems vor allem von der Definition der applikatorischen Objekte abhängig ist. Die Entwurfstätigkeit umfasst im wesentlichen

- — die Erarbeitung der abstrakten Sichten von applikatorischen Objekten durch die syntaktische und semantische Definitionen der Objektfunktionen (Methoden) und
- — die Festlegung der Informationen (Daten), die durch diese Methoden zwischen den Objekten und der Aussenwelt fliessen (Botschaften).

Als Ziel bei diesem Entwurf wird der interne Aufbau der Objekte sowie die Schnittstelle nach aussen bestimmt. Für die Produktion der auf diese Art definierten applikatorischen Objekte, übergibt die Systementwurfsgruppe einen Auftrag an die *Objektfertigungsgruppe*.

Das durch die Systementwurfsgruppe beschriebene System, welches aus applikatorischen Objekten besteht, hat einen ausgesprochen hierarchischen Charakter: Das oberste Objekt entspricht dem System als Ganzes, es folgen mehrere Klassen, die durch Abstraktion des Gesamtsystems gebildet werden (siehe dazu nocheinmal Abb.3). Innerhalb der Klassen befinden sich weitere applikatorische Objekte. Da Objekte allgemein aus Objekten bestehen, gilt der gleiche rekursive Zusammenhang für die applikatorischen Objekte. Die meisten applikatorischen Objekte werden aus Teilobjekten zusammengesetzt sein, die teilweise wiederum applikatorische Objekte darstellen, teilweise auch Standard-, Struktur- oder Elementarobjekte sind. Die Definition der einzelnen applikatorischen Objekte eines Softwaresystems ergibt zwangsläufig auch den hierarchischen Objektaufbau dieses Systems.

● *Die Objektfertigungsgruppe*

Die Objektfertigungsgruppe erhält ihre Aufträge von der Systementwurfsgruppe. Zur Herstellung der applikatorischen Objekte benutzt die Objektfertigungsgruppe eine Bibliothek von sogenannten Normobjekten (Elementarobjekte, Standardobjekte und höhere Strukturobjekte). Gegebenenfalls wird es nötig sein, neue Normobjekte zu entwerfen und zu implementieren. Zu diesem Zweck stehen der Objektfertigungsgruppe Spezialisten z.B. aus der Systemgruppe, der Datenbankgruppe oder der Netzwerkgruppe zur Verfügung. Die Objektfertigungsgruppe hat auch die Aufgabe, die implementierten Objekte durch ein spezielles, für jedes Objekt erstelltes Testbett sicher auszutesten, wenn eine formale Objektverifikation nicht möglich oder sinnvoll ist. Innerhalb der Objektfertigungsgruppe wird es in vielen Fällen eine Revisionsstelle geben, die bestimmte Objekte gemäss den betrieblichen Vorschriften überprüft.

Die Planungs-, Führungs- und Kontrollmechanismen in einer grossen Objektfertigungsgruppe, die gleichzeitig an mehreren umfangreichen Projekten arbeitet, sind komplex. Neben der präzisen Einhaltung vorgegebener Objektschnittstellen, gilt es, die Objektfertigung so zu gestalten, dass die richtigen Objekte zur richtigen Zeit fertig sind, dass kritische Pfade und Flaschenhälse erkannt werden und dass die fachliche und zeitliche Arbeitskapazität zufriedenstellend und kostengünstig genutzt wird. Dies sind jedoch alles Probleme, die im Gebiet der *Industriebetriebswirschaftslehre* bestens bekannt sind. Sie betreffen z.B. die qualitative und quantitative Kapazitätsplanung des Personal- und Maschineneinsatzes etc. Die manuellen und computergestützten Methoden der Produktionssteuerung für Einzelfertigung (z.B. die Netzplantechnik) können praktisch unverändert für die Objektfertigung übernommen werden. Die Komponenten der beschriebenen Objekthierarchie stehen in direktem Zusammenhang mit Begriffen aus der betrieblichen Fertigung:

Elementarobjekt	→	Rohmaterial
Standardobjekt	→	Normteile
Strukturobjekt	→	Normbaugruppen
applikatorische Objekte	→	spezifisch gefertigte Teile

In der Objektfertigung finden wir ein weites Spektrum von Informatikern, vom Programmieranfänger bis zum hochbezahlten Spezialisten. Sie werden entsprechend ihren Fähigkeiten an der Herstellung von Objekten mit verschiedenem Komplexitätsgrad beschäftigt. Der objektorientierte Ansatz fördert die arbeitsteilige Softwareproduktion, da jedes Objekt aus seinen Teilobjekten völlig autark aufgebaut und ausgetestet werden kann. Dadurch kann auch ein noch wenig ausgebildeter Informatiker schon bald produktiv arbeiten, indem er mit der Implementierung von einfachen Objekten beginnt (z.B. einfache Bildschirm- oder Listenobjekte).

Bei einer nach den heute üblichen, funktionalen Gesichtspunkten aufgebauten Modularisierung ist es wegen der Modul-Interdependenzen selten sinnvoll, mehrere Programmierer an einem einzigen Programm arbeiten zu lassen. Jedes Mitglied eines Programmierteams muss mit allen anderen Mitgliedern Kontakte pflegen, damit technische Absprachen (z.B. die Steuerung des Programmflusses) getroffen werden können. Dieser Kommunikationsaufwand mindert die Produktivität. Andererseits ist aber ein Anfänger durch ein ganzes Programm meistens überlastet, wenn er dafür allein verantwortlich ist. Dies trifft besonders zu, wenn er sich mit der Implementierung von Datenbeständen zu befassen hat, auf die andere Programmierer mit ihren Programmen ebenfalls zugreifen müssen (z.B. die Kundenstammdaten einer Firma).

- *Die Wartungsgruppe*

Neben der Systementwurfsgruppe und der Objektfertigungsgruppe existiert eine Instanz, die Modifikationen an den Objekten nach der Übernahme dieser Objekte in den Betrieb durchführt. Wir nennen diese Instanz *Wartungsgruppe*. Die Wartungsgruppe erhält Modifikationsanträge und Fehlermeldungen aus dem Betrieb des Softwaresystems. Je nach Umfang und Art der erforderlichen Änderungen, werden die Objekte entweder innerhalb der Gruppe umgeändert, an die Objektfertigungsgruppe zur völligen Überarbeitung gegeben oder sogar der Systementwurfsgruppe zur weiteren Behandlung überlassen. Wichtig ist, dass Änderungen innerhalb eines Objektes keinerlei Auswirkungen auf andere Objekte haben, wenn die Syntax und Semantik der Botschaften (Schnittstellen), die für ein Objekt gültig sind, unverändert bleiben. Zum erneuten Test eines Objektes, nach dessen Änderungen, wird das gleiche zum Objekt gehörende Testbett verwendet, das bei der ersten Produktion dieses Objektes erstellt wurde. Gegebenenfalls kann das modifizierte Objekt wieder einer Revision unterzogen werden.

Wenn bei der Entwicklung von Softwaresystemen nach dem objektorientierten Ansatz vorgegangen wird, kann das Organigramm einer EDV-Abteilung wie in Abb.5 aussehen:

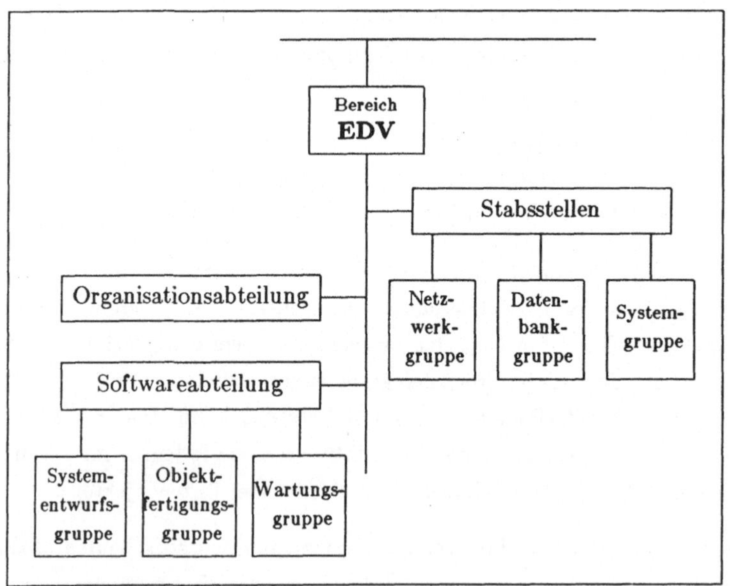

Abb.5 Organigramm bei einer objektorientierte Projektorganisation

5. Schlussbemerkungen

Das Konzept des objektorientierten Ansatzes beruht auf wenigen Prinzipien, die aber äusserst konsequent verfolgt werden. Ein Softwaresystem besteht aus einzelnen Objekten, wobei alle Objekte autonom sind, gleich behandelt werden und auf die gleiche Art Botschaften senden können. Infolge dieser Gleichbehandlung aller Objekte bestehen keine Interdependenzen, wie bei einer funktionalen Modularisierung, bei der die Gliederung der Module vorwiegend nach der physischen Aufteilung des Systems vorgenommen wird. Die Objekte sind damit Mittelpunkt der Programme. Durch den objektorientierten Ansatz kann die Technik der Datenabstraktion im Rahmen einer Projektorganisation leichter angewendet werden als bei einem funktionalen Vorgehen.

Die vorgestellte Projektorganisation ist keine neue Erfindung, da sie in der IBWL seit langem bekannt ist. Der objektorientierte Ansatz ebnet den Weg zur Anwendung dieser bewährten Organisationsform auch im Softwarebereich. Damit die für eine derartige Projektorganisation notwendige Art der Systemgestaltung und Programmierung durchgeführt werden kann, sind einige Informatikvoraussetzungen erforderlich. Dazu zählen ausser einer neuen Art zu Denken, die Umschulung des Fachpersonals sowie die Verwendung geeigneter Programmiersprachen und neuer computergestützter Systeme (z.B. Entwurfssysteme, Programmiersysteme) zur Produktion von Software. Selbstverständlich sollen solche Software-Entwicklungssysteme auf dem objektorientierten Ansatz basieren. Gesichtspunkte, die diese Voraussetzungen betreffen, wurden hier bewusst nicht behandelt. Siehe dazu z.B. einige der Artikel in [Sto-83].

Dank

Viele der Ideen in dieser Arbeit stammen von R. Marty. Ihm möchte ich an dieser Stelle für seine Anregungen herzlich danken.

Literaturverzeichnis

[Ada-82]   U.S. Department of Defense; Ada Programming Language, Washington, April 1982, in: Horowitz E. (ED), Programming Languages - A Grand Tour, Springer Verlag 1983, pp.417-658.

[Byte-81]   Byte Magazine, August 1981, 14 Artikel zu Smalltalk-80.

[Dah-68]   Dahl O.J., Myhrhaug B., Nygaard K.; SIMULA 67 - Common Base Language, Technical Report Norwegian Computing Center, May 1968.

[Gol-77]   Goldberg A., Kay A.; Personal Dynamic Media, *IEEE Computer Vol.10 No.3*, March 1977, pp.31-41.

[Gol-83]   Goldberg A., Robson D.; Smalltalk-80, The Language and its Implementation, Addison-Wesley Publishing Company, 1983.

[Gut-77]   Guttag J.V.; Abstract Data Types and the Development of Data Structures, *Comm. ACM Vol.20 No.6*, June 1977, pp.396-404.

[Hoa-68]   Hoare C.A.R.; Record Handling, in: *Symbol Manipulation Languages and Techniques, Bobrow I.G. (Ed)*, North Holland Publishing Company, 1968, pp.262-284.

[Kras-83]   Krasner G.; (Ed); Smalltalk-80; Bits of History, Words of Advice, Addison-Wesley Publishing Company, 1983.

[Lam-77]   Lampson B.W. et al.; Report on the Programming Language Euclid, *ACM SIGPLAN Notices Vol.12 No.2*, Feb. 1977.

[Lis-81]   Liskov B. et al.; CLU Reference Manual, *Lecture Notes in Computer Science No.144*, Springer Verlag, 1981.

[Nau-63]   Naur P. (Ed); Revised Report on the Algorithmic Language ALGOL 60, *Comm. ACM Vol.6 No.1*, Jan 1963, pp.1-17.

[Org-83]   Organick E.I.; A Programmer's View of the Intel 432 System, McGraw-Hill Book Company, 1983.

[Par-72]   Parnas D.L.; On the Criteria to be Used in Decomposing Systems into Modules, *Comm. ACM Vol.15 No.12*, Dez. 1972, pp.330-336.

[Ren-82]   Rentsch T.; Object Oriented Programming, *ACM SIGPLAN Notices VOL.17 No.9*, Sept 1982, pp.51-57.

[Sto-83]   Stoyan H., Wedekind H. (Ed); Objektorientierte Software- und Hardwarearchitekturen, Tagung II/1983 des German Chapter of the ACM, Teubner Verlag, 1983.

[War-79]   Warren S.K., Abbe D.; Rosetta Smalltalk - A Conversational Extensible Microcomputer Language, *ACM SIGSMALL Newsletter Vol.5 No.2*, 1979, pp.36-45.

[Wir-66]   Wirth N., Hoare C.A.R.; A Contribution to the Development of ALGOL, *Comm. ACM Vol.9 No.6*, June 1966, pp.413-431.

[Wir-82]   Wirth N.; Programming in Modula-2, Springer Verlag, 1982.

[Wul-76]   Wulf W., London R.L., Shaw M.; An Introduction to the Construction and Verification of Alphard Programs, *IEEE Transactions on Software Engineering Vol.2 No.4*, Dez. 1976.

[Wul-81]   Wulf W.A., Levin R., Harbison S.P.; HYDRA/C.mmp An Experimental Computer System, McGraw-Hill Book Company, 1981.

Konzepte zur Strukturierung und Generierung adaptierbarer Anwendungssoftwaresysteme

W. Altmann

sd & m GmbH
Führichstraße 70
8000 München 80

B. Bartsch-Spörl

Interface Concilium
Gesellschaft für Softwaretechnologie
und DV-Systeme
Arabellastraße 30
8000   München 81

Zusammenfassung

Dieser Beitrag reflektiert Erfahrungen der Autoren mit der Architektur großer Anwen-
wendungssoftwaresysteme und Problemen der Anpaßbarkeit derartiger Systeme an unterschiedliche Umgebungen.

Dazu wird im ersten Teil eine weitgehend anwendungsunabhängige Schichtenstruktur für
dialogorientierte Softwaresysteme vorgestellt und schwerpunktmäßig auf Konzepte zur
Verwaltung von Anwendungsdaten und zur Systemfehlerbehandlung eingegangen.

Des weiteren beschäftigt sich dieser Beitrag mit dem Thema der Parametrisierung von
Softwaresystemen im Hinblick auf leichte und schnelle Anpaßbarkeit der Software an
unterschiedliche Hardware- und Software-Umgebungen.

Zuletzt werden die Auswirkungen der vorgestellten Strukturierungskonzepte auf die
Änderbarkeit eines in der Entwicklung bzw. im Betrieb befindlichen Softwaresystems
behandelt.

Inhaltsverzeichnis:

3   Bereitstellung von Anlagenprogrammsystemen
4   Auswirkungen der Systemarchitektur auf den Lebenszyklus
     von Software-Produkten

1   <u>Einleitung</u>

Die Entwicklung großer Softwaresysteme ist trotz aller Fortschritte auf dem Sektor
des Software-Engineering in den letzten Jahren noch immer ein außerordentlich komple-
xes und aufwendiges Unternehmen, dessen Erfolg von einer ganzen Reihe von Faktoren
mitbestimmt wird.

Zu den wichtigsten und kritischsten Faktoren gehört dabei, ob es gelingt, das Gesamt-
problem in hinreichend kleine und sich gegenseitig möglichst wenig beeinflussende
Bausteine zu zerlegen, um so das entstehende Software-Produkt in sämtlichen Phasen
seines Lebenszyklus überschaubar und gut handhabbar zu machen.

2   <u>Strukturierung von Anwendungssoftware</u>

Die Realisierung großer Projekte erfordert nicht nur in der Software-Entwicklung,
sondern auch in vielen anderen Bereichen eine Zerlegung der Aufgabenstellung in klei-
nere Teilaufgaben.

Unterschiede zwischen der Software-Entwicklung und vergleichbaren Vorhaben im Maschi-
nen- oder Anlagenbau sind darin zu sehen, daß Software als immaterieller Werkstoff
besonders schwer faßbar, prüfbar und quantifizierbar ist. Zudem ist die Disziplin des
Software-Engineering noch vergleichsweise jung und viele Ansätze auf diesem Sektor
erlangen erst im Laufe von Jahren die erforderliche praktische Erprobung und den nötigen Reifegrad.

Eine umfangreiche Aufgabenstellung muß nach problemadäquaten Kriterien zerlegt werden,
um die Komplexität beherrschbar und eine arbeitsteilige Realisierung durch ein Team
von gleichzeitig an derselben Aufgabenstellung arbeitenden Mitarbeitern durchführbar
zu machen.

Zudem ist ein Projekt wesentlich besser planbar und kontrollierbar, wenn es aus Teilaufgaben mit bekannten Abhängigkeiten untereinander besteht, die sowohl an ihrer
zeitlichen als auch von ihrer fachlichen Ausdehnung die Kapazität eines Bearbeiters
nach Möglichkeit nicht übersteigen [5] .

Die Kriterien, nach denen ein Gesamtsystem in Bausteine zerlegt wird, werden sowohl durch die gegebene Problemstellung als auch durch die Software-Entwicklungsumgebung und die gewählte Modularisierungsphilosophie bestimmt.

Die Autoren arbeiten in einer sehr fortschrittlichen Software-Entwicklungs-Umgebung [6] mit dem Konzept der Datenabstraktion als Modularisierungsprinzip [1] . Die Zerlegung von Systemen wird in dieser Umgebung hauptsächlich geprägt von den Gesichtspunkten

- funktionelle Abgeschlossenheit
- Hierarchisierung und
- Strukturierung in aufeinander aufbauende Schichten.

Die Zerlegung eines Systems in Moduln verläuft je nach Größe des Systems in mindestens zwei Schritten, wobei das System baumartig zunächst in sogenannte Komponenten und danach weiter in Moduln unterteilt wird [1] .

Betrachtet man sich die bei teilweise sehr verschiedenen Aufgabenstellungen aus dem Bereich der dialogorientierten Anwendungssoftwaresysteme nach den geschilderten Kriterien entstandenen Systemzerlegungen, so stellt man fest, daß die Resultate strukturell immer wieder ähnlich aussehen und daß sich die anwendungsbedingten Unterschiede erst in den Anwendungsdaten, der Dialogführung und den angebotenen Funktionen im Detail bemerkbar machen.

Die von der konkreten Anwendung abstrahierte Struktur einer Systemzerlegung soll im folgenden als "Systemarchitektur" bezeichnet werden. Sie bildet sozusagen das Rückgrat des Systementwurfs, von dessen Tragfähigkeit und Anpaßbarkeit an sich verändernde Umgebungen die weitere Entwicklungs- und Lebensdauer eines Softwareproduktes ganz wesentlich geprägt wird.

2.1   Schichtenstruktur

Ganz grob lassen sich die entstandenen Architekturen in folgende vier hierarchisch übereinanderliegende Schichten untergliedern:
(Die Hierarchie ist im wesentlichen durch eine "benutzt" - Relation zwischen Moduln definiert [2]).

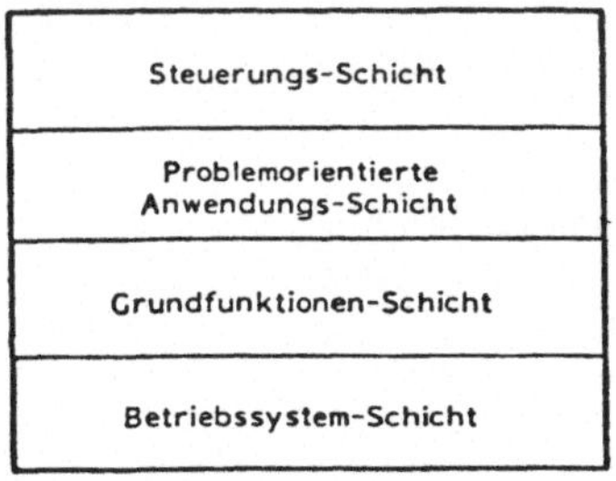

Abbildung 1

Die oberste Steuerungsschicht besteht im wesentlichen aus einem System-Monitor, der die jeweils als nächstes auszuführenden Aufgaben auswählt, anstößt und überwacht.

Die Anwendungsschicht realisiert die eigentliche Aufgabe des Software-Systems, wie z. B. "Reisebuchungen ausführen" oder "Bestellungen registrieren".

Sie läßt sich untergliedern in

- anwendungsorientierte Dialog- bzw. E/A-Steuerung,
- Benutzerfunktionen,
- Anwendungs-Datenbasis und
- Anwendungs-Dienstleistungen.

Die Dialogsteuerung für Dialogsysteme (z. B. in Form von Interakttionsdiagrammen [3]) bzw. die E/A-Steuerung für Stapelsysteme beschreiben die Ablaufstrukturen an der Benutzerschnittstelle.

Die Benutzerfunktionen definieren die verfügbaren Dialog- bzw. Stapelanwendungen.

Die Anwendungs-Datenbasis sorgt für eine anwendungsgerechte Bereitstellung der benötigten Anwendungsdaten, wie z. B. der Ausgabe der Artikelbezeichnung eines über seine Nummer identifzierbaren Postens einer Bestellung.

Die Anwendungs-Dienstleistungen enthalten die von mehreren Anwendungen gemeinsam benutzten Funktionen, wie z.B. Umrechnungsfunktionen für Fremdwährungen oder ganz allgemeine Dienstleistungen wie z. B. Auskunftsfunktionen für Uhrzeiten oder Kalenderdaten.

Die Grundfunktionenschicht definiert eine virtuelle Maschine, die sogenannte Applikationsmaschine, die die Anwendungsschicht von sich verändernden Hard- und Softwaregegebenheiten weitgehend unabhängig machen soll.

Die Applikationsmaschine besteht im wesentlichen aus den Teilen

- virtuelle E/A-Schnittstelle (mit Formularunterstützung)
  (virtuelles Bildschirmterminal/ virtueller Drucker/
  virtueller Arbeitsplatz)

- Anwendungsdatenverwaltung und

- Dateisystem (mit Transaktions-Mechanismus)

Virtuelle E/A Schnittstellen

Virtuelle Geräte dienen dazu, die Anwendungssoftware von den verwendeten realen Datenendgeräten unabhängig zu machen, sie stellen "Modellgeräte" bereit. Diese Modelle abstrahieren von den verschiedenen Varianten einer Klasse verwandter (realer) Geräte und verstärken deren Intelligenz. Für die Anwendungsprogramme werden somit Funktionen angeboten, die u. U. von einigen der realen Geräte gar nicht erbracht werden.

Die gegenüber den Anwendungsprogrammen einheitliche Softwareschnittstelle wird durch das virtuelle Gerät auf die verschiedenen realen Geräte abgebildet (Mapping), d. h. das virtuelle Gerät übernimmt die routinemäßigen Gerätesteuerungen und ermöglicht so eine bequeme Programmierung.

Eine Konsequenz hieraus ist, daß gewisse Besonderheiten bestimmter realer Geräte von der Anwendungssoftware nicht "ausgereizt" werden können. Hierdurch wird gewährleistet, daß die Anwendungsprogramme unverändert mit verschiedenen realen Geräten (einer durch das Modellgerät definierten Klasse) arbeiten können. Es ist lediglich eine Neugenerierung oder Rekonfigurierung des Systems erforderlich.

Anwendungsdatenverwaltung

Die Anwendungsdatenverwaltung zieht zwischen den Moduln der Anwendungs-Datenbasis und dem Dateisystem eine separate Schicht ein.

Diese stellt einen für die gesamte Vorgehensweise typischen Baustein dar und soll deswegen im folgenden etwas näher erläutert werden.

In großen Anwendungssystemen werden, bedingt durch das anfallende Volumen, die von den einzelnen Moduln zu bearbeitenden Daten in Dateien gehalten. Die Hauptaufgabe der Anwendungsdatenverwaltung besteht darin, die anwendungsspezifischen Zugriffswünsche aller Moduln derart in Zugriffe auf die real vorhandenen Dateien umzusetzen, daß einerseits

-   jedem "Datenmodul" die Modellvorstellung vermittelt wird, seine Daten seien in einer privaten Datei untergebracht, deren Datensätze er jederzeit einrichten, lesen, verändern und löschen kann,

und andererseits

-   die durch eine Realisierung der Datenverwaltung in entsprechend vielen Dateien entstehenden Konsistenz-Probleme und Performance-Verluste auf ein Minimum beschränkt werden.

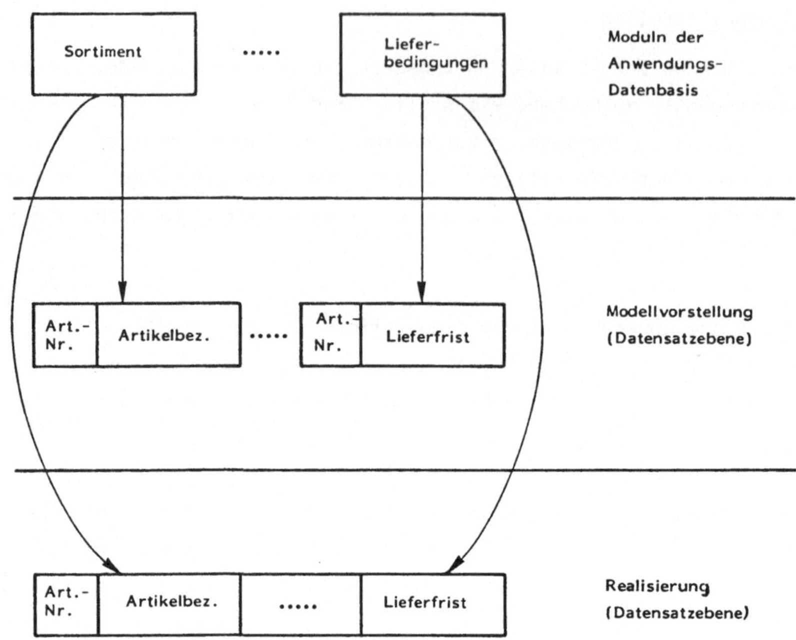

Abbildung 2

Die erste Forderung steht im Einklang mit den Prinzipien der Datenabstraktion und erlaubt den Moduln einen sehr einfachen Zugriff auf ihre Moduldaten, während die zweite Forderung dazu dient, diese Modellierung mit den zusätzlichen Randbedingungen Datenintegrität und Performance in Einklang zu bringen.

Die Anwendungsdatenverwaltung ist im Entwurfsstadium zunächst als konzeptionelle Komponente darstellbar, die den Zugriff der Anwendungsdatenmoduln auf ihre in Dateien gespeicherten privaten Moduldaten organisiert.

Sie wird im nächsten Schritt weiter zerlegt in eine Anzahl von real zu implemtierenden Moduln. Die Aufgabenstellung und Anzahl dieser Moduln orientiert sich an allen im System vorhandenen Dateien, deren Datensätze aus Moduldaten mehrerer Moduln zusammengesetzt sind.
(Ein Beispiel hierfür wäre ein Modul Artikelstammdatenverwaltung, der Artikelstammsätze mit Einzeldaten wie Artikelnummer, Artikelbezeichnung, Preis, Lieferkonditionen u. a. m. verwaltet und der von Moduln wie z. B. Sortiment, Preisgestaltung und Lieferbedingungen benötigt wird.)
Der Zugriff auf Datensätze dieser Art sieht typischerweise so aus, daß mehrere Moduln kurz hintereinander auf verschiedene Teile des gleichen Satzes zugreifen. Um nun zu verhindern, daß ein Satz vor Durchführung der letzten schreibenden Veränderung zurückgeschrieben wird, kann man in der darüberliegenden Dialogschicht sogenannte

Kontrollzugriffsoperationen zu benutzen, um der Anwendungsdatenverwaltung den Beginn und das Ende jeder Folge von Zugriffen verschiedener Moduln auf den gleichen Datensatz zu signalisieren.

Das Zusammenspiel der verschiedenen Modularten z. B. bei der Ausführung einer Bestellung läßt sich durch folgende Skizze veranschaulichen:

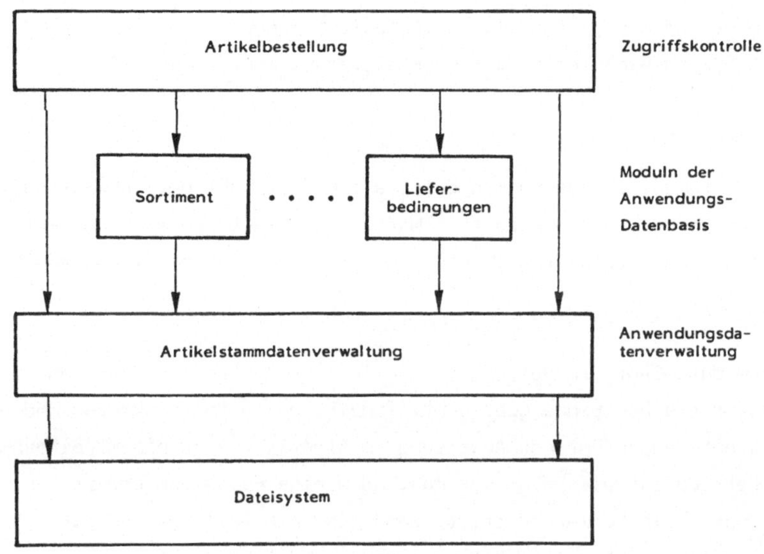

Abbildung 3

Mit Hilfe der Kontrollzugriffsoperationen wird sichergestellt, daß jeder Datensatz für den Zugriff aller zugriffsberechtigten Moduln nur einmal geholt, bei Bedarf gleichzeitig gesperrt und nur nach erfolgreich abgeschlossener Veränderung wieder zurückgeschrieben wird.

Die Anwendungsdatenverwaltung ist außerdem in der Lage, die Einhaltung von Zugriffsberechtigungen oder Reihenfolgebedingungen sowohl bezüglich der "Identität" von Moduln als auch bezüglich der verschiedenen Operationen zu prüfen.

Dateisystem

Das Dateisystem muß zur Wahrung der Integrität der häufig außerordentlich wertvollen Anwendungsdaten mit einem Transaktionsmechanismus ausgestettet sein, um sicherzustellen, daß logisch eine Einheit bildende Veränderungen der Datenbasis, von denen aber verschiedene physikalische Einheiten der Datenbasis betroffen sein können, entweder vollständig oder überhaupt nicht ausgeführt werden [4] .

Die zuunterst gelegene Betriebssystemschicht bildet die Basis für die Realisierung der Grundfunktionen und hat mit ihren Schnittstellen und ihren Eigenschaften einen wesentlichen Einfluß auf die Struktur und die Komplexität der Applikationsmaschine.

2.2 Orthogonal zur Schichtenstruktur liegende Konzepte

Drei weitere die Systemarchitektur mitbestimmende Konzepte, die nicht innerhalb einer der beschriebenen Schichten angesidelt werden können, sondern sich durch fast alle Schichten "hindurchziehen", sind die Systemfehlerbehandlung, der Anlauf bzw. Wiederanlauf und die System-Generierung und -Installierung (vergl. Kap. 3).

Systemfehlerbehandlung

Im Rahmen der Wartungsvorsorge können bereits zum Zeitpunkt der Entwicklung Vorkehrungen getroffen werden, die die spätere Wartung und Weiterentwicklung erleichtern. Einen wesentlichen Beitrag hierzu leistet das folgende Systemfehlerbehandlungskonzept.

Jedes DV-System durchläuft im Betrieb eine Folge von Zuständen. ("Zustand" ist hier im automatentheoretischen Sinne gebraucht: Inhalte der Datenstrukturen und der Zeiger auf die nächste auszuführende Anweisung im Algorithmus zu einem Zeitpunkt.) Im fehlerfreien Betrieb ist die Folge von Zuständen eine Folge von erwarteten Zuständen. Wenn im System ein Fehler auftritt, wenn also ein Teil des Systems - Hardware oder Software - sich nicht spezifikationsgemäß verhält, erfolgt ein Übergang von einem erwünschten zu einem unerwünschten Zustand des Systems.

In einem sorgfältig modularisierten und spezifizierten System gibt es viele Aussagen über den Zustand, die immer oder an kritischen Punkten gelten (Invarianten). Durch Überprüfung dieser Aussagen ist es möglich, Vorkehrungen zu treffen für den Fall, daß einer jener unerwünschten Zustände eingetreten ist, für die die überprüfte Aussage nicht mehr gilt. Diese unerwarteten unerwünschten Zustände sind die Systemfehler. Je mehr und je genauere Überprüfungen das System enthält, desto früher werden Systemfehler erkannt. Je früher sie erkannt werden, desto weniger unterscheidet sich der unerwünschte Zustand vom entsprechenden erwünschten, und desto weniger wird die Sicherheit des Systems gefährdet.

Zur Sicherheit des Systems gehören drei Aspekte:

1.   Das System darf nicht "abstürzen" (Ausfallsicherheit).

2.   Die Daten im System dürfen nicht korrumpiert werden (Datensicherheit).

3.   Es muß möglich sein, einen Fehler zu finden, ohne sein erneutes Auftreten oft

beobachten zu müssen (Diagnosesicherheit).

Der folgende Systemfehlermechanismus ermöglicht die Konstruktion besonders sicherer Systeme durch frühe Erkennung von Systemfehlern. Welche Konsequenzen aus einem erkannten Systemfehler am besten zu ziehen sind, hängt davon ab, welcher Aspekt der Systemsicherheit der wichtigste ist. Der grundlegende Systemfehlermechanismus ist aber in jedem Fall derselbe.

In jedem Modul werden an geeigneten Stellen Invarianten überprüft, um das Auftreten eines unerwünschten Zustandes zu erkennen. Diese Überprüfungen heißen deshalb Detektoren.

Wenn ein Detektor einen unerwünschten Zustand festgestellt hat, verzweigt das Programm in einem sogenannten Abnormalteil. Dort wird die Situation protokolliert (Diagnosesicherheit) und entweder die Auswirkung des Fehler kompensiert (Herstellung eines erwünschten Zustandes im Handler) oder die Situation wird dem aufrufenden Modul gemeldet (Trap).

Wenn ein gerufener Modul einen Systemfehler meldet, dann verfährt der rufende Modul genauso, wie wenn ein Detektor in seinem Code angesprochen hätte. Nach jedem Aufruf eines Unterprogramms befindet sich deshalb im rufenden Programm ein Trap, das auf Systemfehlermeldungen des gerufenen Unterprogramms anspricht wie ein Detektor auf die Verletzung von Invarianten.

Die Fehlermeldung beschränkt sich jeweils auf eine dem Abstraktionsniveau angemessene Schilderung der Situation, die Fehlerbehandlung entscheidet erst, ob eine Behebung versucht wird, oder ob der Systemfehler weitergemeldet wird. Wenn ein Systemfehler über viele Stufen der Aufrufhierarchie weitergemeldet wird, entstehen auch entsprechend viele Einträge im Protokoll, so daß die Entstehung der Situation über alle Stufen verfolgt werden kann. Wenn auch auf der obersten Stufe keine Behebung möglich ist, muß versucht werden, verbleibende Maßnahmen von einem anderen Prozeß aus zu unternehmen.

Wenn beim Versuch, einen Systemfehler zu beheben, erneut ein Systemfehler auftritt, darf das nicht zu einer endlosen Schachtelung von Fehlern und Behebungsversuchen führen. Im Fehlerprotokoll wird deshalb auch festgehalten, ob bereits eine Behandlung im Gang ist. Solange das der Fall ist, darf keine erneute Fehlerbehandlung angestoßen werden.

Der Anlauf bzw. Wiederanlauf haben die Aufgabe, ein System erstmalig bzw. nach normalen Abschaltvorgängen oder unvorhergesehenen Störungen in einen ordnungsgemäßen

Betriebszustand zu versetzen.

Das Thema System-Generierung und Installierung wird im nächsten Kapital ausführlicher behandelt.

Insgesamt ergibt sich folgende allgemeine Systemarchitektur:

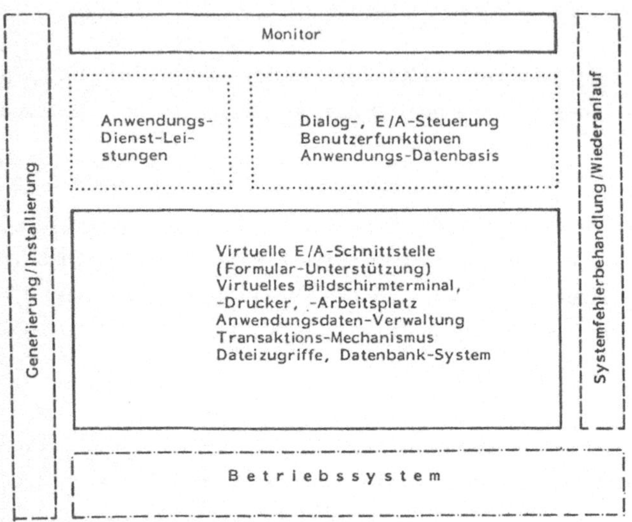

Abbildung 4

Legende: .... Anwendungs-Schicht

_______ Applikationsmaschine

-.-.-.- Betriebssystem

------- Support-Software

3 Bereitstellung von Anlagenprogrammsystemen

Große Anwendungssoftware-Systeme müssen in der Regel für eine Vielzahl von Installationen bereitgestellt werden. Dabei treten prinzipiell zwei Probleme auf:

1. Wodurch wird gewährleistet, daß die gesamte Software entsprechend den Kundenanforderungen ohne größeren Aufwand adaptiert werden kann?

2. Wie kann sichergestellt werden, daß nur "sichere" Ausgaben eines Anlagenprogrammsystems (APS) zum Kunden gelangen?

Eine Antwort auf die erste Frage kann gefunden werden, wenn bereits während des Entwicklungsprozesses auf die Generier- und Konfigurierbarkeit (Parametrisierung) des

Systems geachtet wird. Das zweite Problem wird erheblich reduziert, wenn man zur
Bereitstellung eines APS ein Software-Generiersystem in Verbindung mit einer Projekt-
bibliothek bzw. einer Generierungsdatenbank verwendet.

Parametrisierung

Die Parametrisierung der Software kann durch systemcharakterisierende, installationsabhängige oder technische Daten erfolgen.

Die Parametrisierung des Systems kann dabei wirksam werden entweder offsite bei der
Bereitstellung eines ladbaren Systems auf einem geeigneten Trägermedium (Band, Plat-
te) - dieser Vorgang wird als System-Generierung bezeichnet - oder onsite bei der
Übernahme des ladbaren Systems auf die Kundenanlage - dieser Vorgang wird als System-
Installierung bezeichnet.

Systemcharakterisierende Daten sind SW-Parameter, durch die ein System eindeutig definiert ist und die für alle Installationen gleich sind.

Installationsabhängige Daten sind einstellbare Software-Parameter, deren konkrete
Werte von dem jeweils projektierten Kundensystem abhängen. Die Einstellung kann sowohl bei der System-Generierung als auch bei der -Installierung erfolgen.

Technische Parameter sind einstellbare SW-Parameter, deren Abhängigkeit durch die
konkrete, interne Realisierung bedingt ist, die aber nicht von einer speziellen Kun-
deninstallation abhängen. Die Einstellung kann sowohl bei der System-Generierung als
auch bei der -Installierung erfolgen.

SW-Parameter, die während der Installierung eingestellt werden, können sowohl offsite als auch onsite modifiziert werden (Konfigurationsparameter), im Gegensatz zu
SW-Parametern, die ausschließlich während der Generierung (Generierungsparameter)
eingestellt werden können.

Die Parametrisierung kann dann besonders kostengünstig vorgenommen werden, wenn diese Parameter zentral gehalten werden und eine Referenzierung in den Software-Bausteinen entsprechend dokumentiert ist.

Software-Generiersystem

Die Aufgabe eines Software-Generiersystems (SWGS) besteht darin, aus einer Menge von
Software-Bausteinen, die für ein definiertes System entwickelt wurden, ein vollstän-
diges, in sich konsistentes Software-Paket für eine bestimmte Installation (APS) zu

erzeugen. Aktivitäten hierzu werden offsite auf der Entwicklungs- bzw. Generier-Anlage durchgeführt.

In dieser Phase werden Versionen eines APS generiert für eine neue Installation (Neu-Generierung), die Erweiterung einer bestehenden Installation (Erweiterungs-Generierung) oder die Verbesserung einer bestehenden Installation (Update-Generierung).

Zur Erweiterungs-Generierung gehören HW- und SW-Ergänzungen, die von der Projektierung her noch nicht vorgeleistet sind. Die bis dahin angefallenen Benutzerdaten sind zu übernehmen. Bei der Update-Generierung ist es unter Umständen notwendig, eine Transformation von Benutzer-Datenbeständen durchzuführen.

Anhand der Neu-Generierung ist im folgenden die Wirkungsweise eines SWGS dargestellt.

Die Neu-Generierung hat die Aufgabe für die verschiedenen Installationen eines Systems unter Zuhilfenahme einer entsprechenden Installationsbeschreibung (Eingangs-Daten des SWGS) ein APS sowie Installierungs-Unterlagen (Ergebnis-Daten) für den Betreiber des Systems zur Verfügung zu stellen.

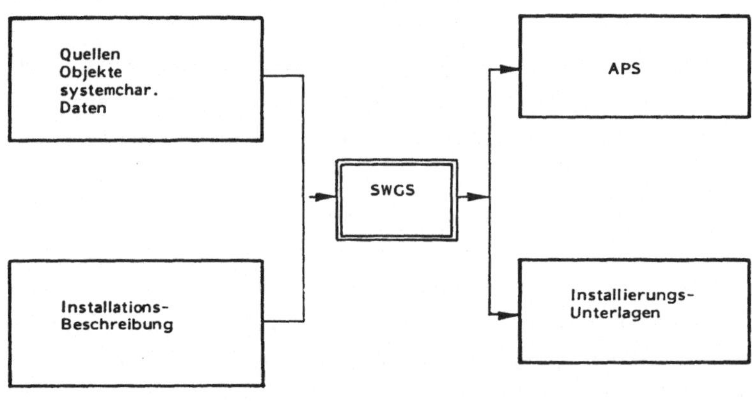

Abbildung 5

Installations-Beschreibungen beinhalten eine komplette Beschreibung aller für die Bereitstellung eines APS benötigten Objekte (ev. Quellen) und Dateien für Installations- bzw. Konfigurationsparameter sowie deren gegenseitige Abhängigkeiten. Sie ermöglichen eine automatische Überprüfung der Konsistenz von Anlagen-Programm-Systemen.

Die Beschreibung einer Installation erfolgt in zwei Stufen:

1. Beschreibung der SW-Konfiguration als Zusammenstellung der zugehörigen Installierungs-Einheiten,

2. Beschreibung der Installierungs-Einheiten.

Die Installierungs-Einheiten setzen sich zusammen aus Lade-Einheiten und Installierungs-Dateien.

Die Lade-Einheiten sind die ladbaren Code-Segmente. Für sie muß eine Darstellung
der benötigten Übersetze- und Binde-Kommandos für die Code- und Objekt-Dateien angegeben werden.
Installierungs-Dateien enthalten Konfigurationsparameter. Diese werden z.T. durch
einen Transformator/Generator aus Installierungs-Daten erzeugt, z. T. durch die Ent-
wickler direkt zur Verfügung gestellt.

4   Auswirkungen der Systemarchitektur auf den Lebenszyklus
     von Software-Produkten

Für Software-Produkte, die über viele Jahre hinweg im Einsatz sind, ist eine strenge
Abgrenzung derjenigen Systemteile, die geräte- und/oder systemsoftware-spezifische
Importschnittstellen enthalten, von großer Wichtigkeit für die "Überlebensfähigkeit"
des Systems in realer, sich wandelnder Umgebung.

Der Aufbau der Anwendungssoftware auf eine die Einflüsse der Systemsoftware neutra-
lisierende Applikationsmaschine garantiert, daß der eigentliche Kern der Anwendungssoftware auf neuere Versionen desselben Systems, auf neue Systemsoftware und sogar
auf Rechner anderer Hersteller mit vertretbarem Aufwand portabel gestaltet wird.

So müssen bei Änderungen in der Systemsoftware lediglich diejenigen Moduln der
Applikationsmaschine, die die veränderten Systemfunktionen importieren, in ihrer
Konstruktion entsprechend angepaßt werden.

Das Konzept der viruellen Ein-/Ausgabegeräte sorgt dafür, daß beim Überwechseln auf
neue E/A-Geräte, deren Eigenschaften innerhalb des durch das Modellgerät definierten Spektrums liegen, keine Änderungen an der Anwendungssoftware vorzunehmen sind.
Für den Fall, daß neue E/A-Geräte den Rahmen des Modellgeräts sprengende Eigenschaften besitzen und diese auch genutzt werden sollen, ist eine lokal gut begrenzbare
Erweiterung bzw. Änderung des Modellgerätes durchzuführen.

Änderungen am Formularaufbau sind ohne Eingriffe in die eigentliche Software nur über Änderungen der Formulardefinitionen möglich und selbst größere Änderungen an der Eingabefeldstruktur und/oder der Dialogführung lassen sich mit relativ wenig Änderungsaufwand beim Virtuellen Terminal und in der Dialogschicht schnell und sicher in das System einbauen.

Änderungen an der Datensatzstruktur der Anwendungsdaten können für die darüberliegenden Moduln unsichtbar innerhalb der Anwendungsdatenverwaltungsschicht realisiert werden.

Bei der Systemfehlerbehandlung ist die - textmäßige - Trennung von Algorithmus und Fehlerbehandlung wichtig, da erfahrungsgemäß im Zuge längerer Betriebserfahrung die Fehlerbehandlung häufiger überarbeitet wird. Würde man dabei jeweils in den Algorithmus eingreifen, liefe man unnötigerweise Gefahr, durch unachtsame Änderungen neue Fehler zu programmieren.

Wenn ein System nach langjährigem Einsatz weitgehend fehlerfrei ist, können zur Verminderung des dynamischen Aufwands Detektoren, die überflüssig erscheinen, - beispielsweise mit Hilfe eines kompilierbaren Kommentars - abgeschaltet werden.

Zu den entscheidenden Vorteilen einer klar gegliederten Software-Architektur zählt, daß sich bei Änderungen der Benutzerwünsche sowohl während des Entwicklungsprozesses als auch in der Wartungsphase sehr schnell feststellen läßt,

- in welcher Schicht bzw. in welchen Schichten überhaupt Änderungen vorgenommen werden müssen,

- welche Moduln in welchen Teilprodukten wie stark von dieser Änderung betroffen sind,

- wie sich die Änderung im Terminplan niederschlägt.

Bei einer derart klar gegliederten Architektur, die man mit einem wohlgeordneten Regal vergleichen könnte, kann es nicht mehr vorkommen, daß beim Auftreten eines Wartungsfalles niemand mit Sicherheit sagen kann, ob eine Änderung überhaupt durchführbar ist und in welcher Größenordnung der erforderliche Aufwand liegen wird.

Ein weiterer Vorteil derartiger Architekturen besteht darin, daß die relative Unab-

hängigkeit vieler Bausteine von der konkret zu realisierenden Anwendung ihre Wiederverwendbarkeit für weitere ähnlich gelagerte Aufgabenstellungen zur Folge hat.

Dabei ist die Wahrscheinlichkeit für die Wiederverwendbarkeit von Bausteinen umso
größer, je weiter diese vom Benutzer und von der Hardware-Basis entfernt, d. h. z.B.
in den mittleren Schichten von Abbildung 1 liegen.

In diesem Zusammenhang ist es oft schwierig zu erfahren, was an für eine neue Aufgabe
verwendbaren Bausteinen innerhalb einer Organisation vorhanden ist. Dieses Problem
läßt sich unserer Erfahrung nach nur mit einem rechnergestützten System zur Verwaltung der beim Software-Entwicklungsprozeß entstehenden Teilprodukte (Projektbiblio-
thek) [7] zufriedenstellend lösen.

Schlußbemerkung

Es soll noch erwähnt werden, daß sich die vorgestellten Konzepte auch bei der Kon-
zeption und Realisierung heterogener, verteilter Rechnersysteme bewährt haben, wobei
jedoch auf die bei verteilten Systemen zusätzlich zu berücksichtigenden Aspekte an
dieser Stelle nicht eingegangen worden ist.

Literatur:

1. W. ALTMANN: Modularisierung und Spezifikation großer Softwaresysteme,
   3. Fachgespräch der Fachgruppe Software Engineering der GI, April 82, Aachen

2. W.BARTUSSEK: Hierarchische Strukturen in der Praxis des Systementwurfs und der
   Realisierung, 3. Fachgespräch der Fachgruppe Software Engineering der GI,
   April 82, Aachen

3. B. BARTSCH-SPÖRL, H.-M. MEYER, K. PINKERT: Einsatz von Interaktionsdiagrammen
   zur Beschreibung und Realisierung von Dialogabläufen, Notizen zum Interaktiven
   Programmieren 8 (March 82), 39-48

4. P. DADEM: Synchronisieren in verteilten Datenbanken: Ein Überblick Teil 1,
   Informatik-Spektrum 4,3, 1981, 175-184

5. E. DENERT: Software Engineering: Experience and Convictions, Lecture Notes in
   Computer Science, Vol. 123, Springer 1981, 16-35

6. E. DENERT,W. HESSE, H. NEUMAIER: S/E/TEC - an environment for the production of
   reliable software, Lecture Notes in Computer Science, Vol. 123, Springer 1981,
   65-84

7. G. GREITER, G. KUGEL, J. LANGE, G. MERBETH, H. RACH, B. REINECK: Die Projekt-
   bibliothek PAPICS, Softlab GmbH, Interner Bericht 1982

Anschrift der Autoren

Prof. C.A.R. H O A R E
Computing Laboratory
Oxford University
8-11 Keble Road
Oxford OX1 3QD
England

Dr.J.J. H O R N I N G
XEROX PARK
3333 Cojote Hill Road
Palo Alto, CA 94304
U S A

Dr. W. A L T M A N N
TRIUMPH-ADLER AG für Büro-
und Informationstechnik
Hundingstr. 11 b
D-8500 Nürnberg 80

R. A M M E R
P. M E I N E N
G. R E H M A N N
Softlab GmbH
Arabellastr. 13
D-8000 München 81

M. B U D D E
Ch. K N A B E
W. S I M O N S M E I E R
PSI GmbH
Heilbronnerstr. 10
D-1000 Berlin 31

Dr. H. B U R K H A R T
Y. C H A O
M. M O S E R
Institut für Elektronik
ETH-Zentrum
CH-8092 Zürich

P. G R O G O N O
V.S. A L A G A R
Dept. of Computer Science
Concordia University
1455 deMaisonneuve Blvd. West
Montreal, Quebec H3G 1M8
Canada

Dr. J.D. I C H B I A H
Alsys
29. Avenue de Versailles
F-78170 La Celle Saint - Cloud

Prof. Dr. J.W. S C H M I D T
Fachbereich Informatik
Johann Wolfgang Goethe-Universität
D-6000 Frankfurt

W. H E N H A P L
G. S N E L T I N G
Institut für praktische Informatik
Alexanderstr. 24
D-6100 Darmstadt

B. H O H L F E L D
AEG-Telefunken
Forschungsinstitut Ulm
Postfach 1730
D-7900 Ulm

Th. L E T S C H E R T
Technische Hochschule Darmstadt
Programmiersprachen & Uebersetzer
Fachbereich 20
Alexanderstr. 24
D-6100 Darmstadt

B. M E R G L E R
Institut für Informatik
der Universität Zürich
Postfach
CH-8035 Zürich

U. M O E N C K E
B. W E I S G E R B E R
Prof. Dr. R. W I L H E L M
Fachbereich 10 - Informatik
Universität des Saarlandes
D-6600 Saarbrücken

F. M U E L L E R
Fachbereich 10 - Informatik
Universität des Saarlandes
D-6600 Saarbrücken

Dr. H. P A R T S C H
Institut für Informatik
Technische Universität München
Postfach 20 24 20
D-8000 München 2

H.D. R O M B A C H
K. W E G E N E R
FB Informatik
Universität Kaiserslautern
Postfach 3049
D-6750 Kaiserslautern

Dr. R. S C H O E N B E R G E R
Landis&Gyr AG
CH-6301 Zug

H.E. S E N G L E R
URW Unternehmensberatung
Harksheider Str. 102
D-2000 Hamburg 65

Dr. B. B A R T S C H - S P O E R L
Interface Concilium
Gesellschaft für Software-
technologie und DV-Systeme
Arabellastr. 30

D-8000 München 81